Elizabeth Peel, PhD
Victoria Clarke, PhD
Jack Drescher, MD
Editor

British Lesbian, Gay, and Bisexual Psychologies: Theory, Research, and Practice

British Lesbian, Gay, and Bisexual Psychologies: Theory, Research, and Practice has been co-published simultaneously as *Journal of Gay & Lesbian Psychotherapy*, Volume 11, Numbers 1/2 2007.

*Pre-publication
REVIEWS,
COMMENTARIES,
EVALUATIONS . . .*

"**I**NDISPENSABLE to those working in the areas of practice, public policy, academia, and social activism. Employing a wide range of variously critical approaches to the study of lesbians, gay men, and bisexuals, this exciting new collection highlights cutting-edge research from the United Kingdom. Most importantly, this text will pertain to the experiences of a diverse sample of lesbians, gay men, and bisexuals, featuring as it does a focus on communities such as LGB young people, gay men with learning difficulties, and gay athletes. Standing alongside the chapters focusing on therapeutic practice with LGB individuals, this diverse range of topics demonstrates the key importance of this text in the ongoing development of a critical LGB psychology in the United Kingdom."

Damien W. Riggs, PhD
Postdoctoral Fellow
The University of Adelaide, Australia
Editor
Gay and Lesbian Issues
and Psychology Review

The Haworth Medical Press®
An Imprint of The Haworth Press, Inc.

British Lesbian, Gay, and Bisexual Psychologies: Theory, Research, and Practice

British Lesbian, Gay, and Bisexual Psychologies: Theory, Research, and Practice has been co-published simultaneously as *Journal of Gay & Lesbian Psychotherapy*, Volume 11, Numbers 1/2 2007.

Monographs from the *Journal of Gay & Lesbian Psychotherapy*

For additional information on these and other Haworth Press titles, including descriptions, tables of contents, reviews, and prices, use the QuickSearch catalog at http://www.HaworthPress.com.

1. *Addictions in the Gay and Lesbian Community*, edited by Jeffrey R. Guss, MD, and Jack Drescher, MD (Vol. 3, No. 3/4, 2000). *Explores the unique clinical considerations involved in addiction treatment for gay men and lesbians, groups that reportedly use and abuse alcohol and substances at higher rates than the general population.*

2. *Gay and Lesbian Parenting*, edited by Deborah F. Glazer, PhD, and Jack Drescher, MD (Vol. 4, No. 3/4, 2001). *Richly textured, probing. These papers accomplish a rare feat: they explore in a candid, psychologically sophisticated, yet highly readable fashion how parenthood impacts lesbian and gay identity and how these identities affect the experience of parenting. Wonderfully informative. (Martin Stephen Frommer, PhD, Faculty/Supervisor, The Institute for Contemporary Psychotherapy, New York City).*

3. *Sexual Conversion Therapy: Ethical, Clinical, and Research Perspectives*, edited by Ariel Shidlo, PhD, Michael Schroeder, PsyD, and Jack Drescher, MD (Vol. 5, No. 3/4, 2001).*"This is an important book. . . . an invaluable resource for mental health providers and policymakers. this book gives voice to those men and women who have experienced painful, degrading, and unsuccessful conversion therapy and survived. The ethics and misuses of conversion therapy practice are well documented, as are the harmful effects." (Joyce Hunter, DSW, Research Scientist, HIV Center for Clinical & Behavioral Studies, New York State Psychiatric Institute/ Columbia University, New York City)*

4. *The Mental Health Professions and Homosexuality: International Perspectives*, edited by Vittorio Lingiardi, MD, and Jack Drescher, MD (Vol. 7, No. 1/2, 2003). *"Provides a worldwide perspective that illuminates the psychiatric, psychoanalytic, and mental health professions' understanding and treatment of both lay and professional sexual minorities." (Bob Barrett, PhD, Professor and Counseling Program Coordinator, University of North Carolina at Charlotte)*

5. *Transgender Subjectivities: A Clinician's Guide*, edited by Ubaldo Leli, MD, and Jack Drescher, MD (Vol. 8, No. 1/2, 2004). *"Indispensable for diagnosticians and therapists dealing with gender dysphoria, important for researchers, and a direct source of help for all individuals suffering from painful uncertainties regarding their sexual identity." (Otto F. Kernberg, MD, Director, Personality Disorders Institute, Weill Medical College of Cornell University)*

6. *Handbook of LGBT Issues in Community Mental Health*, edited by Ronald E. Hellman, MD, and Jack Drescher, MD (Vol. 8, No. 3/4, 2004). *"Comprehensive . . . Richly strewn with data, useful addresses of voluntary and other organizations, and case histories." (Michael King, MD, PhD, Professor of Primary Care Psychiatry, Royal Free and University College Medical School, London)*

7. *A Gay Man's Guide to Prostate Cancer*, edited by Gerald Perlman, PhD, and Jack Drescher, MD (Vol. 9, No. 1/2, 2005). *"Excellent. . . . highly recommended. Patients reading this book will find themselves here, and professionals will learn what they need to help their patients as they struggle with these emotional topics." (Donald Johannessen, MD, Clinical Assistant Professor of Psychiatry, NYU School of Medicine)*

8. *Barebacking: Psychosocial and Public Health Approaches*, edited by Perry N. Halkitis, PhD, Leo Wilton, PhD, and Jack Drescher, MD (Vol. 9, No. 3/4, 2005). *An examination of the psychological, social, and health issues involving intentional unprotected gay or bisexual sex.*

9. *Crystal Meth and Men Who Have Sex with Men: What Mental Health Care Professionals Need to Know,* edited by Milton L. Wainberg, MD, Andrew Kolodny, MD, and Jack Drescher, MD (Vol. 10, No. 3/4, 2006). *"This comprehensive book captures not just the extent of the problem and how to recognize it, it offers excellent clinical interventions and treatments. . . . invaluable." (Robert Paul Cabaj, MD, Director, San Francisco Department of Public Health's Community Behavioral Health Services Member, Mayor's Task Force on Methamphetamine Abuse, San Francisco)*

10. ***British Lesbian, Gay, and Bisexual Psychologies: Theory, Research, and Practice,*** edited by Elizabeth Peel, PhD, Victoria Clarke, PhD, and Jack Drescher, MD (Vol. 11, No. 1/2, 2007). *A comprehensive examination of the latest developments in lesbian, gay, and bisexual psychological and psychotherapeutic theory, research, and practice in the United Kingdom.*

British Lesbian, Gay, and Bisexual Psychologies: Theory, Research, and Practice

Elizabeth Peel, PhD
Victoria Clarke, PhD
Jack Drescher, MD
Editors

British Lesbian, Gay, and Bisexual Psychologies: Theory, Research, and Practice has been co-published simultaneously as *Journal of Gay & Lesbian Psychotherapy*, Volume 11, Numbers 1/2 2007.

The Haworth Medical Press®
An Imprint of The Haworth Press, Inc.

www.HaworthPress.com

Published by

The Haworth Medical Press®, 10 Alice Street, Binghamton, NY 13904-1580 USA

The Haworth Medical Press® is an imprint of The Haworth Press, Inc., 10 Alice Street, Binghamton, NY 13904-1580 USA.

British Lesbian, Gay, and Bisexual Psychologies: Theory, Research, and Practice has been co-published simultaneously as *Journal of Gay & Lesbian Psychotherapy*, Volume 11, Numbers 1/2 2007.

The development, preparation, and publication of this work has been undertaken with great care. However, the publisher, employees, editors, and agents of The Haworth Press and all imprints of The Haworth Press, Inc., including The Haworth Medical Press® and Pharmaceutical Products Press®, are not responsible for any errors contained herein or for consequences that may ensue from use of materials or information contained in this work. With regard to case studies, identities and circumstances of individuals discussed herein have been changed to protect confidentiality. Any resemblance to actual persons, living or dead, is entirely coincidental.

The Haworth Press is committed to the dissemination of ideas and information according to the highest standards of intellectual freedom and the free exchange of ideas. Statements made and opinions expressed in this publication do not necessarily reflect the views of the Publisher, Directors, management, or staff of The Haworth Press, Inc., or an endorsement by them.

Library of Congress Cataloging-in-Publication Data

British lesbian, gay, and bisexual psychologies : theory, research, and practice / Elizabeth Peel, Victoria Clarke, Jack Drescher, editors.
    p. cm.
    "Co-published simultaneously as Journal of gay & lesbian psychotherapy, volume 11, numbers 1/2 2007."
    Includes bibliographical references and index.
    ISBN-13: 978-0-7980-3251-5 (hard cover : alk. paper)
    ISBN-10: 0-7890-3251-1 (hard cover : alk. paper)
    ISBN-13: 978-0-7890-3252-2 (soft cover : alk. paper)
    ISBN-10: 0-7890-3252-X (soft cover : alk. paper)
    1. Gays–Mental health–Great Britain. 2. Lesbians–Mental health–Great Britain. 3. Bisexuals–Mental Health–Great Britain. 4. Psychotherapy–Great Britain. 5. Homosexuality–Psychological aspects. I. Peel, Elizabeth. II. Clarke, Victoria, Ph.D. III. Drescher, Jack, 1951-
RC451.4.G39B75 2007
616.89'14008664–dc22

                                              2005032687

The HAWORTH PRESS *Inc*
Abstracting, Indexing & Outward Linking
PRINT *and* ELECTRONIC BOOKS & JOURNALS

This section provides you with a list of major indexing & abstracting services and other tools for bibliographic access. That is to say, each service began covering this periodical during the the year noted in the right column. Most Websites which are listed below have indicated that they will either post, disseminate, compile, archive, cite or alert their own Website users with research-based content from this work. (This list is as current as the copyright date of this publication.)

Abstracting, Website/Indexing Coverage . . . . Year When Coverage Began

- ****Academic Search Premier (EBSCO)****
  <http://search.ebscohost.com> 2001

- ****Expanded Academic ASAP (Thomson Gale)**** 1993

- ****Expanded Academic ASAP - International (Thomson Gale)**** 1993

- ****Expanded Academic Index (Thomson Gale)**** 1995

- ****InfoTrac Custom (Thomson Gale)**** 1998

- ****InfoTrac OneFile (Thomson Gale)**** 1998

- ****MasterFILE Premier (EBSCO)****
  <http://search.ebscohost.com> 2006

- ****ProQuest Academic Research Library (ProQuest CSA)****
  <http://www.proquest.com> 1993

- ****Psychological Abstracts (PsycINFO)****
  <http://www.apa.org> 2001

- ****Research Library (ProQuest CSA)****
  <http://www.proquest.com> 2006

- ****Social Work Abstracts (NASW)****
  <http://www.silverplatter.com/catalog/swab.htm> 1993

(continued)

(continued)

(continued)

Bibliographic Access

- **Cabell's Directory of Publishing Opportunities in Psychology** *<http://www.cabells.com>*

- **Magazines for Libraries (Katz)**

- **MedBioWorld** *<http://www.medbioworld.com>*

- **MediaFinder** *<http://www.mediafinder.com/>*

- **Ulrich's Periodicals Directory: The Global Source for Periodicals Information Since 1932** *<http://www.bowkerlink.com>*

Special Bibliographic Notes related to special journal issues (separates) and indexing/abstracting:

- indexing/abstracting services in this list will also cover material in any "separate" that is co-published simultaneously with Haworth's special thematic journal issue or DocuSerial. Indexing/abstracting usually covers material at the article/chapter level.
- monographic co-editions are intended for either non-subscribers or libraries which intend to purchase a second copy for their circulating collections.
- monographic co-editions are reported to all jobbers/wholesalers/approval plans. The source journal is listed as the "series" to assist the prevention of duplicate purchasing in the same manner utilized for books-in-series.
- to facilitate user/access services all indexing/abstracting services are encouraged to utilize the co-indexing entry note indicated at the bottom of the first page of each article/chapter/contribution.
- this is intended to assist a library user of any reference tool (whether print, electronic, online, or CD-ROM) to locate the monographic version if the library has purchased this version but not a subscription to the source journal.
- individual articles/chapters in any Haworth publication are also available through the Haworth Document Delivery Service (HDDS).

As part of Haworth's continuing commitment to better serve our library patrons, we are proud to be working with the following electronic services:

AGGREGATOR SERVICES

EBSCOhost

Ingenta

J-Gate

Minerva

OCLC FirstSearch FirstSearch

Oxmill

SwetsWise SwetsWise

LINK RESOLVER SERVICES

1Cate (Openly Informatics)

ChemPort (American Chemical Society) ChemPort·

CrossRef

Gold Rush (Coalliance)

LinkOut (PubMed)

LINKplus (Atypon)

LinkSolver (Ovid)

LinkSource with A-to-Z (EBSCO)

Resource Linker (Ulrich)

SerialsSolutions (ProQuest) SerialsSolutions

SFX (Ex Libris) $S·F·X$

Sirsi Resolver (SirsiDynix) SirsiDynix

Tour (TDnet)

Vlink (Extensity, formerly Geac) ((extensity))

WebBridge (Innovative Interfaces) WebBridge

British Lesbian, Gay, and Bisexual Psychologies: Theory, Research, and Practice

CONTENTS

ABOUT THE EDITORS

Elizabeth Peel, PhD, is a lecturer in psychology at Aston University, Birmingham, UK. Her research interests are in the areas of critical social psychology and critical health psychology. Dr. Peel has been editor of *Lesbian & Gay Psychology Review*, the journal of the Lesbian and Gay Psychology Section of the British Psychological Society. She has published articles on heterosexism, same-sex relationships, and diabetes and is editor (with Victoria Clarke) of *Out in Psychology: Lesbian, gay, bisexual, trans and queer perspectives* (Wiley), 2007.

Victoria Clarke, PhD, is a senior lecturer in social psychology at the University of the West of England, Bristol, UK. She has published a number of articles on lesbian and gay parenting and same-sex relationship and co-edited two special issues of *Feminism & Psychology* on marriage (with Sara-Jane Finlay and Sue Wilkinson). She is editor (with Elizabeth Peel) of *Out in Psychology: Lesbian, gay, bisexual, trans and queer perspectives* (Wiley), 2007.

Jack Drescher, MD, is Editor-in-Chief of the *Journal of Gay & Lesbian Psychotherapy*. He is a Training and Supervising Analyst at the William Alanson White Institute and Adjunct Assitant Professor at New York University's Postdoctoral Program in Psychotherapy and Psychoanalysis. He is a Distinguished Fellow of the American Psychiatric Association and Past Chair of the Committee on GLB Issues as well as a Past President of APA's New York County District Branch. He is a member of many distinguished professional organizations, including the Group for the Advancement of Psychiatry, the American College of Psychiatrists and the New York Academy of Medicine. Dr. Drescher is author of *Psychoanalytic Therapy and the Gay Man* (The Analytic Press) and editor of a score of books dealing with gender, sexuality and public health. He is also editor of the Bending Psychoanalysis Book Series (The Analytic Press). Dr. Drescher is in private practice in New York City.

SECTION 1:
INTRODUCING LGB PSYCHOSOCIAL THEORY AND PRACTICE IN THE UK

Introduction to LGB Perspectives in Psychological and Psychotherapeutic Theory, Research and Practice in the UK

Elizabeth Peel, PhD
Victoria Clarke, PhD
Jack Drescher, MD

Elizabeth Peel is Lecturer in Psychology, School of Life & Health Sciences, Aston University, Birmingham B4 7ET, UK (E-mail: e.a.peel@aston.ac.uk).

Victoria Clarke is Senior Lecturer in Social Psychology, School of Psychology, Faculty of Applied Sciences, University of the West of England, Frenchay Campus, Bristol BS16 1QY, UK (E-mail: Victoria.Clarke@uwe.ac.uk). Jack Drescher is Editor-in-Chief of the *Journal of Gay & Lesbian Psychotherapy*.

The editors wish to thank Anna Sandfield for organising the one-day *Sexuality and Identity* conference held in November 2003 at Aston University, Birmingham, UK that formed the basis of this volume. The Guest Editors would like to thank the following people who kindly reviewed the submissions: Mark Andersen, Phyllis Annesley, Christopher Bennett, Catherine Butler, Trevor Butt, Isabel Clare, Adrian Coyle, Kamaldeep Dhillon, Barbara Duncan, Guy Faulkner, Hannah Frith, Rosie Harding, Colleen Heenan, Craig Hutchinson, Katherine Johnson, Susan King, Vikki Krane, Peter Martin, Jeremy Monsen, Hazel Platzer, Ian Rivers, Katrina Roen, Susan Speer and John Waite.

[Haworth co-indexing entry note]: "Introduction to LGB Perspectives in Psychological and Psychotherapeutic Theory, Research and Practice in the UK." Peel, Elizabeth, Victoria Clarke, and Jack Drescher. Co-published simultaneously in *Journal of Gay & Lesbian Psychotherapy* (The Haworth Medical Press, an imprint of The Haworth Press, Inc.) Vol. 11, No. 1/2, 2007, pp. 1-6; and: *British Lesbian, Gay, and Bisexual Psychologies: Theory, Research, and Practice* (ed: Elizabeth Peel, Victoria Clarke, and Jack Drescher) The Haworth Medical Press, an imprint of The Haworth Press, Inc., 2007, pp. 1-6. Single or multiple copies of this article are available for a fee from The Haworth Document Delivery Service [1-800-HAWORTH, 9:00 a.m. - 5:00 p.m. (EST). E-mail address: docdelivery@haworthpress.com].

We are delighted to welcome readers to this collection of papers showcasing current developments in lesbian, gay and bisexual (LGB) psychological and psychotherapeutic theory, research and practice in the United Kingdom. This is our second foray into the international arena, having published in Volume 7 of *Journal of Gay & Lesbian Psychotherapy* a special volume entitled *"The Mental Health Professions and Homosexuality: International Perspectives* (issued in monograph volume as Lingiardi and Drescher, 2003). In that previous collection, our lone UK contributor, the late Daniel Twomey (2003), focused on psychoanalytic perspectives about and attitudes toward homosexuality in the UK. This volume expands upon that earlier contribution and introduces readers to a wider range of British mental health approaches.

When reading these papers, it is worth keeping in mind some important distinctions between our two countries: (1) in contrast to the US, mental health services are subsidized in the UK by the government's National Health Service (NHS); (2) British national policy is becoming increasingly gay-affirmative–including the adoption of same-sex civil partnerships–while US policies at the Federal level are resisting such affirmation; (3) research intended to address the mental health needs of LGBT populations is increasingly likely to influence policy-making regarding the British health-care system, while similar research in the US (and much research openly dealing with sexual matters or sexual minorities) is under attack by social conservatives at the federal, state and local levels.

This collection opens with Clarke and Peel's "LGBT Psychosocial Theory and Practice" which offers a critical review of the (recent) history of UK LGB psychology and psychotherapy, focusing on key publications, and outlining the current terrain, highlighting similarities and differences between the UK and the US contexts.

The remaining papers are organised into two thematic sections and exemplify psychosocial perspectives in UK LGB psychological and psychotherapeutic theory, research and practice. Section 2 explores theoretical frameworks in UK therapeutic practice. As John Gonsiorek (2000) notes in his forward to the second volume of the UK-produced *Pink Therapy* series (Davies and Neal, 2000), the prominence given to different schools of therapy in the UK stands in contrast with the strongly integrative (or eclectic) approaches that are the norm in the US.

Section 2 begins with Darren Langdridge's "Gay Affirmative Therapy: A Theoretical Framework and Defence." While gay affirmative therapy (GAT) provides a framework for clinical practice that is supportive of lesbian, gay and bisexual identities, a number of humanistic and existential psychotherapists seek to avoid imposing specific expectations on their clients and consequently have challenged the applicability of using a GAT framework for their practice. Langdridge examines their arguments and suggests a solution consistent with enabling therapists to recognise and work with the twin impacts of the psychotherapist and social world on the construction of a client's sexual identity.

Next is Martin Milton's "Being Sexual: Existential Contributions to Psychotherapy with Gay Male Clients." This paper outlines an existential-phenomenological (E-P) approach to psychotherapy and considers some of its core concepts, the stance taken to understanding sexuality and the implications for therapeutic practice with gay male clients. Colin Clarke's "Facilitating Gay Men's Coming Out: An Existential-Phenomenological Exploration" further examines, from an E-P approach, the core issues facing male clients in confronting their anxiety about whether or not to "come out" as gay.

Section 2 concludes with Aaron Balick's "Gay Subjects Relating: Object Relations Between Gay Therapist and Gay Client." Balick discusses the development of object relations theory in Britain. His paper examines object relations in the context of its unique challenges for gay male therapists working with gay male clients in what he refers to as "the gay therapeutic dyad."

Section 3 explores sexual minority identities and their needs for support and community. It begins with Malley and Tasker's " 'The Difference that Makes a Difference': What Matters to Lesbians and Gay Men in Psychotherapy." In order to determine what aspects of psychotherapy lesbians and gay men find helpful, the authors conducted a postal survey with a community sample of lesbians and gay men in the UK who had used counselling or psychotherapy services. Content analysis of the responses of 365 lesbians and gay men revealed that issues related to sexual identity were important in addition to generic qualities of the therapeutic relationship. Lesbians and gay men also listed friends, family of choice, and family of origin, and complementary or "alternative" therapies as important sources of support aside from psychotherapy.

Sonja Ellis further explores sexual minority populations in "Community in the 21st Century: Issues Arising from a Study of British Lesbians and Gay Men." Historically, lesbians and gay men created "communities" because their oppressed status often rendered them invisible to each other. In the UK this led to a wide range of organised social activities and venues, including lesbian-organised Women's Centres and, following the HIV/AIDS crisis of the 1980s, a range of health-based organisations and groups available to gay men. However, with the mainstreaming of lesbian and gay culture–combined with the ever-increasing commercialisation of lesbian and gay venues–many "non-scene" venues and organised social activities for lesbians and gay men disappeared. Drawing on data from an interview-based study with UK lesbians and gay men, Ellis's paper highlights the ways in which these changes have affected the lives and lifestyles of lesbians and gay men, resulting in the social exclusion of certain individuals and groups.

Colm Crowley, Rom Harré and Ingrid Lunt shift the focus to youth in "Safe Spaces and Sense of Identity: Views and Experiences of Lesbian, Gay and Bisexual Young People." Given that empirical data on the life experiences of contemporary school-age LGB young people in Britain is sparse, they report preliminary findings of a study conducted at a recently-initiated LGB youth Summer School. The aim was to elicit the young people's views and experiences relating to their need for support such as that offered by the Summer School. Themes drawn from participants' interviews are presented and key issues included: being positioned as different by their majority heterosexual peers; feelings of isolation and loneliness in their peer groups and families; difficulties in finding others like themselves for companionship; and the importance of meeting more LGB people of their own age.

In "Gay Men with Learning Disabilities: UK Service Provision," Sören Stauffer-Kruse notes that although the UK's NHS offers many services for people with learning disabilities, sexuality issues are often overlooked. The paper explores how gay men with learning disabilities (GMLD) experience a complex set of increased difficulties in forming a functioning identity. Stauffer-Kruse also offers suggestions as to how practitioners could offer the best psychological service to GMLD.

The final paper in this volume is Brendan Gough's "Coming Out in the Heterosexist World of Sport: A Qualitative Analysis of Web Postings by Gay Athletes." There is very little published on how gay athletes come out to their sporting peers yet coming out is likely to present some unique challenges for those who do. Gough reports on a preliminary study based on an analysis of eight online accounts provided by North American gay athletes for a web-based newsletter. Using qualitative research methods, several themes emerged: (1) sport as distraction from sexuality; (2) invisibility and isolation within sport; (3) coming out to the team: difficult but rewarding; and (4) becoming politicised: challenging heterosexism within sport. Gough's discussion centres on the challenges and opportunities facing gay men within sporting contexts and the implications of the analysis for possible psychological interventions with gay athletes. The need for further qualitative research in this area is also underlined.

To readers, a number of these contributions may appear sociological rather than psychological in nature; however, all of the contributions fit firmly in the cannon of LGB psychology in the UK. A reason why some of the contributions may appear sociological is their reliance on qualitative methods and discursive and constructionist approaches. The papers by Crowley et al., Ellis and Gough illustrate the use of qualitative perspectives in UK LGBT psychology. Crowley et al.'s and Ellis's papers are examples of experiential qualitative approaches–ones that emphasise participants' subjective understandings. Experiential approaches are grounded in an epistemology and view of language that assumes language reflects reality. Experiential qualitative researchers inspect participants' language for evidence of their underlying thoughts, feelings and beliefs. For instance, Ellis is interested in her participants' thoughts and feelings about their access to, or lack of access to, LGB community and support settings. By contrast, discursive and constructionist perspectives–such as those used by Gough–assume that language constructs reality. Gough is not interested in what feelings gay athletes' stories reflect, rather he is interested in how the stories constitute the coming out process and are used to negotiate a viable position as a gay athlete in the heterosexist world of sport.

Qualitative researchers in the UK rely both on more traditional methods of data collection (such as interviews, focus groups and qualitative surveys) and on less traditional methods–such as Gough's use of coming out stories posted on a website for gay athletes. Qualitative researchers–particularly discursive and constructionist researchers–also work with a broad definition of text that incorporates traditional social science texts as well as a wide range of cultural texts including television shows (Clarke and Kitzinger, 2004; Speer and Potter, 2000), parliamentary debates (Ellis and Kitzinger, 2002), newspaper articles (Alldred, 1998), and teaching and training sessions (Kitzinger, 2000; Kitzinger and Peel, 2005; Peel, 2002). As discursive studies, in particular, rely on detailed examinations of text, sample sizes tend to be significantly smaller than in more conventional qualitative research. Furthermore, because discursive psychologists view representation, generalisability, reliability and validity as wedded to a mainstream research agenda, they reject traditional sampling concerns.

We anticipate that this collection will serve for newcomers to LGB psychological and psychotherapeutic theory, research and practice in the UK as a useful introduction to work in the area, and for those already familiar with the UK context, as an interesting survey of current developments. There is limited literature of collaboration between LGB-affirmative psychologists and psychotherapists in the US and in the UK. This volume has been a start and we hope that it will foster the possibility of increasing transatlantic dialogue in the future.

REFERENCES

Alldred, P. (1998), Making a mockery of family Life? Lesbian mothers in the British media. *J. Lesbian Studies*, 2:9-21.

Clarke, V. & Kitzinger, C. (2004), Lesbian and gay parents on talk shows: Resistance or normalisation? *Qualitative Research in Psychology*, 1(3):195-217.

Davies, D. & Neal, C., eds. (2000), *Pink Therapy 2: Therapeutic Perspectives on Working with Lesbian, Gay and Bisexual Clients*. Buckingham: Open University Press.

Ellis, S. J. & Kitzinger, C. (2002), Denying equality: An analysis of arguments against lowering the age of consent for sex between men. *J. Community & Applied Social Psychology*, 12:167-180.

Gonsiorek, J. (2000), Foreword. In: *Pink Therapy: A Guide for Counsellors and Therapists Working with Lesbian, Gay and Bisexual Clients*, eds., D. Davies & C. Neal. Buckingham: Open University Press, pp. xiii-xviii.

Kitzinger, C. (2000), Doing feminist conversation analysis. *Feminism & Psychology*, 10(2):163-193.

Kitzinger, C. & Peel, E. (2005), The de-gaying and re-gaying of AIDS: Contested homophobias in lesbian and gay awareness training. *Discourse & Society*. 16(2): 173-197.

Lingiardi, V. & Drescher, J., eds. (2003), *The Mental Health Professions and Homosexuality: International Perspectives*. New York: The Haworth Press, Inc.

Peel, E. (2002), Lesbian and gay awareness training: Challenging homophobia, liberalism and managing stereotypes. In: *Lesbian & Gay Psychology: New Perspectives*, eds., A. Coyle & C. Kitzinger. Oxford: BPS Blackwell, pp. 255-274.

Speer, S. & Potter, J. (2000), The management of heterosexist talk: Conversational resources and prejudiced claims. *Discourse & Society*, 11(4):543-572.

Twomey, D. (2003), British psychoanalytic attitudes toward homosexuality. *J. Gay & Lesbian Psychotherapy*, 7(1/2):7-22. Reprinted in: *The Mental Health Professions and Homosexuality: International Perspectives*, eds. V. Lingiardi & J. Drescher. New York: The Haworth Press, Inc., pp. 7-22.

doi:10.1300/J236v11n01_01

LGBT Psychosocial Theory and Practice in the UK: A Review of Key Contributions and Current Developments

Victoria Clarke, PhD
Elizabeth Peel, PhD

SUMMARY. This paper outlines the recent history of LGBT psychology and psychotherapy in the United Kingdom, focusing on key publications,[1] and the current terrain, highlighting similarities and differences between the UK and the US contexts.[2] The paper is divided into four sections: the first focuses on the early development of the field in the late 1960s. The second section explores the 1980s–a decade that witnessed the publication of two key texts that had a strong influence on the development of the field and, in particular, on the development of critical and discursive approaches. The third section details the rapid changes that occurred in the 1990s including the establishment of a Lesbian and Gay Psychology Section within the British Psychological Society. The final

---

Victoria Clarke is Senior Lecturer in Psychology, School of Psychology, Faculty of Applied Sciences, University of the West of England, Frenchay Campus, Bristol BS16 1QY, UK (E-mail: Victoria.Clarke@uwe.ac.uk).

Elizabeth Peel is Lecturer in Psychology, School of Life & Health Sciences, Aston University, Birmingham B4 7ET, UK (E-mail: e.a.peel@aston.ac.uk).

The authors thank Dominic Davies and Martin Milton for their helpful comments on an earlier version of this paper.

[Haworth co-indexing entry note]: "LGBT Psychosocial Theory and Practice in the UK: A Review of Key Contributions and Current Developments." Clarke, Victoria, and Elizabeth Peel. Co-published simultaneously in *Journal of Gay & Lesbian Psychotherapy* (The Haworth Medical Press, an imprint of The Haworth Press, Inc.) Vol. 11, No. 1/2, 2007, pp. 7-25; and: *British Lesbian, Gay, and Bisexual Psychologies: Theory, Research, and Practice* (ed: Elizabeth Peel, Victoria Clarke, and Jack Drescher) The Haworth Medical Press, an imprint of The Haworth Press, Inc., 2007, pp. 7-25. Single or multiple copies of this article are available for a fee from The Haworth Document Delivery Service [1-800-HAWORTH, 9:00 a.m. - 5:00 p.m. (EST). E-mail address: docdelivery@haworthpress.com].

7

section considers the current terrain and the similarities and differences in the theoretical commitments of researchers and practitioners working in the UK and in the US. doi:10.1300/J236v11n01_02 *[Article copies available for a fee from The Haworth Document Delivery Service: 1-800-HAWORTH. E-mail address: <docdelivery@haworthpress.com> Website: <http://www. HaworthPress.com> © 2007 by The Haworth Press, Inc. All rights reserved.]*

KEYWORDS. Bisexual, critical psychology, gay, history, homosexuality, Hopkins, Kitzinger, lesbian, LGBT psychology, LGBT psychotherapy, Richardson and Hart, social constructionism, United Kingdom

EARLY BEGINNINGS

Lesbian and gay[3] scholarship began in Britain in the late nineteenth and early twentieth centuries. Edward Carpenter and Havelock Ellis founded the British Society for the Study of Sex Psychology in 1914 (Coyle and Wilkinson, 2002).[4] Havelock Ellis (1897), among others, challenged the nineteenth century view of homosexuality as sinful, immoral and criminal, and presented homosexuality as an inborn, normal variation.

The work of Ellis and others significantly predated the beginnings of US work in this area; however, the development of an affirmative lesbian and gay psychology in the US outpaced that in the UK in the second half of the twentieth century. More than a decade after Evelyn Hooker (1957) published her landmark article on the projective test findings of *non-patient* gay men, a British-based clinical psychologist, June Hopkins, published an equally groundbreaking paper on the lesbian personality in the *British Journal of Psychiatry* (Hopkins, 2002/ 1969; see also Clarke, 2002a). Although Hopkins' paper was not the first British psychological publication on lesbians, it was amongst the first, if not the first, to offer an affirmative psychological perspective on lesbians. Hopkins' aim was to attempt to "fill the void in objective investigation into the personality factors of lesbians" (2002/1969: 40). As a number of the contributors to a recent reappraisal of Hopkins' work note, her work was interesting because unlike most other lesbian and gay research at the time it focused specifically on lesbians and highlighted differences between lesbians and heterosexual women, and between lesbians and gay men (Malley, 2002a; Peel, 2002). In *The Lesbian Personality*, Hopkins wrote that

the following terms are suggested as appropriately descriptive of the lesbian personality in comparison to her heterosexual female counterpart: 1. More independent. 2. More resilient. 3. More reserved. 4. More dominant. 5. More bohemian. 6. More self-sufficient. 7. More composed. (2002/1969, p. 40)

When Hopkins was working as a clinical psychologist in the 1960s, the Rorschach protocol was used as a diagnostic tool to "detect" homosexuality (see Clarke and Hopkins, 2002). In *Lesbian Signs on the Rorschach*, Hopkins demonstrated that "homosexual signs" on the Rorschach were not useful in detecting lesbianism and that there were three "lesbian signs" that distinguished between lesbians and heterosexual women. As we document below, an emphasis on the differences between heterosexuals, lesbians and gay men is a significant theme in UK lesbian and gay psychological and psychotherapeutic theory, research and practice.

As Hopkins herself notes, she was one of very few British psychologists studying lesbians and gay men from an affirmative perspective in the 1960s and 1970s, and after her papers were published there was a significant lull in lesbian and gay psychological output until the 1980s (Clarke and Hopkins, 2002; see also Furnell, 1986).

THE 1980s: ESTABLISHING A CRITICAL TERRAIN

Shortly after publishing a paper on the differences between lesbians and gay men in the *Bulletin of the British Psychological Society* (Hart and Richardson, 1980), John Hart and Diane Richardson produced a book: *The Theory and Practice of Homosexuality* (1981; see also Hart, 1982, 1984; Richardson, 1978, 1984; Richardson and Hart, 1980). This edited collection offered psychosocial perspectives on lesbian and gay identities, the lesbian and gay lifespan and the presenting problems of lesbians and gay men seeking professional help. The authors considered the major theoretical models relating to homosexuality and the treatment implications of such theories. Hart and Richardson were critical of the male bias in the literature on homosexuality, and–like Hopkins–were careful to distinguish the differences in the experience of homosexual women and men. They also emphasised the importance of placing homosexuality in a social context, and of acknowledging the political implications of (all) theories of homosexuality. Richardson (1981a) called for "an explicit recognition of the close relationship between the politics and science of homosexuality" (p. 37).

In relation to therapy and counselling, Hart (1981) argued that it was difficult to see how the conditions for successful therapy for lesbian and gay clients could be achieved by therapists who personally hold pathological models of homosexuality or who are anxious about their own sexuality. Hart was critical of US mental health professionals who advocated treatment of homosexuality and argued that evidence from "born that way" studies does not provide a basis for social engineering efforts with homosexuals. Parallel to Richardson's call for reflexivity in research on homosexuality, Hart urged "professionals . . . [to] cease to see themselves as neutral technicians and instead recognize their role as moral agents" (Hart, 1981, p. 66). He also emphasised the limitations of individual therapy in compensating for the adverse experiences of homosexuals in our society.

Following a thoroughgoing review of psychological theories of homosexuality, Richardson and Hart (1981) outlined an alternative theory of the development and maintenance of a homosexual identity that emphasised personal choice, the possibility of change throughout the life span, and the meanings of homosexuality for the individual. They argued that the development, maintenance and meaning of homosexuality are unique for each individual and occur by a complex interaction of various factors specific to the individual. Their model placed homosexuality firmly within a political arena, in contrast to the work they reviewed which theorised homosexuality as if it were apart from moral debates. Richardson and Hart viewed their model as helpful for practitioners in acknowledging the possible development of a positive homosexual identity. The publication of their text marked the beginnings of a critical (post-positivist) approach to lesbian and gay psychology.

Although critical approaches such as that used by Hart and Richardson were crucial to the development of lesbian and gay psychology in the UK, some of the early pioneering studies were so, precisely because of their reliance on more mainstream psychological theories and methods. One such study—of children of lesbian mothers—was first discussed by Richardson (1981b) in *The Theory and Practice of Homosexuality*. Two years after the publication of this milestone text, Golombok, Spencer and Rutter (1983) published their similarly groundbreaking study. This was a landmark publication in research on lesbian and gay parenting (D'Augelli, 2002) and has been widely recognised for its significant contribution to changing the tide of judicial opinion on lesbian custody in the UK and elsewhere (Clarke, 2002b). This paper examined the psychosocial experiences of the children of lesbian mothers. As D'Augelli (2002) notes, it demonstrated the need for lesbian and gay psychologists to focus on social units as well as on individual lesbians and gay men. It also documented the existence of lesbian mothers and their children at a time when these families were neither part of the wider social landscape nor part of the agenda of researchers studying "normal" families. Susan Golombok, in collaboration with Fiona Tasker, completed a follow-up to the initial study in the late 1990s (Tasker and Golombok, 1997). Theirs was the first longitudinal study of children in lesbian families to be published. The initial publication by Golombok et al. and subsequent papers by Golombok and Tasker sit firmly within a positivist-empiricist framework—and, by emphasising the similarities between lesbian mothers and heterosexual mothers, a liberal-humanistic framework as well.

In 1986, paper in the *Bulletin of the British Psychological Society* called attention to lesbian and gay psychology as a neglected area of British research (Furnell, 1986). Furnell, the author of an early paper on gay identity development (1985), noted that issues of the treatment and aetiology of (male) homosexuality dominated British research until the late 1970s and "compared with the wealth of empirical studies emerging from the United States over the last 15 years, there is a definite dearth of such research on gay and lesbian issues by British psychologists" (p. 41).[5] Indeed, according to Furnell, the British literature in the mid-1980s resembled the US literature in the late 1960s and early 1970s. Other issues of concern to British psychologists identified by Furnell included the assessment of sexual orientation, the psychological characteristics of homosexuals, heterosexuals' attitudes toward homosexuals, counselling and therapy, psychoanalytic discussions of homosexuality, and the personal and social dimensions of lesbian and gay experience. Furnell noted that compared to a substantial American literature, on homophobic attitudes there was little British research on heterosexuals' attitudes toward homosexuals. He accounted for the lack of research on this and other topics partly in terms of the lack of a self-identified UK group of lesbian and gay psychologists. This state of affairs was a marked contrast to the American Psychological Association's then-recent establishment of Division 44 (Society for the Psychological Study of Lesbian and Gay Issues)[6] to provide encouragement and support for new research and publications.

One of the papers Furnell discussed under the heading of the personal and social dimensions of lesbian and gay experience and lifestyles was a Q-methodological study of lesbian identities (Kitzinger and Stainton-Rogers, 1985). This was one of a number of publications on lesbian identities—including the now classic text, *The Social Construction of*

Lesbianism (Kitzinger, 1987; see also Clarke and Peel, 2004; Peel and Clarke, 2005)–produced by Celia Kitzinger from the mid-1980s onwards. Like Hopkins' earlier study, Kitzinger's research focused specifically on lesbians and highlighted differences between lesbians and heterosexual women, and between lesbians and gay men (Rothblum, 2004). As Kitzinger and Coyle (2002) note, Hart's and Richardson's work at the beginning of the decade laid some of the groundwork for Kitzinger's critical agenda. Kitzinger rejected the hierarchal, liberal-humanistic models of lesbian and gay identity formation developed by psychologists in the US (e.g., Cass, 1979). Instead, she offered a social constructionist account of lesbian *identities*. According to Kitzinger, a social constructionist approach to identity is concerned with how people construct, negotiate and interpret their experience–the focus is on people's accounts per se, rather than on inspecting them for what they reveal about underlying emotions, thoughts and feelings, or on assessing their truth-value. Kitzinger presented five distinct accounts of lesbian identity: personal fulfillment, true love, personal sexual orientation, political/feminist and personal inadequacy. Kitzinger's goal was to recognise the existence of numerous "truths" about lesbians and to explore the meanings and implications of each. Kitzinger explicitly acknowledged that the political/feminist lesbian account is "the account on which I have relied most heavily in constructing my own account of lesbianism and as such constitutes the context from within which I assess and discuss the other four accounts" (Kitzinger, 1986, p. 164).

The Social Construction of Lesbianism incorporated a critical discussion of the then-emerging field of affirmative lesbian and gay psychology–a field dominated by the work of US psychologists and therapists. Kitzinger was critical of the liberal-humanistic and positivist-empiricist frameworks underlying much affirmative lesbian and gay psychology, and concepts such as "homophobia" and "internalised homophobia." Kitzinger (1987) called for a radical, feminist, critical, social constructionist lesbian and gay psychology that deconstructed the ideologies underlying research in this area, and the "mystique surrounding social science itself" (p. 188). She argued that the concept of homophobia "depoliticises lesbian and gay oppression by suggesting that it comes from the personal inadequacy of particular individuals suffering from a diagnosable phobia" (Kitzinger, 1997, p. 211). Lesbian and gay (mainstream) psychology, she maintained, replaces political explanations (in terms of structural oppression) with personal explanations (in terms of the workings of the psyche). Kitzinger was equally critical of the concept of internalised homophobia; she argued that if some people are unhappy about being lesbian or gay, this is a perfectly reasonable response to oppression. "Internalised" homophobia, according to Kitzinger, shifts the focus of concern away from the oppressor and back onto the victims of oppression.

In the same year that *The Social Construction of Lesbianism* was published, a group of US-based lesbian psychologists published *Lesbian Psychologies* (Boston Lesbian Psychologies Collective, 1987), an edited collection that explicitly relied on many of the concepts and theories that Kitzinger rejected (e.g., the chapter by Margolies, Becker and Jackson-Brewer on internalised homophobia). This development clearly signalled the differences between the theoretical commitments of lesbian and gay psychologists and therapists in the UK and those in the US. As Coyle (2004) notes, and as we discuss further below, social constructionism is now a defining feature of lesbian and gay psychology[7] in the UK and one that differentiates it from lesbian and gay psychology in the US. Russell and Gergen (2004) consider why the force of Kitzinger's critique has yet to be fully realised in the US. They argue that in relation to the discipline of psychology as a whole, social constructionist and other postmodern approaches remain marginal.[8] Further, because lesbian and gay psychology has developed in a hostile context, lesbian and gay psychologists seek to counter this by using traditional research methods–dismantling the master's house by using the master's tools.

1990S: ACHIEVING RECOGNITION

The early 1990s was a period of rapid development for lesbian and gay psychology and psychotherapy in the UK. In 1990, the official publication of the British Psychological Society, *The Psychologist*, published a paper by Celia Kitzinger (1990a) that drew attention to the rampant heterosexism in British psychology and how it affects lesbian and gay staff and students in psychology departments. The European Association of Lesbian, Gay and Bisexual Psychologists was established two years later in 1992; one year later, homosexuality was removed from the *International Classification of Diseases*– a diagnostic manual used in Europe–two decades after the removal of homosexuality per se from the American Psychiatric Association's *Diagnostic and Statistical Manual (DSM)* (Kitzinger and Coyle, 2002; Nakajima, 2003). In 1994, Charles Neal founded the Association for

Lesbian, Gay, and Bisexual Psychologies (ALGBP-UK), which affiliated to ALGP-Europe.[9]

By the mid-1990s, lesbian and gay psychological theory and research were gaining significant momentum (and recognition in social psychology–see Kitzinger, 1989, 1990b); however, the literature on affirmative psychotherapeutic practice was only beginning to develop (Annesley and Coyle, 1998). Neal and Davies (1996) argued that the declassification of homosexuality per se as a mental illness in 1973 allowed gay affirmative models of therapy to develop in the US much earlier than in the UK. The work that constituted the springboard for their book–the first volume of the Pink Therapy series (*Pink Therapy: A Guide for Counsellors and Therapists Working with Lesbian, Gay and Bisexual Clients*)–was almost exclusively North American. This collection was predated by a small number of individual papers (e.g., Hart, 1982, 1984; Richardson and Hart, 1980), and publications produced by people involved in voluntary sector organisations (Furnell, 1986); however, it stands as the first significant UK publication to address affirmative therapeutic practice. The text covered lesbian, gay and bisexual development and life-span issues, religion and spirituality conflicts, alcohol and substance misuse, homophobia and heterosexism, and developing a model of affirmative therapeutic practice.

A Lesbian and Gay Psychology Section (a BPS Section is roughly equivalent to an APA Division) was finally established within the BPS in 1998, after nearly a decade of campaigning and three rejected proposals (two for a Psychology of Lesbianism Section and one for a Lesbian and Gay Psychology Section) (Wilkinson, 1999; Comely et al., 1992). Membership of the Section is open to all members of the BPS, and Section members include researchers, teachers, clinical psychologists, counselling psychologists, and students.[10] Although there are a number of US journals, including this one, that focus on LGBT perspectives, the Section publishes the only LGBT psychology journal of which we are aware–*Lesbian & Gay Psychology Review*.[11] It also awards annual undergraduate and graduate prizes and organises conferences, symposia and other events.[12]

In the US, it is mostly psychiatrists, psychologists and clinical social workers who practice counselling and therapy (with lesbian and gay clients and their families). In the UK, counselling and therapy are not part of the remit of social workers, and there is an important distinction between the National Health Service (NHS) and the private (and voluntary) sector. The majority of counsellors and psychotherapists work in the voluntary sector or in private practice, whereas psychiatrists and psychologists have a monopoly in the NHS. As yet, there is little in the way of professional infrastructure specifically for counsellors and psychotherapists working with lesbian and gay clients in the UK. Neither the British Association for Counselling and Psychotherapy nor the United Kingdom Council for Psychotherapy has groupings for those therapists and counsellors. LGBT psychiatrists also lack a professional body; however, there is a Gay and Lesbian Association of Doctors and Dentists (GLADD) (see *www.gladd.dircon.co.uk*).

In the years following the establishment of the Lesbian and Gay Psychology Section, a number of landmark texts were published. These included the second and third volumes in the *Pink Therapy* series (Davies and Neal, 2000; Neal and Davies, 2000) in 2000 and, in 2002, *Lesbian & Gay Psychology: New Perspectives* (Coyle and Kitzinger, 2002)–the first ever British edited and authored book on lesbian and gay psychology and psychotherapy–and a special European issue of the *Journal of Community & Applied Social Psychology* (Coyle and Wilkinson, 2002). These and other developments perhaps substantiate Furnell's (1986) argument that the dearth of lesbian and gay psychological research in the UK in the mid-1980s, compared to that produced in the US, can be explained by the lack of a professional network.

THE CURRENT TERRAIN

The rapidly developing field of LGBT psychology and psychotherapy in the UK and the more established field in the US engage with similar concerns, and both fields are defined by a commitment to justice for, and the well-being of, LGBT persons. Work in the UK focuses on: coming out (Davies, 1996a; Markowe, 1996, 2002) and identity (Kitzinger and Wilkinson, 1995); health (Fish and Wilkinson, 2000; Wilkinson, 2002); sexual health and HIV/AIDS (Flowers et al., 1997); development and life-span issues (Rivers, 1997); relationships (Barker, 2004; Kitzinger and Coyle, 1995; Simon, 1996); family and parenting (Barrett and Tasker, 2002; Hargaden and Llewellin, 1996); homophobia and heterosexism (Braun, 2000; Ellis, 2001; Gough, 2002; Hegarty, 2002; Peel, 2001); diversity within LGBT communities (Bennett and Coyle, 2001); methodological and theoretical concerns (Fish, 2000; Judd and Milton, 2001); LGBT affirmative therapeutic practice (Malley, 2002b); and evaluations of clinical psychology, counselling and psychotherapy services (Annesley and Coyle, 1998). There are some different concerns, for instance, interrogating representations of non-heterosexuals in the larger cultural context and in psychology (Alldred, 1996; Clarke and Kitzinger, 2004; Ellis and Kitzinger, 2002). In relation to practice, psychotherapists and counsellors in the UK–unlike those working in the US–are likely to employ particular theoretical frameworks (such as psychoanalysis, cognitive-behavioural therapy, existential therapy, systemic therapy) for working with LGBT (and heterosexual) clients. However, the most significant difference lies in the theories and methods used, and in the questions asked, by some LGBT researchers and practitioners in the UK.

Some LGBT psychology in the UK is essentialist, positivist-empiricist, quantitative and liberal; for instance, Tasker's (2002) work on lesbian and gay parenting. However, a significant proportion of work is constructionist, discursive, qualitative, and critical, such as Clarke's (2002c) work on lesbian and gay parenting. As Kitzinger and Coyle (2002) note, the contrast between Tasker's essentialist and Clarke's social constructionist approach to lesbian and gay parenting is striking. Tasker compares children from lesbian mother families with children from heterosexual mother families in relation to family and peer relationships, mental health and psychosexual development. Tasker offers facts about family life and so contributes to positive representations of lesbian parenting. By contrast, Clarke interrogates representations of lesbian and gay parenting in popular media and in psychological research, and does so not from a presumably neutral/objective position of a scientific psychologist, but from a politically engaged, lesbian feminist stance. Whereas essentialist work like Tasker's is concerned with generating "scientific evidence" about whether or not children in lesbian families grow up psychologically healthy, constructionist work like Clarke's is concerned with the political/ideological costs, benefits and effects of making this kind of argument. Furthermore, whereas Tasker emphasises the similarities between children in lesbian families and children in heterosexual mother families, Clarke explores the effects, costs and benefits of emphasising similarities and offers an alternative to sameness discourse in the shape of radical lesbian feminist accounts of lesbian parenting.

As Coyle and Wilkinson (2002) note, debates about essentialism versus social constructionism are a feature of LGBT psychology in the UK (see Kitzinger, 1995, for an overview). These theoretical differences map onto methodological differences, with positivist/essentialist work mostly based on quantitative data and constructionist work mostly based on qualitative data (although not all qualitative work is social constructionist–see, for instance, Touroni and Coyle, 2002). Coyle and

Wilkinson (2002) argue that LGBT psychological research in the UK looks epistemologically and methodologically much like social psychology and could loosely be described as social psychological in nature. LGBT psychology in the UK is also closely associated with qualitative methods (Coyle, 2000). Coyle argues that qualitative approaches offer many benefits to LGBT psychology, including the concerted engagement with context and the subjectivities of participants.

Furthermore, much LGBT psychology in the UK fits firmly in the canon of critical psychology. Critical psychology is a developing area of research, theory and therapeutic practice in the UK (and elsewhere). The label "critical psychology" is regarded as an "umbrella term" (Walkerdine, 2001) for a wide variety of radical perspectives on the discipline. As the editors of a key collection (Prilleltensky and Fox, 1997) outlined, critical psychologists "believe that psychology's traditional practices and norms hinder social justice, to the detriment of individuals and communities in general and of oppressed groups in particular" (p. 3). Critical psychologists, echoing Richardson and Hart (1981) and Kitzinger (1987), argue that psychology (both mainstream and critical) is not a neutral endeavour conducted by researchers and practitioners detached from the larger social and political context. The theories and practices of mainstream psychology are value-laden and reinforce an unjust status quo. By contrast, the central themes of critical psychology are the pursuit of social justice, the promotion of the well-being of communities and in particular of oppressed groups, and changing the status quo of society and of psychology (Sloan, 2000).[13] Critical psychology rejects the individualism, humanism, and positivistic traditions of mainstream psychology (see Spears, 1997). Recent critical psychology collections include contributions by LGBT psychologists (e.g., Kitzinger, 1997, 1999), and recent critical psychology textbooks discuss LGBT psychology (Gough and McFadden, 2001; Hepburn, 2002). Gough and McFadden's (2001) *Critical Social Psychology* includes a chapter on sexualities and psychology that outlines social constructionist perspectives on homosexuality and the limitations of liberal-humanistic explanations of homosexuality. A chapter on prejudice encourages critical thinking on antihomosexual discourse. They note that LGBT scholars such as Celia Kitzinger have:

> been among the most cogent and vociferous critics of mainstream psychological theories and methods which have furnished "norms" around gender and sexuality with scientific authority and contributed to the marginalisation of women and homosexuality. (p. 6)

A recent decision by the editor of *The Psychologist*–the official publication of the BPS–to publish a homophobic letter caused outrage among LGBT psychologists (see Accoroni et al., 2004). However, incidents such as this are now relatively rare. Less rare is the exclusion of non-heterosexuals from psychological research across a whole range of topics. Kitzinger (1996) and others (e.g., Peel, 2001b) have interrogated in particular the exclusion of lesbian experience in feminist psychology. Likewise, most counselling, therapy and clinical psychology training programmes in the UK offer limited coverage of lesbian and gay issues in their course content, yet significant numbers of lesbians, gay men and bisexuals present for counselling and therapy (Neal and Davies, 1996).

The broader social/political context for LGBT psychology and psychotherapy (and for lesbians and gay men) in the UK is significantly different from that in the US. The UK is, broadly speaking, a more liberal and secular society than the US–the far right/Christian right is less visible and less prevalent in the UK. The LGBT rights movement in the UK has won significant victories in the last few years including the right for same-sex couples to adopt jointly.[14] The Gender Recognition Act of 2004 affords trans persons a number of rights, including the right to be issued with a new birth certificate that records their gender of choice. The Employment Equality (Sexual Orientation) Regulations of 2003 ban discrimination on the basis of sexual orientation in employment and vocational training (see www.hmso.gov.uk). Lesbian mothers are rarely likely to lose custody of their children simply because they are lesbian (Harne et al., 1997); however, gay men may still face considerable difficulties in the courts (Stonewall, 2004).

The provisions of the Civil Partnership Act 2004, offering same-sex couples many of the rights and responsibilities of marriage, came into force at the end of 2005. By contrast, although some US states recognise same-sex relationships, Federal legislation on same-sex partnership is highly unlikely.

Political differences are clearly evident in the domain of conversion therapy. Whereas a number of organisations in the US (both religious and scientific/psychological) promote conversion therapy, there is only one in the UK of which we are aware–the True Freedom Trust (www. truefreedomtrust.co.uk)–a member of the US-based Exodus International. A recent study conducted with 30 UK psychologists and psychiatrists (most of whom had worked in the NHS) suggests that those professionals who did provide conversion "treatment" for lesbians and gay men from the 1950s to the 1970s now tend to view same-sex sexuality as mentally healthy (King, Smith and Bartlett, 2004). This suggests that conversion therapy is more of a historical than a contemporary phenomenon in the UK. Moreover, the treatment of homosexuality has always been more common in the US than in the UK (see Hart, 1981; see also Ellis's, 1997, commentary on homophobia and psychoanalysis).

CONCLUSION

Although LGBT psychologists and psychotherapists in the UK and in the US share the same broad commitment to facilitating the well-being of, and social justice for, lesbians, gay men, bisexual and trans people, they differ in terms of their approach to achieving these goals. Whereas US psychotherapists mostly work within "integrative" models and US psychologists favour mainstream theories and methods, the majority of practitioners in the UK are strongly committed to particular theoretical frameworks, and within psychology critical and discursive approaches are achieving increasing prominence.

NOTES

1. This is by no means an exhaustive survey of LGBT psychology in the UK–to illustrate the development of LGBT psychology in the UK and the distinctiveness of the UK approach, we have chosen to organise this brief history around a discussion of key publications. The publications we have selected are those acknowledged as key contributions in reviews of research or in broader discussions of LGBT psychology in the UK. Furnell (1986) provides a more detailed survey of work in the UK between 1965 and 1985–although his focus is not specifically, as is ours, on *affirmative* lesbian and gay psychology.

2. It is important to note that we write this history as two academic LGBT psychologists; therefore, the history of LGBT psychology offered in the paper may be more complete than the history of LGBT psychotherapy.

3. We have chosen to mostly use the term "lesbian and gay psychology" in the historical sections because UK psychologists have only very recently begun seriously to engage with bisexual and trans perspectives and experiences. Just one of the UK produced collections on psychology/psychotherapy (Coyle and Kitzinger, 2002; Coyle and Wilkinson, 2002; Davies and Neal, 1996, 2000) incorporates trans (Neal and Davies, 2002). However, more recently, there have been a number of explorations of bisexual and trans concerns in *Lesbian & Gay Psychology Review*–the journal of the British Psychological Society (BPS) Lesbian & Gay Psychology Section (see below)– and the latest symposia and papers at BPS conferences have incorporated these issues (e.g., Clarke and Peel, 2004). Our usage of "LGBT psychology" in the latter sections reflects these developments and signals a more inclusive future for work in the area in the UK.

4. See Kitzinger and Coyle (2002) for a more detailed account of the early history of lesbian and gay scholarship in the UK.

5. Furnell identified 165 papers and books published in Britain between 1965 and 1985; however, as noted above he did not explicitly distinguish between affirmative and non-affirmative work.

6. Now called the Society for the Psychological Study of Lesbian, Gay and Bisexual Issues.

7. A concerted engagement with social constructionist approaches and approaches that emphasise understanding individuals in relation to their social and relational contexts–for example, systemic approaches (see Malley, 2002b)–and how individuals make sense of their world is also a feature of lesbian and gay counselling and therapy in the UK (see Simon and Whitfield, 2000).

8. While social constructionism may be marginal to psychological theorizing in the US, it has become increasingly important to lesbian and gay psychoanalytic authors in the US since the 1990s. For example, see Domenici and Lesser (1995), Magee and Miller (1997), Drescher (1998), Schwartz (1998) and Lesser and Schoenberg (1999).

9. ALGBP-UK folded four years later due to a lack of support for its fourth annual conference.

10. A number of contributors to this collection, including the editors, are current or past Section committee members.

11. Non-Section and non-BPS members may subscribe to *Lesbian & Gay Psychology Review;* non-members may also subscribe to the Section listserv; see www. bps.org.uk/lesgay/lesgay_home.cfm

12. This collection grew out of a one-day conference on sexuality and identity organised by the West Midlands (regional) Branch of the BPS.

13. However, there is no necessary relationship between criticality and social change. Kitzinger (1997) argues that although much LGBT psychology does not share the features of critical psychology outlined above, discourses of liberal individualism and of positivist empiricism–prevalent in North American lesbian and gay psychology–are powerful and persuasive discourses that can be used to influence policymakers and create social change.

14. Of course LGBT people in the UK still do face significant challenges; see www.stonewall. org.uk for an up-to-date overview.

REFERENCES

Accoroni, A., Adams, N., Babbs, N., Burn, A., Butler, C., Davidson, O., & Van Dijkhuizen, M. (2004), Unjustified publication? *The Psychologist*, 17(2):64.

Alldred, P. (1996), 'Fit to parent'? Developmental psychology and 'non-traditional' families. In: *Challenging Women: Psychology's Exclusions, Feminist Possibilities*, eds. E. Burman, P. Alldred, C. Bewley, B. Goldberg, C. Heenan, D. Marks, J. Marshall, K. Taylor, R. Ullah & S. Warner. Buckingham: Open University Press, pp. 141-159.

Annesley, P. & Coyle, A. (1998), Dykes and psychs: Lesbian women's experiences of clinical psychology services. *Changes: An International Journal of Psychology & Psychotherapy*, 16:247-258.

Barker, M. (2004), This is my partner, and this is my . . . partner's partner: Constructing a polyamorous identity in a monogamous world. *International Journal of Constructivist Psychology*, 18:75-88.

Barrett, B. & Tasker, F. (2002), Gay fathers and their children: What we know and what we need to know. *Lesbian & Gay Psychology Review*, 3(1):3-10.

Bennett, C.J. & Coyle, A. (2001), A minority within a minority: Identity and well-being among gay men with learning disabilities. *Lesbian & Gay Psychology Review*, 2(1):9-15.

Boston Lesbian Psychologies Collective, eds. (1987), *Lesbian Psychologies: Explorations and Challenges*. Chicago, IL: University of Illinois Press.

Braun, V. (2000), Heterosexism in focus group research: Collusion and challenge. *Feminism & Psychology*, 10(1):133-140.

Cass, V.C. (1979), Homosexual identity formation: A theoretical model. *J. Homosexuality*, 4(3):219-235.

Clarke, V., ed. (2002a), 'The Lesbian Personality': A Reappraisal of June H. Hopkins' milestone work. Special Issue, *Lesbian & Gay Psychology Review*, 3(2).

Clarke, V. (2002b), Sameness and difference in research on lesbian parenting. *J. Community & Applied Social Psychology*, 12:210-222.

Clarke, V. (2002c), Resistance and normalisation in the construction of lesbian and gay families. In: *Lesbian & Gay Psychology: New Perspectives*, eds., C. Kitzinger & A. Coyle. Oxford: BPS Blackwell, pp. 98-116.

Clarke, V. & Hopkins, J. (2002), Victoria Clarke in conversation with June Hopkins. *Lesbian & Gay Psychology Review*, 3(2):44-47.

Clarke, V. & Peel, E., eds. (2004), Celia Kitzinger–Speaking radically about lesbianism. *Feminism & Psychology*, 14(4):485-490.

Clarke, V. & Peel, E. (Conveners) (2004), *LGBT Psychology: The State of the Art [Symposium]*. The British Psychological Society Psychology of Women Section Conference, July 7-9, Brighton, UK.

Comely, L, Kitzinger, C., Perkins, R. & Wilkinson, S. (1992), Lesbian psychology in Britain: Back in the closet? *Off Our Backs*, March, pp. 16-17.

Coyle, A. (2004), Subverting psychology and prioritizing politics: Reflections on *The Social Construction of Lesbianism* from an irritated youth. *Feminism & Psychology*, 14(4):507-510.

Coyle, A. (2000), Qualitative research and lesbian and gay psychology in Britain. *Lesbian & Gay Psychology Section Newsletter*, 4: 2-5.

Coyle, A. & Kitzinger, C. eds. (2002), *Lesbian & Gay Psychology: New Perspectives*. Oxford: BPS Blackwell.

Coyle, A. & Wilkinson, S. (2002), Introduction: Social psychological perspectives on lesbian and gay issues in Europe: The state of the art. *J. Community & Applied Social Psychology*, 12:147-152.

D'Augelli, A. (2002), Forward: The cutting edges of lesbian and gay psychology. In: *Lesbian & Gay Psychology: New Perspectives*, eds., C. Kitzinger & A. Coyle. Oxford: BPS Blackwell, pp. xiii-xvi.

Davies, D. (1996a), Working with people coming out. In: *Pink Therapy: A Guide for Counsellors and Therapists Working with Lesbian, Gay and Bisexual Clients*, eds., D. Davies & C. Neal. Buckingham: Open University Press, pp. 66-88.

Davies, D. & Neal, C., eds. (1996c), *Pink Therapy: A Guide for Counsellors and Therapists Working with Lesbian, Gay and Bisexual Clients*. Buckingham: Open University Press.

Davies, D. & Neal, C., eds. (2000), *Pink Therapy 2: Therapeutic Perspectives on Working with Lesbian, Gay and Bisexual Clients*. Buckingham: Open University Press.

Domenici, T. & Lesser, R.C., Eds. (1995), *Disorienting Sexuality: Psychoanalytic Reappraisals of Sexual Identities*. New York: Routledge.

Drescher, J. (1998), *Psychoanalytic Therapy and the Gay Man*. Hillsdale, NJ: The Analytic Press.

Ellis, H. (1897), *Studies in the Psychology of Sex, Vol 1: Sexual Inversion*. London: Wilson and Macmillan.

Ellis, M.L. (1997), Challenging Socarides: New psychoanalytic responses. *Feminism & Psychology*, 7(2):289-97.

Ellis, S.J. (2001), Doing being liberal: Implicit prejudice in focus group talk about lesbian and gay human rights issues. *Lesbian & Gay Psychology Review*, 2(2):43-49.

Fish, J. (2000), Sampling issues in lesbian and gay psychology: Challenges in achieving diversity. *Lesbian & Gay Psychology Review*, 1:32-38.

Fish, J. & Wilkinson, S. (2000), Lesbians and cervical screening: Preliminary results from a UK survey of lesbian health. *Psychology of Women Section Review*, 2:45-68.

Flowers, P., Smith, J.A., Sheeran, P. & Beail, N. (1997), Health and romance: Understanding unprotected sex in relationships between gay men. *British J. Health Psychology*, 2:73-86.

Furnell, P.J. (1985), Relationships and emotional experience in a process of gay identity development: A case study based on personal construct theory. *British J. Guidance & Counselling*, 13:248-265.

Furnell, P.J. (1986), Lesbian and gay psychology: A neglected area of British research. *Bulletin British Psychological Society*, 39:41-47.

Golombok, S., Spencer, A. & Rutter, M. (1983), Children in lesbian and single-parent households: Psychosexual and psychiatric appraisal. *Child Psychology & Psychiatry*, 24:551-572.

Gough, B. (2002), 'I've always tolerated it but . . . ': Heterosexual masculinity and the discursive reproduction of homophobia. In: *Lesbian & Gay Psychology: New Perspectives*, eds., C. Kitzinger & A. Coyle. Oxford: BPS Blackwell, pp. 219-238.

Gough, B. & McFadden, M. (2001), *Critical Social Psychology: An Introduction*. New York, NY: Palgrave.

Hargaden, H. & Llewellin, S. (1996), Lesbian and gay parenting issues. In: *Pink Therapy: A Guide for Counsellors and Therapists Working with Lesbian, Gay and Bisexual Clients*, eds., D. Davies & C. Neal. Buckingham: Open University Press, pp. 116-130.

Harne, L. & Rights of Women (1997), *Valued Families: The Lesbian Mothers' Legal Handbook, 2nd edition*. London: The Women's Press.

Hart, J. (1981), Theoretical explanations in practice. In: *The Theory and Practice of Homosexuality*, eds., J. Hart & D. Richardson. London: Routledge & Kegan Paul, pp. 38-67.

Hart, J. (1982), Counselling problems arising from the social categorisation of homosexuals. *Bulletin British Psychological Society*, 39:198-200.

Hart, J. (1984), Therapeutic implications of viewing sexual identity in terms of essentialist and constructionist theories. *J. Homosexuality*, 9:39-51.

Hart, J. & Richardson, D. (1980), The differences between homosexual men and women. *Bulletin British Psychological Society*, 33:451-454.

Hart, J. & Richardson, D., eds. (1981), *The Theory and Practice of Homosexuality*. London: Routledge & Kegan Paul.

Hegarty, P. (2002), "It's not a choice, it's the way we're built": Symbolic beliefs about sexual orientation in the United States and in Britain. *Journal of Community & Applied Social Psychology*, 12:1-14.

Hepburn, A. (2002), *An Introduction to Critical Social Psychology*. London: Sage.

Hooker, E. (1957), The adjustment of the male overt homosexual. *J. Projective Techniques*, 21:18-31.

Hopkins, J. (2002/1969), The lesbian personality. *Lesbian & Gay Psychology Review*, 3(2):40-43. [Originally published in *British J. Psychiatry*, 115:1433-1436.]

Judd, D. & Milton, M. (2001), Psychotherapy with lesbian and gay clients: Existential-phenomenological contributions to training. *Lesbian & Gay Psychology Review*, 2(1):16-22.

King, M., Smith, G. & Bartlett, A. (2004), Treatments of homosexuality in Britain since the 1950s: An oral history: The experience of professionals. *British Medical J.*, 328(4737):429.

Kitzinger, C. (1986), Introducing and developing Q as a feminist methodology: A study of accounts of lesbianism. In: *Feminist Social Psychology: Developing Theory and Practice*, ed., S. Wilkinson. Buckingham: Open University Press, pp. 151-172.

Kitzinger, C. (1987), *The Social Construction of Lesbianism*. London: Sage.

Kitzinger, C. (1989), Liberal humanism as an ideology of social control: The regulation of lesbian identities. In: *Texts of Identity*, eds., K. Gergen & J. Shotter. London: Sage, pp. 82-98.

Kitzinger, C. (1990a), Heterosexism in psychology. *The Psychologist*, 3:391-392.

Kitzinger, C. (1990b), The rhetoric of pseudoscience. In: *Deconstructing Social Psychology*, eds., I. Parker & J. Shotter. London: Routledge, pp. 61-75.

Kitzinger, C. (1995), Social constructionism: Implications for lesbian and gay psychology. In: *Lesbian, Gay, and Bisexual Identities over the Lifespan: Psychological Perspectives*, eds., A.R. D'Augelli & C.J. Patterson. New York, NY: Oxford University Press, pp. 136-161.

Kitzinger, C. (1996), The token lesbian chapter. In: *Feminist Psychologies: International Perspectives*, ed., S. Wilkinson. Buckingham: Open University Press, pp. 119-144.

Kitzinger, C. (1997), Lesbian and gay psychology: A critical analysis. In: *Critical Psychology: An Introduction*, eds., D. Fox & I. Prilleltensky. London: Sage, pp. 202-216.

Kitzinger, C. (1999), Lesbian and gay psychology: Is it critical? *Annual Review Critical Psychology*, 1(1):50-66.

Kitzinger, C. & Coyle, A. (2002), Introducing lesbian and gay psychology. In: *Lesbian & Gay Psychology: New Perspectives*, eds., A. Coyle & C. Kitzinger. Oxford: BPS Blackwell, pp. 1-29.

Kitzinger, C. & Stainton-Rogers, R. (1985), A Q-methodological study of lesbian identities. *European J. Social Psychology*, 15:167-188.

Kitzinger, C. & Wilkinson, S. (1995), Transitions from heterosexuality to lesbianism: The discursive production of lesbian identities. *Developmental Psychology*, 31(1): 95-104.

Lesser, R.C. & Schoenberg, E., eds. (1999), *That Obscure Subject of Desire: Freud's Female Homosexual Revisited*. New York: Routledge.

Magee, M. & Miller, D. (1997), *Lesbian Lives: Psychoanalytic Narratives Old and New*. Hillsdale, NJ: The Analytic Press.

Malley, M. (2002a), 'I wish I'd written that': An appreciation of 'The Lesbian Personality.' *Lesbian & Gay Psychology Review*, 3(2):54-56.

Malley, M. (2002b), Systematic therapy with lesbian and gay clients: A truly social approach to psychological practice. *J. Community & Applied Social Psychology*, 12:237-241.

Margolies, L., Becker, M. & Jackson-Brewer, K. (1987), Internalized homophobia: Identifying and treating the oppressor within. In: *Lesbian Psychologies: Explorations and Challenges*, eds., Boston Lesbian Psychologies Collective. Chicago, IL: University of Illinois Press, pp. 229-241.

Markowe, L.A. (1996), *Redefining the Self: Coming Out as Lesbian*. Cambridge: Polity Press.

Markowe, L.A. (2002), Coming out as lesbian. In: *Lesbian & Gay Psychology: New Perspectives*, eds., A. Coyle & C. Kitzinger. Oxford: BPS Blackwell, pp. 63-80.

Nakajima, G.A. (2003), The emergence of an international lesbian, gay, and bisexual psychiatric movement. *J. Gay & Lesbian Psychotherapy*, 7(1/2):165-188. Reprinted in: *The Mental Health Professions and Homosexuality: International Perspectives*, eds., V. Lingiardi & J. Drescher. New York: The Haworth Press, Inc., pp. 65-188.

Neal, C. & Davies, D. (1996), Introduction. In: *Pink Therapy: A Guide for Counsellors and Therapists Working with Lesbian, Gay and Bisexual Clients*, eds., D. Davies & C. Neal. Buckingham: Open University Press, pp. 1-7.

Neal, C. & Davies, D., eds. (2000), *Pink Therapy Vol. 3: Issues in Therapy with Lesbian, Gay, and Bisexual and Transgender Clients*. Buckinghamshire: Open University Press.

Peel, E. (2001a), Mundane heterosexism: Understanding incidents of the everyday. *Women's Studies International Forum*, 24:541-554.

Peel, E. (2001b), Neglect and tokenism: Representations of violence against lesbians in textbooks. *Psychology of Women Section Review*, 3(1):14-19.

Peel, E. (2002), 'The Lesbian Personality' three decades on. *Lesbian & Gay Psychology Review*, 3(2):2-53.

Prilleltensky, I. & Fox, D. (1997), Introducing critical psychology: Values, assumptions, and the status quo. In: *Critical Psychology: An Introduction*, eds., D. Fox & I. Prilleltensky. London: Sage, pp. 2-20.

Richardson, D. (1978), Do lesbians make good parents? *Community Care*, 224:16-17.

Richardson, D. (1981a), Theoretical perspectives on homosexuality. In: *The Theory and Practice of Homosexuality*, eds., J. Hart & D. Richardson. London: Routledge & Kegan Paul, pp. 5-37.

Richardson, D. (1981b), Lesbian mothers. In: *The Theory and Practice of Homosexuality*, eds., J. Hart & D. Richardson. London: Routledge & Kegan Paul, pp. 149-158.
Richardson, D. (1984), The dilemma of essentiality in homosexual theory. *J. Homosexuality*, 9:79-90.
Richardson, D. & Hart, J. (1980), Gays in therapy: Getting it right. *New Forum: J. Psychology & Psychotherapy Association*, 6(3):58-60.
Richardson, D. & Hart, J. (1981), The development and maintenance of a homosexual Identity. In: *The Theory and Practice of Homosexuality*, eds., J. Hart & D. Richardson. London: Routledge & Kegan Paul, pp. 73-92.
Rivers, I. (1997), Lesbian, gay and bisexual development: Theory, research and social issues. *J. of Community & Applied Social Psychology*, 7(5):329-343.
Rothblum, E. (2004), 'Out'standing in her field: Looking back at Celia Kitzinger's *The Social Construction of Lesbianism. Feminism & Psychology*, 14(4):503-506.
Russell, G. & Gergen, K.J. (2004), The social construction of lesbianism: Resistance and reconstruction. *Feminism & Psychology*, 14(4):511-514.
Schwartz, A.E. (1998), *Sexual Subjects: Lesbians, Gender, and Psychoanalysis*. New York: Routledge.
Simon, G. (1996), Working with people in relationships. In: *Pink Therapy: A Guide for Counsellors and Therapists Working with Lesbian, Gay and Bisexual Clients*, eds., D. Davies & C. Neal. Buckingham: Open University Press, pp. 101-113.
Simon, G. & Whitfield, G. (2000), Social constructionist and systemic therapy. In: *Pink Therapy 2: Therapeutic Perspectives on Working with Lesbian, Gay and Bisexual Clients*, eds., D. Davies & C. Neal. Buckingham: Open University Press, pp. 144-162.
Sloan, T., ed. (2000), *Critical Psychology: Voices for Change*. Basingstoke: Macmillan.
Spears, R. (1997), Introduction. In: *Critical Social Psychology*, eds., T. Ibáñez & L. Íñiguez. London: Sage, pp. 1-26.
Stonewall (2004), Equal as Parents [document]. Accessed 5 January 2005: http://www.stonewall.org.uk/docs/equal_as_parents.pdf
Tasker, F. (2002), Lesbian and gay parenting. In: *Lesbian & Gay Psychology: New Perspectives*, eds., A. Coyle & C. Kitzinger. Oxford: BPS Blackwell, pp. 81-97.
Tasker, F. & Golombok, S. (1997), *Growing Up in a Lesbian Family: Effects on Child Development*. New York, NY: The Guilford Press.
Touroni, E. & Coyle, A. (2002), Decision-making in planned lesbian parenting: An interpretative phenomenological analysis. *J. Community & Applied Social Psychology*, 12:194-209.
Walkerdine, V. (2001), Editorial. *International J. Critical Psychology*. Retrieved from the World Wide Web 3 September 2002: http://www.l-w-bks.co.uk/journals/archive/ctri-psych/Crit-psych1_Editorial.html
Wilkinson, S. (1999), The struggle to found the lesbian and gay psychology section. *Lesbian & Gay Psychology Section Newsletter*, 2:3-5.
Wilkinson, S. (2002). Lesbian health. In: *Lesbian & Gay Psychology: New Perspectives*, eds., A. Coyle & C. Kitzinger. Oxford: BPS Blackwell, pp. 117-134.

doi:10.1300/J236v11n01_02

SECTION 2:
EXPLORING THEORETICAL FRAMEWORKS IN UK THERAPEUTIC PRACTICE

Gay Affirmative Therapy:
A Theoretical Framework and Defence

Darren Langdridge, PhD

SUMMARY. Gay affirmative therapy (GAT) has recently emerged in an attempt to rectify previously discriminatory psychotherapeutic practice with lesbians, bisexuals and gay men. GAT aims to achieve this by providing a framework for practice which is affirmative of lesbian, gay

Darren Langdridge is Lecturer in Social Psychology at The Open University, and a practicing existential psychotherapist. He is author of *Phenomenological Psychology: Theory, Research and Method* (2005, Pearson Education).

Address correspondence to: Dr. Darren Langdridge, Faculty of Social Sciences, The Open University, Walton Hall, Milton Keynes, MK7 6AA, UK (E-mail: d.langdridge@open.ac.uk).

[Haworth co-indexing entry note]: "Gay Affirmative Therapy: A Theoretical Framework and Defence." Langdridge, Darren. Co-published simultaneously in *Journal of Gay & Lesbian Psychotherapy* (The Haworth Medical Press, an imprint of The Haworth Press, Inc.) Vol. 11, No. 1/2, 2007, pp. 27-43; and: *British Lesbian, Gay, and Bisexual Psychologies: Theory, Research, and Practice* (ed: Elizabeth Peel, Victoria Clarke, and Jack Drescher) The Haworth Medical Press, an imprint of The Haworth Press, Inc., 2007, pp. 27-43. Single or multiple copies of this article are available for a fee from The Haworth Document Delivery Service [1-800-HAWORTH, 9:00 a.m. - 5:00 p.m. (EST). E-mail address: docdelivery@haworthpress.com].

and bisexual identities. This "positive framework" is clearly challenging for psychotherapies which seek to avoid imposing specific expectations on their clients, and a number of humanistic and existential psychotherapists have challenged the applicability of such a framework for their practice. This paper examines these arguments and suggests that Ricoeur's formulation of hermeneutic phenomenology may provide a solution. It is argued that incorporating a version of a hermeneutic of suspicion and critique of the illusions of the subject into psychotherapeutic practice would enable therapists to recognise and work with the twin impact of the psychotherapist and social world on the construction of a client's sexual identity. doi:10.1300/J236v11n01_03 *[Article copies available for a fee from The Haworth Document Delivery Service: 1-800-HAWORTH. E-mail address: <docdelivery@haworthpress.com> Website: <http://www.HaworthPress.com> © 2007 by The Haworth Press, Inc. All rights reserved.]*

KEYWORDS. Bisexual, ethics, existential psychotherapy, gay affirmative therapy, hermeneutic phenomenology, homosexuality, humanistic psychotherapy, lesbian, Ricoeur, subjectivity

INTRODUCTION

The antigay practices of many psychotherapies, now thankfully mostly on the wane, have resulted in a very uneasy relationship between those identifying as lesbian, gay or bisexual (LGB)[1] and the psychotherapeutic professions. Perhaps partly because of these problems there has been increasing interest in affirmative practice, particularly within humanistic and existential psychotherapies,[2] for and with members of LGB communities. However, these developments have not been without opposition. Whilst most humanistic and existential psychotherapists recognise the need to avoid discriminatory practice with LGB clients, they are less certain of the need for affirmative practice.

Existential and humanistic psychotherapies have much in common. They both reject diagnostic labelling, clinical formulations and any notion of cure. Instead they focus on the subjective experience of the client and trust in their ability to effect change in the client's world. Undoubtedly, the most important commonality is a phenomenological focus on the world of the client and how it appears to the therapist. It is this common focus that leads some practitioners working within the existential and humanistic psychotherapies to raise doubts about the applicability of gay affirmative therapy. This is due to the belief that a politically motivated therapy necessarily entails the projection of the therapist's agenda onto the client and also possibly the premature foreclosure of ways of living for the client.

This paper first examines the two major types of affirmative therapy applicable for existential and humanistic psychotherapies currently on offer for LGB clients.[3] The paper then moves on to explore the debate for and against such affirmative practices. In a discussion of Ricoeur's (1981) arguments about the need for a hermeneutic of suspicion and critique of the illusions of the subject, the theoretical case is made for a form of LGB affirmative practice applicable for humanistic and existential psychotherapies. It is argued that such a strong form of LGB affirmative practice is theoretically sound and practically desirable as it enables clinicians to recognise and work with the twin impact of the psychotherapist and social world on the construction of a client's sexual identity.

THE GROWTH OF AFFIRMATIVE THERAPIES

In recent years, there has been a growth in gay affirmative psychotherapies, of various kinds, in both the UK and US. In the UK, the most significant development in the field of LGB affirmative therapies can be found in the *Pink Therapy* series (Davies and Neal, 1996, 2000; Neal and Davies, 2000). The handbooks of Perez, DeBord and Bieschke (2000) and Ritter and Terndrup (2002) represent similar summary statements of the state of LGB affirmative therapy in the US. There are similarities between LGB affirmative therapies and feminist and multi-cultural therapies (Fassinger, 2000; Milton, 2000a) and the growth in LGB affirmative therapies mirrors the growth in black and feminist affirmative psychotherapies.

However, LGB affirmative theory and practice is relatively new. As Brown (2000) puts it, "in 1973, the notion that psychologists might be interested in serving the needs of lesbian, gay or bisexual (LGB) clients in an affirmative manner was unknown" (p. xi). The foundations for gay affirmative practice were built with and alongside the lesbian and gay civil rights movement in the 1970s and 1980s. The removal of homosexuality per se from lists of mental disorders (Bayer, 1981; Nakajima, 2002), the increase in lesbian and gay "affirmative" scholarship, and the growing belief in equality for lesbians and gay men, were important factors in this history. However, it was not until the late 1980s that LGB affirmative therapies began to be properly formulated and discussed within the psychotherapeutic community. Most recently, there has been a rapid growth of interest in affirmative psychotherapy, broadly understood, and with this the publication of an increasing number of scholarly books and papers addressing the topic (see, for instance, Buhrke, 1989; Carl, 1990; Davies and Neal, 1996, 2000; Drescher, 1998; Greene and Herek, 1994; Isay, 1989; Neal and Davies, 2000; Perez, DeBord and Bieschke, 2000; Ritter and Terndrup, 2002; Stein and Cohen, 1986 and all issues of the *Journal of Gay & Lesbian Psychotherapy* from 1989).

Ethically Affirmative Therapy

There are two distinguishable forms of affirmative psychotherapy in use amongst humanistic and existential psychotherapists in the UK and US today–one "weak" and one "strong." The weak version could be thought of as "ethically affirmative" therapy; it is concerned with a form of practice with LGB clients which is ethical in the full sense of that term.[4] This results in a form of therapy where LGB identities are valued equally with heterosexual identities, giving due consideration to LGB cultures and the unique problems that such clients may bring to therapy. The strong version, termed here "LGB affirmative" therapy, adopts a more radical notion in which a therapist may engage in affirming responses to elements in the expression of LGB identities. The therapist not only recognises and values an LGB identity, but also uses positive affirmation to directly ameliorate the effects of heterosexism.

What I call ethically affirmative therapy is also usually termed gay affirmative therapy in the literature (Hancock, 1995; Perez, DeBord and Bieschke, 2000). However, the two forms of therapy should be distinguished because ethically affirmative therapy is nothing more than ethically appropriate therapy with LGB clients. That is, any practitioner engaging with clients who are lesbian, gay or bisexual should be practicing in accordance with these guidelines if their practice is ethical. This is the case with humanistic and existential therapies, where most practitioners need little more than education and information about the specific needs of LGB clients and communities.

For example, while Hancock (1995) and Perez et al. (2000) refer to their therapeutic work as gay affirmative therapy, none[5] of them specifically advocate significant theoretical and/or technical modifications to the therapeutic process. Instead, these authors highlight the many problems that resulted in poor practice with LGB clients in the past and provide thoughtful suggestions, based on empirical research, for improving practice.[6] It is appropriate to term this practice ethically affirmative, rather than gay affirmative, because, arguably, it is unethical to practice with LGB clients without knowledge of the kind provided by these authors. Within this form of practice, a gay identity may be valued equally with a heterosexual identity but it is not affirmed in the sense of being strengthened, supported or made firm. To take such a stance would require significant modifications to practice that enable and encourage the therapist to directly tackle the impact of heterosexism and homonegativity in ways that foster the development of LGB identities and behaviours.

LGB Affirmative Therapy

Davies (1996), drawing on Clark (1987), presented one of the earliest, and probably the clearest, statements about what is entailed in gay affirmative therapy for UK therapists. Davies (1996) begins by outlining what he terms the core condition of respect. This includes respect for the personal integrity of the client, respect for lifestyle and culture of the client and respectful attitudes and beliefs from the therapist. These conditions raise similar expectations to the ethically affirmative therapies described above. It is when Davies draws on and advocates Clark's (1987) "Twelve Guidelines for Retraining" and "Ground Rules for Helping" that he presents a strong LGB affirmative therapy (see Table 1) that is distinct from ethically affirmative practice.

Clearly, many of the guidelines presented in Davies (1996) make sense in the context of any ethical therapy with LGB clients. There are, however, a few guidelines which are controversial and which some therapists (Cross, 2001; du Plock, 1997; Goldenberg, 2000) find irreconcilable with existential and humanistic theoretical orientations. These include Davies's 11th and 12th recommendations, that the therapist actively encourage and affirm LGB thoughts and feelings and attempt to reduce clients' feelings of shame and guilt. Davies's aim is for the therapist to use his or her authority to try to counter the internalised homonegative values of society. This is clearly a more active strategy for affirmation than ethically affirmative therapies. All of Davies's guidelines used together are intended to produce a strong affirmative therapy, which not only recognises an LGB identity but also positively encourages such an identity. He goes on to suggest that an affirmative therapist should also fulfil an educative role with LGB clients, especially concerning HIV awareness and safety issues. Davies argues that affirmative therapists should introduce discussions of safety issues with their clients.

TABLE 1. Summary of Guidelines for LGB Affirmative Practice from Clark (1987)

1. Therapists need to interrogate themselves for their own LGB feelings.

2. Do not enter into arrangements which imply LGB identities to be pathological or undesirable.

3. Recognise and work with the oppression all LGB people have experienced.

4. Work to deprogramme internalised stereotypes of LGB people.

5. Work to explore awareness of feelings, especially anger, amongst LGB clients.

6. Actively support body-self and body impulses.

7. Encourage the development of a LGB support network.

8. Support LGB clients in engaging in consciousness raising activities.

9. Work towards a peer relationship with the LGB client.

10. Encourage the LGB clients to develop their own valuing system, mindful of the risk of relying on society's systems for self-validation.

11. Work to lessen shame and guilt around LGB thoughts and feelings.

12. Use the weight of your authority to affirm LGB thoughts and feelings.

Note: The guidelines of Clark listed above are from Davies (1996). In producing this edited list of recommendations for gay affirmative practice, the language of Clark (1987), and, to a lesser extent, Davies (1996), has been modified to better reflect current terminology about sexuality.

More recently, Ritter and Terndrup (2002) have offered comprehensive guidelines for gay affirmative practice with LGB clients, predominantly based on empirical research. The affirmative nature of their practice is most obvious when examining their suggestions for psychotherapeutic interventions. They recommend working to reduce feelings of stigma related to difference, validating probable identities, recognising the reality of heterosexist oppression and encouraging pride in such identities. In addition, the authors recommend providing information and education on LGB communities/resources, relationship formation and sexuality.[7]

Criticism of Affirmative Therapy

LGB affirmative therapies are not entirely without their critics. While those discussed here support and value ethical and equal practice with LGB clients, they have nevertheless voiced theoretical criticisms of the notion that humanistic and existential psychotherapies should actively encourage LGB identities and their behavioural sequelae. For example, du Plock (1997), Cross (2001) and Goldenberg (2000) all voice similar concerns about the risk of affirmative therapies restricting a client's power to work through and create their own meaning within the therapeutic relationship. One of their concerns is that gay affirmative therapies might limit and prematurely foreclose the sexual identity work of an LGB client.

These criticisms derive from a belief in the central role of therapeutic neutrality in existential and humanistic psychotherapeutic practice. These therapies encourage the therapist to adopt a naïve attitude and to approach a client with an open mind and questioning stance.[8] Existential and humanistic therapists therefore find advocating or affirming *anything* in advance of encountering a particular client to be at odds with the foundations of their therapeutic theories. As Cross (2001) puts it, "the construction of self can only be impoverished when derived from a role manufactured external to the individual, however enlightened or liberal that role may appear" (p. 337).

THEORETICAL FRAMEWORK AND DEFENCE OF AFFIRMATIVE THERAPY

Whilst authors advocating an LGB affirmative approach have made a clear practical case for such practice (e.g., Milton, 2000a, 2000b), they have not answered the theoretical criticisms above. Is there a theoretical incompatibility between LGB affirmative practice and existential and humanistic therapies? What follows are some arguments in favour of LGB affirmative practice which take into account the impact of heterosexism on LGB individuals as well as the need to recognise the power of the social world. This is followed by a theoretical defence of LGB affirmative practice and the presentation of a model of LGB affirmative practice that draws on the hermeneutic phenomenology of Paul Ricoeur.

Countering the Pervasive Power of Heterosexism and Internalised Homonegativity

One of the leading figures in UK existential psychotherapy, Ernesto Spinelli (1996), has attempted to develop an existential theory of sexuality. Toward this end, he emphasises the "chosen" nature of sexuality. He draws on Isay's (1989) arguments about gay children experiencing a sense of "otherness" and extends this idea to heterosexuality. Whilst

Spinelli (1989) is persuasive in his arguments against a bio-reproductive basis for human sexuality, he, like Cross (2001) and du Plock (1997), underemphasizes the role of social forces in the construction of sexualities. Whilst one may choose one's identity, this choice is not equally clear or easy, particularly if the sexuality one is choosing is condemned by the social world into which one is thrown (Heidegger, 1962).[9] The "otherness" described by Isay may be experienced by heterosexual individuals if, for instance, they express particular dissident sexualities (such as a sadomasochistic sexual identity). However, by and large, their heterosexuality is the "ground," rather than the "figure" in their sexual being-in-the-world.

This is not the case with lesbian, gay or bisexual identities, where feelings of otherness require a decision to confront or deny that which the individual discovers and/or creates in him- or herself. Nor is this decision a simple or easy one when an individual finds him- or herself in a world in which people are routinely condemned for expressing the very same sexual identity. The impact of heterosexism and homonegativity on people who are lesbian, gay or bisexual is well-documented (see Ritter and Terndrup, 2002). These attitudes have an adverse impact on the psychosocial development of lesbians, gay men and bisexuals. The negativity associated with prejudice can be internalised and directly turned against the self, even in the absence of an external aggressor or oppressor (Malyon, 1982). This internalised homonegativity has also been conceptualized as a universal developmental outcome for lesbians, gay men and bisexuals (Shidlo, 1994).

In light of these environmental forces, it is unrealistic (and perhaps even unethical) to expect an LGB client to do all of the work of countering such prejudice alone. The impact of the social world on clients and their perception of their sexuality cannot and must not be underestimated. The therapist is in a uniquely privileged position to directly have an impact on the world of another person in an affirmative way. Through the direct affirmation of LGB identities, therapists can work with clients by helping them to resist the external and internal homonegativity they inevitably encounter.

Ricoeur's Hermeneutic Phenomenology and the Critique of the Illusions of the Subject

Ricoeur is one of the leading living phenomenological philosophers (Clark, 1990). Whilst his work (1974, 1981, 1984, 1985, 1988, 1992) is primarily concerned with interpreting text, his theory of interpretation may be relevant for understanding and elaborating the therapeutic process (Langdridge, 2004; van Deurzen, 1997). Ricoeur's theory of interpretation can be applied to the therapeutic encounter to make a theoretical case for LGB affirmative therapy within existential and humanistic practice. His work is grounded in an existential phenomenological tradition, which forms the foundation of both existential and humanistic theory and practice. It also recognises and values much that is already present in existential and humanistic theories, so it is not necessary to substantially re-work these theories. Finally, his work provides a way of moving between the neutrality of existential and humanistic therapies and the demands of gay affirmative therapy to provide a direct, politically motivated, corrective to the homonegativity encountered by LGB people in this late modern world.

Ricoeur (1981) calls *appropriation* the means by which we attempt to explicate meaning. However, this is not a simple task, for we inevitably struggle against cultural distance and possibly historical alienation. That is, when attempting to understand what a client means, one is often, though not always, faced with the twin difficulty of understanding the client from the standpoint of a different culture and/or period in history. Appropriation is the act of capturing the meaning being expressed by a client, but not necessarily through identification of the intentions of the client.[10] The purpose of appropriation is to gain an understanding of a client's world. This is not done from the perspective of being "inside" the client, and seeing the world as he or she does, but from the perspective of being "in front of" him or her in a way that expands the therapist's own way of seeing the world. A therapist needs to understand the client both at "face-value," as one does in any phenomenological encounter, and also through the use of a hermeneutic, or method of interpretation, which enables the therapist to see beyond the surface to hidden meanings beyond.

In contrast to Gadamer (1975), Ricoeur does not simply believe that expanding knowledge entails capturing meaning at "face-value." Instead, Ricoeur believes that empathy and suspicion are both necessary for the appropriation of meaning. He identifies two essential approaches for understanding meaning: a *demythologising* (or empathic) element and a *demystifying* (or suspicious) element. Demythologising is the process of empathic engagement where a therapist seeks to identify meaning through a fusion of horizons. One engages with the client bringing one's own *pre-understanding* (Heidegger, 1962), one's own way of seeing the world, into play.[11]

The demystifying moment, in contrast, is one of suspicion. It is a revolutionary act where one seeks to identify the meaning hidden beneath the surface–for here the real significance of a client's discourse is never immediate and transparent. Ricoeur (1970) identifies Freud, Marx and Nietzsche as the three "masters of suspicion." With each of them, meaning is never apparent, but instead lies beneath the surface in need of unmasking. Their hermeneutics of suspicion extended to uncovering unconscious motivation, economic modes of production, and the will to power, respectively.[12]

Another key idea is the critique of what Ricoeur refers to as the *illusions of the subject*. Ricoeur is careful to recognise the potential errors of interpretation of appropriation and provides a corrective in his work. The principal error that may occur is in understanding appropriation as a form of subjectivism (or subjectivist existentialism) in which the therapist's subjectivity is projected onto the client. Here, the worldview of the therapist dominates that of the client through the active projection of the therapist's way of *being-in-the-world* onto the client. Whilst existential and humanistic therapies prize their neutrality, it is naïve of the critics of affirmative therapies to think it possible to speak from "nowhere." One always speaks from "somewhere" and the mechanism through which this error is corrected involves subjecting the subject itself to a hermeneutic critique; that is, turning the hermeneutic (method of interpretation) of choice onto the therapist first and foremost.[13]

The case being made here is that it is necessary to engage in a multi-layered (empathic and suspicious) analysis of all discourse.[14] That is, both client and therapist should be subjected to a demythologising (or empathic) process and a demystifying (or suspicious) process. By recognising the therapist's own role in recovering meaning within the therapeutic encounter and then putting this forward for criticism along with the interpretation of the client, the client should him/herself act as co-critic of the illusions of subjectivity. Should too much of the therapist be projected into the therapeutic encounter, a sceptical client will not find the meaning-recollection persuasive or resonant. Too little and the therapist and client may find themselves limited to an empathic engagement with little or no suspicion about the client or social world into which both are thrown.

A Hermeneutic of Choice

If one accepts the need to critique the illusions of the subject and to subject the client to a hermeneutic of suspicion as well as a hermeneutic of meaning-recollection, then the question arises about what specific hermeneutic should be employed in such work? The most obvious hermeneutic for LGB affirmative practice would be one grounded in existing LGB (affirmative) theory and research that seeks to identify successful outcomes for LGB individuals. Empirical research on the experience of living as a lesbian, gay man or bisexual is increasing and provides a possible framework for a theory of affirmative practice.

What would this mean in clinical practice? The most important research underlying affirmative practice concerns itself with the effects of heterosexism on LGB people and their mental health. Heterosexism and negative stereotyping affect all LGB men and women and their impact can be profound and damaging (DiPlacido, 1998; Herek, Cogan and Gillis, 2000; Shidlo, 1994). Heterosexism can lead to a sense of victimisation, social withdrawal, anxiety, denial of group membership and a self-hating dominant group identification (Ritter and Terndrup, 2002). An affirmative therapist will directly challenge negative self-attributions and encouragingly affirm positive self-attributions about a person's sexual identity. Attention will also need to be paid to the risks of withdrawal and denial of group membership. The evidence is clear that satisfaction with one's sexual identity is positively correlated with openness around one's sexual identity, especially with one's own family (Brown, 1989). However, many LGB people feel considerable anxiety over the risks of coming-out and may instead "strike a devil's bargain in which a stilted or distant relationship is weighed against the possibility of no relationship at all" (Brown, 1989, p. 67).[15]

A gay affirmative therapist will need to tread a careful balance here, between affirmation of the benefits of coming-out versus the risks of such a strategy for a particular client. It would generally be advisable to ensure that clients have sufficient support networks in place before taking the risk of coming-out to their parents, that they are aware of the possibility of negative as well as positive responses, and that they know how best to deal with any negativity that they might encounter. There is much more work to be done to adequately realise the ways an affirmative therapist might best use the available LGB literature within the therapeutic process and this is something that those who choose to work from this perspective might seek to explore further.

A more comprehensive survey of affirmative techniques can be found in Ritter and Terndrup's *Handbook of Affirmative Therapy* (2002). There they provide a comprehensive review of the relevant literature for working with LGB clients and propose a framework for LGB affirmative therapy that builds on these findings. They outline a five-phase therapeutic process for affirmative therapists engaged with clients struggling with their sexual identities. They describe likely client behaviours and also suggested psychotherapeutic interventions based on the available literature.

For instance, in phase 1, they suggest that a client might talk about feeling socially different, alienated and alone. They suggest the therapist empathise with the feelings of alienation and fear and actively attempt to destigmatise feeling socially different. The phases build progressively towards the affirmation of a positive lesbian, gay or bisexual identity where the client feels pride in his/her new identity, recognition of heterosexist oppression, and identification with marginalized others. Use of LGB affirmative research in this way informs practice and provides a method of interpretation that informs therapist choice about which aspects of a client's identity work they might need to affirm within the therapeutic process. The hermeneutic for LGB affirmative practice in this case is one founded on a liberationist politics of respect for difference which seeks to encourage and value LGB identities.

An alternative to the hermeneutic discussed above, one that is arguably more radical,[16] would be to engage a queer hermeneutic within the therapeutic process. That is, one would expose oneself (through a critique of the illusions of subjectivity) and one's clients (through a hermeneutic of suspicion) to a critique from queer theory (Butler, 1991; Fuss, 1991; Sedgwick, 1991). There is inadequate space for a thorough discussion of queer theory and its contested meanings here (see Clarke and Peel, 2007).[17] However, in brief, and for purposes of these arguments, queer theory concerns itself with providing a challenge to fixed identities: heterosexual, bisexual and homosexual alike. The notion of a stable sexual subject is contested and traditional identity politics are challenged as forms of disciplinary regulation. A stable homosexual subject consolidates a heterosexual-homosexual binary, which reinforces particular sexual and social boundaries. Instead it is argued that identities are always multiple and unstable.

Incorporating a queer hermeneutic therefore provides a radical challenge to LGB affirmative (and non-affirmative) practice. There would not be a simple focus on affirming LGB identities but an affirmation of a dynamic notion of identity where sexual subject positions remain contingent and intersect with other psychosocial subject positions. It would be important therefore to encourage a critical questioning of fixed desire in the therapist and client alike with "homo- or bisexual" and "heterosexual" clients. The therapeutic process becomes more clearly political and radical.[18]

It is important, however, that therapists remain mindful of their professional roles and the risk of projecting their subjectivities onto their clients. An LGB or queer critique should not distract existential and humanistic therapists from the main business of appropriating meaning from a client within an empathic phenomenological framework. The client's needs must not be subjugated to those of the therapist's particular political framework. Whilst this is a risk for all affirmative therapies, in many ways this risk may be greatest with a queer affirmative framework. The majority of LGB people may embrace a relatively fixed notion of sexual identity, and a queer therapist will need to be careful to recognise and value this position equally with a more dynamic notion of sexual identity, even when challenging the need for fixed and stable identities themselves.

NOTES

1. Lesbian, gay and bisexual (LGB) people are referred to throughout this paper, but the exclusion of transgendered (T) individuals is recognised. This is simply because the arguments concern existing affirmative practice which has been predominantly concerned with LGB and not T clients. However, the arguments for gay affirmative therapy could be, and should be, extended to transgender affirmative practice.

2. Whilst I recognise that, particularly in the US, existential psychotherapy is generally considered part of the humanistic psychotherapy movement, I distinguish (linguistically) between humanistic and existential psychotherapies in this paper. This is not because I wish to argue strongly that the two traditions should be separated but because I wish simply to respect the strong distinction made between the humanistic and existential psychotherapies in the UK.

3. I recognise the growth in affirmative therapy within other therapeutic orientations but choose to concentrate on humanistic and existential psychotherapies here. This is for a number of reasons. First, different orientations stem from very different theoretical traditions and due to the constraint on space it would be impossible to do justice to them all. Second, and perhaps most importantly, the majority of affirmative practice and discussion around these issues in the UK concerns these particular therapeutic orientations.

4. I say "full sense" here since many psychotherapists have and continue to argue that their practice is ethical when engaged in practices that treat LGB clients and their identities in a lesser way than heterosexual clients. I would argue that for any practice to be considered ethical (in the full sense of the term), it must value and respect all client groups equally.

5. With the exception of Fassinger (2000) who discusses the pros and cons of a number of therapeutic orientations, including systems-cultural approaches which incorporate social and political critiques within the therapeutic process.

6. The authors cover issues such as the impact of homophobia and heterosexism, coming out, identity issues and so on. This form of practice is characterised as that which "challenges the traditional view that homosexual desire and fixed homosexual orientations are pathological" (Malyon, 1982, p. 69, in Hancock, 1995, p. 407).

7. There are many similarities between the gay affirmative therapy of Davies (1996) and that of Ritter and Terndrup (2002), most especially concerning the active affirmation of, even simply probable, LGB identities and behaviours.

8. Person-centred therapists, for instance, traditionally demonstrate unconditional acceptance and attempt to enter a client's frame of reference in order to understand the world from their perspective (Nelson-Jones, 1982). Existential therapists attempt to bracket off their preconceptions and understand the unique way of *being-in-the-world* (Heidegger, 1962) of their clients (van Deurzen, 1997).

9. *Thrownness*, for Heidegger (1962), refers to the way in which we find ourselves in the world with a past that provides us with conventions that enable us to live our life. We are usually unaware of the conventions that frame our experience of the world but the particular sense of being thrown into the world may be revealed through our *attunement*, or our way of finding ourselves thrust into the world.

10. This may be approximated, but through "a fusion of horizons" (Gadamer, 1975) in which knowledge of ourselves is expanded through engagement with the other.

11. This approach originally stems from biblical exegesis where scholars attempted to understand the divine intention behind scripture, but now principally revolves around a notion of the phenomenology of empathy (or meaning-recollection) exemplified in Gadamer's (1975) work.

12. Ricoeur believed these three "masters" demonstrated the inadequacy of gaining understanding through immediate consciousness alone (meaning-recollection)–the project of transcendental phenomenology and of course existential and humanistic psychotherapies.

13. Heidegger (1962) and Ricoeur (1981) both argue that even when attempting to bracket our preconceptions we speak from somewhere, we always occupy an ideological position even if we are unaware of it.

14. Ricoeur sees the critique of subjectivity operating from either a Marxist or Freudian perspective and effectively constitutes a modern form of the critique of "prejudice." Here Marxism and/or Freudianism are not used as frameworks for interpretation but as ways of enabling self-criticism of the therapist. Whilst Ricoeur recognises Freud, Marx and Nietzsche as the masters of suspicion, he does not argue that it is necessary to incorporate such essentialist hermeneutics as psychoanalysis or Marxism into phenomenological practice. These particular hermeneutics of suspicion result in excessive constraints being placed upon the recovery of buried meaning, which is at odds with the existential tradition in which Ricoeur was working.

15. Brown further suggested that problems with internalised homonegativity are likely even where individuals claim they are happy with their familial relationships.

16. I say arguably more radical because there is considerable controversy over the queering of sexual identities and consequent dissolution of sexual identity categories. In this late modern world where identity categories are particularly important, there is no doubt that any attempt to move beyond such categories is radical. Whether this is de-

sirable is another matter and one which each LGB or Q therapist must decide for him-
or herself.

17. See Seidman (1996) for an introduction and discussion from a social scientific
perspective.

18. Although, it is worth noting that in their discussions of schizophrenia, Deleuze
and Guattari (1984) argue that all psychotherapy is inherently political, being marginal, subversive and even potentially revolutionary. Even if therapists choose not to
affirm the exploration of sexual identities by a client it could be argued that they are
making a political choice: a choice for a traditional, arguably conservative, sexual ideology. Advocating a queer position of course recognises a very particular political
quality to one's therapeutic practice, similar to feminist and multicultural systems-cultural therapies (see Fassinger, 2000).

REFERENCES

Bayer, R. (1981), *Homosexuality and American Psychiatry: The Politics of Diagnosis*.
    New York: Basic Books.
Brown, L.S. (1989), Lesbians, gay men and their families: Common clinical issues. *J.
    Gay & Lesbian Psychotherapy*, 1(1): 65-77.
Brown, L.S. (2000), Foreword. In: *Handbook of Counseling and Psychotherapy with
    Lesbian, Gay, and Bisexual Clients*, eds. R.M. Perez, K.A. DeBord & K.J.
    Bieschke. Washington, DC: American Psychological Association, pp. xi-xiii.
Buhrke, R.A. (1989), Incorporating lesbian and gay issues into counselor training: A
    resource guide. *J. Counseling & Development*, 68: 77-80.
Butler, J. (1991), *Gender Trouble*. New York: Routledge.
Carl, D. (1990), *Counseling Same-Sex Couples*. New York: Norton.
Clark, D. (1987), *The New Loving Someone Gay*. Berkeley, CA: Celestial Arts.
Clark, S.H. (1990), *Paul Ricoeur*. London: Routledge.
Clarke, V. & Peel E. (2007), From lesbian and gay psychology to LGBTQ psycholo-
    gies: A journey into the unknown (or unknowable)? In: Out in Psychology: Lesbian,
    Gay, Bisexual, Trans and Queer Perspectives, eds. V. Clarke & E. Peel. Chicester:
    Wiley, pp. 11-35.
Cross, M.C. (2001), The appropriation and reification of deviance: Personal construct
    psychology and affirmative therapy. A response to Harrison. *British J. Guidance &
    Counselling*, 29(3): 337-343.
Davies, D. (1996), Towards a model of gay affirmative therapy. In: *Pink Therapy: A
    Guide for Counsellors and Therapists Working with Lesbian, Gay and Bisexual Cli-
    ents*, eds. D. Davies & C. Neal. Buckingham: Open University Press, pp. 24-40.
Davies, D. & Neal, C., eds. (1996), *Pink Therapy: A Guide for Counsellors and Thera-
    pists Working with Lesbian, Gay and Bisexual Clients*. Buckingham: Open Univer-
    sity Press.
Davies, D. & Neal, C., eds. (2000), *Pink Therapy 2: Therapeutic Perspectives on
    Working with Lesbian, Gay and Bisexual Clients*. Buckingham: Open University
    Press.
Deleuze, G. & Guattari, F. (1984), *Anti-Oedipus: Capitalism and Schizophrenia*. London:
    The Athlone Press.

DiPlacido, J. (1998), Minority stress among lesbians, gay men, and bisexuals: A consequence of heterosexism, homophobia, and stigmatisation. In: *Stigma and Sexual Orientation: Understanding Prejudice Against Lesbians, Gay Men, and Bisexuals*, ed. G.M. Herek. Thousand Oaks, CA: Sage, pp. 138-159.

Drescher, J. (1998), *Psychoanalytic Therapy and the Gay Man*. Hillsdale, NJ: The Analytic Press.

du Plock, S. (1997), Sexual misconceptions: A critique of gay affirmative therapy and some thoughts on an existential-phenomenological theory of sexual orientation. *J. Society for Existential Analysis*, 8(2): 56-71.

Fassinger, R.E. (2000), Applying counseling theories to lesbian, gay, and bisexual clients: Pitfalls and possibilities. In: *Handbook of Counseling and Psychotherapy with Lesbian, Gay, and Bisexual Clients*, eds. R.M. Perez, K.A. DeBord & K.J. Bieschke. Washington, DC: American Psychological Association, pp. 107-131.

Fuss, D., ed. (1991), *Inside/Out*. New York: Routledge.

Gadamer, H. (1975), *Truth and Method*. London: Sheed and Ward.

Goldenberg, H. (2000), A response to Martin Milton. *J. Society for Existential Analysis*, 11(1): 103-105.

Greene, B. & Herek, G.M., eds. (1994), *Lesbian and Gay Psychology: Theory, Research and Clinical Applications*. Newbury Park, CA: Sage.

Hancock, K.A. (1995), Psychotherapy with Lesbians and Gay Men. In: *Lesbian, Gay, and Bisexual Identities Over the Lifespan: Psychological Perspectives*, eds. A.R. D'Augelli & C.J. Patterson. Oxford: Oxford University Press, pp. 398-432.

Heidegger, M. (1962), *Being and Time*. Trans. J. Macquarrie & E. Robinson. Oxford: Blackwell.

Herek, G.M., Cogan, J.C. & Gillis, J.R. (2000), *Psychological Well-Being and Commitment to Lesbian, Gay, and Bisexual Identities*. Paper presented at the 108th annual meeting of the American Psychological Association, Washington, DC.

Isay, R.A. (1989), *Being Homosexual: Gay Men and Their Development*. New York: Avon Books.

Langdridge, D. (2004), The hermeneutic phenomenology of Paul Ricoeur: Problems and possibilities for existential-phenomenological psychotherapy. *Existential Analysis*, 15(2): 243-255.

Malyon, A.K. (1982), Psychotherapeutic implications of internalised homophobia in gay men. In: *Homosexuality and Psychotherapy: A Practitioner's Handbook of Affirmative Models*, ed. J.C. Gonsiorek. Binghamton, NY: The Haworth Press, Inc., pp. 59-69.

Milton, M. (2000a), Is existential psychotherapy a lesbian and gay affirmative therapy? *J. Society for Existential Analysis*, 11(1): 86-102.

Milton, M. (2000b), Existential-phenomenological therapy. In: *Pink Therapy 2: Therapeutic Perspectives on Working with Lesbian, Gay and Bisexual Clients*, eds. D. Davies & C. Neal. Buckingham: Open University Press. pp. 39-53.

Nakajima, G.A. (2003), The emergence of an international lesbian, gay, and bisexual psychiatric movement. *J. Gay & Lesbian Psychotherapy*, 7(1/2): 165-188. Reprinted in: *The Mental Health Professions and Homosexuality: International Perspectives*, eds. V. Lingiardi & J. Drescher. New York: The Haworth Press, Inc., pp. 165-188.

Neal, C. & Davies, D., eds. (2000), *Pink Therapy 3: Issues in Therapy with Lesbian, Gay, Bisexual and Transgender Clients*. Buckingham: Open University Press.

Nelson-Jones, R. (1982), *The Theory and Practice of Counselling Psychology*. London: Cassell.

Perez, R.M., DeBord, K.A. & Bieschke, K.J., eds. (2000), *Handbook of Counseling and Psychotherapy with Lesbian, Gay, and Bisexual Clients*. Washington, DC: American Psychological Association.

Ricoeur, P. (1970), *Freud and Philosophy: An Essay on Interpretation*. Trans. D. Savage. New Haven, CT: Yale University Press.

Ricoeur, P. (1974), *The Conflict of Interpretations*. ed. D. Ihde. Evanston, IL: Northwestern University Press.

Ricoeur, P. (1981), *Hermeneutics and the Human Sciences*. Edited and Trans. J.B. Thompson. Cambridge: Cambridge University Press.

Ricoeur, P. (1984), *Time and Narrative Volume 1*. Trans. K. McLaughlin & D. Pellauer. Chicago, IL: University of Chicago Press.

Ricoeur, P. (1985), *Time and Narrative Volume 2*. Trans. K. McLaughlin & D. Pellauer. Chicago, IL: University of Chicago Press.

Ricoeur, P. (1988), *Time and Narrative Volume 3*. Trans. K. McLaughlin & D. Pellauer. Chicago, IL: University of Chicago Press.

Ricoeur, P. (1992), *Oneself as Another*. Trans. K. Blamey. Chicago, IL: University of Chicago Press.

Ritter, K.Y. & Terndrup, A.I. (2002), *Handbook of Affirmative Psychotherapy with Lesbians and Gay Men*. New York: The Guilford Press.

Sedgwick, E. (1991), *The Epistemology of the Closet*. Berkeley, CA: University of California Press.

Seidman, S., ed. (1996), *Queer Theory/Sociology*. Oxford: Blackwell.

Shidlo, A. (1994), Internalized homophobia: Conceptual and empirical issues in measurement. In: *Lesbian and Gay Psychology: Theory, Research, and Clinical Applications*, eds. B. Greene & G.M. Herek. Thousand Oaks, CA: Sage, pp. 176-205.

Spinelli, E. (1996), Some hurried notes expressing outline ideas that someone might someday utilise as signposts towards a sketch of an existential-phenomenological theory of human sexuality. *J. Society for Existential Analysis*, 8(1): 2-20.

Stein, T.S. & Cohen, C.J., eds. (1986), *Contemporary Perspectives on Psychotherapy with Lesbians and Gay Men*. New York: Plenum Publishing.

Van Deurzen, E. (1997), *Everyday Mysteries: Existential Dimensions of Psychotherapy*. London: Routledge.

doi:10.1300/J236v11n01_03

Being Sexual:
Existential Contributions to Psychotherapy with Gay Male Clients

Martin Milton, CPsychol, AFBPsS, UKCP Reg

SUMMARY. This paper outlines the existential-phenomenological (E-P) approach to psychotherapy and considers some of its core concepts, the stance taken to understanding sexuality and the implications for therapeutic practice with gay male clients. Three previously published case studies are reviewed to provide illustrations of the approach, and the paper concludes by arguing that a non-pathologising view of sexuality is useful in assisting clients in therapy and in assisting therapists and services in understanding their clients without problematising them. doi:10.1300/J236v11n01_04 *[Article copies available for a fee from The Haworth Document Delivery Service: 1-800-HAWORTH. E-mail address: <docdelivery@haworthpress.com> Website: <http://www.HaworthPress.com> © 2007 by The Haworth Press, Inc. All rights reserved.]*

KEYWORDS. Authenticity, construction, Dasein, embodiment, existential, freedom, gay, HIV, homosexuality, phenomenological, psychotherapy, sexual minority

Martin Milton is Senior Lecturer at the University of Surrey and a psychologist specialising in psychotherapy in independent practice.

Address correspondence to: Martin Milton, Department of Psychology, School of Human Sciences, University of Surrey, Guildford, Surrey, GU2 7XH, UK (E-mail: M.Milton@Surrey.ac.uk).

[Haworth co-indexing entry note]: "Being Sexual: Existential Contributions to Psychotherapy with Gay Male Clients." Milton, Martin. Co-published simultaneously in *Journal of Gay & Lesbian Psychotherapy* (The Haworth Medical Press, an imprint of The Haworth Press, Inc.) Vol. 11, No. 1/2, 2007, pp. 45-59; and: *British Lesbian, Gay, and Bisexual Psychologies: Theory, Research, and Practice* (ed: Elizabeth Peel, Victoria Clarke, and Jack Drescher) The Haworth Medical Press, an imprint of The Haworth Press, Inc., 2007, pp. 45-59. Single or multiple copies of this article are available for a fee from The Haworth Document Delivery Service [1-800-HAWORTH, 9:00 a.m. - 5:00 p.m. (EST). E-mail address: docdelivery@haworthpress.com].

INTRODUCTION

As indicated by the May 2004 conference of the Association of Gay and Lesbian Psychiatrists (AGLP) in New York, the debate on psychotherapeutic understandings of gay sexuality continues worldwide (see also reflections from Malta [Bartolo and Borg, 2003], the UK [Davies and Neal, 1996; O'Connor and Ryan, 1993], the US [Isay, 1989; Domenici and Lesser, 1995; Drescher, D'Ercole and Schoenberg, 2003] and Europe [Steffens and Biechele, 2001]). This paper takes up this debate and suggests a contribution that existential-phenomenological (E-P) psychotherapy can make to our understandings of sexuality and the practice of psychotherapy.

While E-P psychotherapy can be used fruitfully in work with a range of sexual minority clients, this paper will focus primarily on work with gay male clients.[1] Before reflecting on the contribution of E-P therapy[2] to client work, this paper will briefly review some of the core concepts underpinning the approach. Readers are referred to other summaries of the existential approach such as Cooper (2003), Spinelli (1989, 1996), du Plock (1997) and Van Deurzen (2002).

EXISTENTIAL-PHENOMENOLOGICAL PSYCHOTHERAPY

Existential-phenomenological psychotherapy is rooted in existential philosophy and phenomenology as much as it is in other therapeutic disciplines.

Existentialism

As a philosophy, existentialism is concerned with the subjective, personal dimension of human existence and it describes the distinctively human mode of being, the ontological "givens" of existence and the clarification of what it means to be alive (Van Deurzen-Smith, 1995). Unlike other therapeutic perspectives used in the British public sector, existential psychotherapy is not concerned with essentialist and compartmentalised views of the person. In broad strokes, an essentialist view of the person assumes that people (and sub-groups of people) can be understood as having a particular nature and this determines what they are, what they can and cannot do (Burr, 1995). An E-P perspective sees people and the challenge of living as an attempt to find a balance between possibility and necessity and, in the process, become "true" to oneself (rather than to just one view of people or a particular sub-group). This has to be considered in relation to the specific contexts in which the individual lives. Thus, an engagement with the struggles and imperfections of life directly facilitates the process of establishing one's own values and sense of self-empowerment (Van Deurzen-Smith, 1997).

The concept of *Dasein* (roughly translated as "Being-in-the-world") is central to the approach. This term stems from a belief that a human being is always *in* the world and always *with* others. Consequently, existential-phenomenology and social constructionism share beliefs regarding the co-construction of experience and the situatedness of existence. In turn, *Authenticity* requires of Dasein a recognition of–and an engagement with–one's limitations such as the ultimate "being-towards-death" (Heidegger, 1927). Authenticity in this regard does not refer to an oft-used sense of being true to some pre-assigned inner "person."[3] By contrast, *Inauthenticity* is seen as a particular response to the anxiety of confronting the world in as open a manner as is possible and is marked by a resignation to convention, conformity and duty, i.e., by doing what people imagine is expected of them (Van Deurzen-Smith, 1988).

According to Sartre (1943), the concepts of choice and freedom in human existence allow us to recognise that, to some degree, we always choose what we become through our actions, which in turn determine our possibilities for the future. Choice and possibility are influenced (or limited) by the contexts within which we are situated. Sartre further contended that humans have no fixed essence but only existence; we exist first and in the process of our existence have to create ourselves. This suggests that we are born into particular worlds and have to generate our own meanings and practices alongside those of others in these worlds. In order to escape from the anxiety of the uncertainty of our nature, we act at being something definite and "fixed" (essentially a nothing pretending to be a something) through a state of "bad faith" or self-deception.

Phenomenology

Phenomenology refers to the study of phenomena (the appearance of things) as they present to our consciousness (Spinelli, 1989). From this perspective, the "reality" that each of us experiences is the result of an inseparable interaction between the raw matter of the physical world and our consciousness of it; our own "reality" is a phenomenal one open to a multiplicity of interpretations and meanings.[4] A phenomenological approach is useful in reconsidering the different experiences of gay sexuality. These experiences are diverse, there being a plethora of self (and social) representations of being attracted to members of one's own gender: e.g., gay person, queer, poof, etc.

Existential-phenomenological psychotherapy therefore concerns itself with how the "givens" of human existence (death, anxiety, meaninglessness, isolation, choice, freedom and responsibility) are negotiated through the interpretations and meanings given to experience–to self, others, the world and our values–and how in turn, this shapes one's sense of reality. Thus it regards all forms of human dilemma, tragedy and suffering (from the normative to the extraordinary) as fundamentally problems about "Being-in-the-world," rather than intrinsic optimal or pathological development.[5] As far as is possible, meaning that is generated through experience is derived from the person's frame of reference and not from the observer's interpretative frame. In the field of psychotherapy, this allows different insights to be explored and thus is useful for a range of client groups–whether one is a gay man in San Francisco with a support network or a refugee from Central Africa feeling isolated in inner London. An E-P perspective recognises that all forms of sexuality are unique, but that identities are developed through the co-construction of meaning. Identities may be useful but they may inevitably fail to capture the richness of the lived experience.

This perspective treats the therapeutic encounter as an invitation for the client to confront and clarify the meaning of what is understood as life's inherent anxieties. It avoids medicalization of the client's problem; any attempt to "cure" people of their experiences or many other aspects of their self would involve "curing" them of life itself (Van Deurzen-Smith, 1988).

In an E-P approach, the therapeutic process is one where the client is assisted in making explicit, beliefs, views and assumptions which have remained implicit and unacknowledged in the development and maintenance of their difficulties (Spinelli, 1994; Strasser, 1999; Strasser and Strasser, 1997). This process involves some degree of challenging, where inconsistencies, contradictions and paradoxes between the client's thinking, feeling and behaviour are noted, pointed out to the client, allowing clarification and exploration. Thus, attending to the experiential lived reality of the client and the ways in which his or her life and sense of self has become confusing, distressing or fragmented, retains a focus upon the complexities of the client's struggles with life. The goal is to allow flexibility, encourage attunement and verification.

To facilitate the exploration of existence, there are three basic principles of the existential-phenomenological method. *Epoche* refers to the setting aside of one's initial assumptions, biases and prejudices within the therapeutic encounter. For example, this would mean accepting that a therapist does not know how a particular "gay" client understands himself as a sexual being, makes sense of his sexual experiences and his entire sense of self. The second principle is one of *description*. When engaging with clients, the therapist aims to facilitate a detailed description of the client's events, experiences and beliefs so that meanings may be identified. Each descriptive element of an event or experience is subjected to the third principle of *horizontalization*, which asks therapists to consider all aspects being described as, at least initially, having equal value/significance so that an initial hierarchy of assumptions is avoided as the client's story unfolds (Spinelli, 1989). While there are limitations to the degree with which each of these three principles may be fully adhered to, they can establish some sound basic guidelines for the practice of E-P psychotherapy.

EXISTENTIAL-PHENOMENOLOGICAL APPROACHES TO SEXUALITY

Binswanger (1963) argued that any understanding of sexuality is insufficient when it ignores "the possibility that these biological needs are . . . enmeshed in a larger meaning-matrix, and therefore, themselves point to something beyond themselves" (p. 75). Laing (1961) criticised "any theory of sexuality which makes the 'aim' of the sexual 'instinct' the achievement of orgasmic potency alone" (p. 85).[6] Such theories treat the sexual other as "a mere object, a means to this end" and overlook the desire to make a difference to the sexual other.

In contrast to psychoanalytic efforts to develop a theory of sexuality per se, existential writers who address sexuality appear to attend to the sexual aspect of existence in order to highlight the struggles people have with fundamental existential issues (see Spinelli, 1997).[7] Merleau-Ponty (1962) has discussed the nature of sexuality most directly, and Spinelli (1997) has argued that in doing so the former "is not interested in the issues of male or female sexuality, sexual orientation, or the socio-political dimensions of sexuality. His is an investigation aimed toward the clarification of sexuality as it is revealed in its intentional dimension" (p. 7). A very particular E-P contribution is the unpacking of the experience of sexuality in both its embodied form (i.e., in relation to the physical experience of sexuality) and its intersubjective form (i.e., in relation to the interpersonal experience of being with another sexually). In contrast to much of the recent literature in British lesbian and gay psychology (see Bell, Kitzinger, Hodges, Coyle and Rivers, 2002; Bennett and Coyle, 2001; Clarke, 2001; Ellis, 1999), the E-P approach focuses on aspects of sexuality that are experiential, rather than political or related to the interpersonal domain.[8]

While an existential approach acknowledges both the personal and the constructed aspects of experience, it attempts to study the phenomenon as it is (Husserl, 1977). Merleau-Ponty (1962) notes that when it comes to sexuality, "we are concerned, not with a peripheral involuntary action, but with an intentionality which follows the general flow of existence and yields to its movements. . . . sexuality is not an autonomous cycle" (p. 157). In line with a view of people as always in relation, Merleau-Ponty notes that sexuality is not independent of meaning. Thus, while sexuality is seen as influenced by biological phenomena, it is also seen as an aspect of life created and manipulated through intentionality.

EXISTENTIAL LITERATURE ON SAME-SEX SEXUALITY: SOME ARGUMENTS AND COUNTER-ARGUMENTS

Where examples of sexual experience are used in the existential literature, some are of heterosexual experience (Frankl, 1967; Kruger, 1979; Yalom, 1980; Sartre, 1981) and some are of gay male experience (Laing, 1961; Sartre, 1981; Strasser and Strasser, 1997). Lesbian experience seems not to feature explicitly.

Boss (1966) discusses same-sex attraction in some detail and views homosexuality as a "perversion." He positions human sexuality in a bio-reproductive framework where heterosexuality is the "healthy norm."[9] He views same-sex sexuality as problematic. Cohn (1997) argues that in doing so, Boss moves away from the phenomenological position to one based on a normative framework. As he puts it, any "view [which] proposes unilinear causal connections between our anatomy and physiology and our way of being . . . entirely ignores context and history. It is, therefore, unphenomenological" (Cohn, 1997, p. 90).

Sartre (1981) writes about same-sex sexuality when he uses the example of "the homosexual" to illustrate the notion of "bad faith." For Sartre, it is not being gay that creates a situation of bad faith; rather, rigidly identifying oneself with one identity leads to an inflexible and limited view of oneself. The limitations that are imposed on the possibilities that exist in life create a state of bad faith.[10]

Same-sex sexuality is also addressed in contemporary existential writings. Cohn (1997) says, "homosexuality is not a 'condition' brought about by specific factors, but a way of being in which whatever is 'given' is most delicately intertwined with our responses" (p. 95). He also argues for the existential perspective that "the attempt to find a particular 'cause' to explain an imprecisely defined area on the wide spectrum of sexuality is quite meaningless" (p. 94).

In fact, as an E-P perspective views the experience of one's sexuality as entirely a matter of intersubjective meaning, it becomes absurd to view gay sexuality as either a "developmental arrest" or a form of psychopathology in need of a "cure."[11] An existential view is that sexuality and the experience of sexual identity must be constructed phenomena and as such cannot be "benchmarked" or viewed as falling short of the "correct" form of sexuality. For example, Spinelli (1997) argues that we "identify ourselves as homosexual, heterosexual or any-kind-of-sexual, not because of past circumstances or biological dictates, but because it is who we say we are" (p. 19). Thus, an E-P perspective can be seen as challenging the affirmative psychotherapeutic view that gay identity is "an equally positive human experience and expression to heterosexual identity" (Davies and Neal, 1996, p. 25). However, if the constructed nature of sexual identity is recognised, one needs to consider that in social, political and psychological terms, the experience of a gay identity is constructed in very different ways than heterosexual identities and experiences (Ellis, 1997). Given the hostility directed at same sex sexual behaviour (Herek and Berrill, 1992), Cohn (1997) notes that "homosexual people are, of course, especially vulnerable in a situation in which they are targets of persecution" (p. 89).[12]

IMPLICATIONS FOR THERAPEUTIC ENGAGEMENT

This section offers some clinical examples of the psychotherapeutic work undertaken by the author where issues related to gay male sexuality have been an aspect of the clinical encounter.[13]

Sean: Coming Out

The therapy with Sean (Milton, 1996) occurred in the context of an outpatient psychological therapies service. In formal psychological and psychiatric terminology the client was functioning well but was seeking therapy to reflect on his sexuality. Sean was anxious that his sexuality would be problematic for his family (whose family honour seemed to rest on him having a wife and many children) and for his career. I therefore deemed it important that his therapy did not replicate these same expectations.

When faced with Sean's agonising over whether he was or was not gay, and whether he could face being openly gay, I asked, *"Does it need a name yet? Or can we just think about what it is you are experiencing?"* The introduction of this idea (based on the Sartrean notion of essence being a product of one's generating of meaning) allowed Sean to escape a rather crippling state of anxiety and allowed him to engage with the specifics of his desires and anxieties in a more curious manner. Sean's reaction of relief and greater reflection also gave us confidence that rejecting, even if only momentarily, diagnostic categories allowed us to focus on what he felt–both at the level of desire but also with regard to the relationships in which he was immersed.

The issue of labelling his sexuality arose mid-way through therapy when Sean asked, as he was leaving a session, whether I was gay. As with many of these "door handle moments," I thought it important that we have more time for discussion and so I said, *"Interesting you ask that just as you are leaving; maybe you should ask me again next week."* As Sean did not raise the issue in the next session, I commented that he had asked me a question the previous week and not come back to it. As we reflected on his previous urge to know and his current apparent anxiety about knowing, it became evident that Sean was partly hoping that if I were gay, I could just tell him how to "sort out" his situation.

Reflection on this dilemma meant that we were able to understand his inauthentic stance (anxiously attending to a sexual identity as the sole defining aspect of himself) as meaningful, even if it might not be particularly helpful to him. By taking up my invitation to adopt a curious stance and accept his dilemma of what to "be" and how open to be about it, Sean was able to become more open to other aspects of his being and the potential of other ways of relating to different contexts in which he lived. The notions of freedom and choice become relevant and both provoke anxiety as well as offer the chance for authentic living.

Clients sometimes read my choosing not to disclose anything overtly as indicative of a particular state (one decided this meant I was gay, because if I was "straight" I would have been shocked and denied it immediately). When we discussed the meaning for Sean if I was gay as well as if I *was not*, he felt I had allowed him a freedom to which he was unaccustomed. Sean again asked me about my own sexuality in the 16th and concluding session of his therapy. At that time, I was less concerned that he was looking for a template of how to be; he had used the therapy to consider his experience a great deal, had instigated a support network, and had been able to discuss his dilemma with friends and his sister. At that point it seemed unhelpful for me to avoid the question so I simply said I was gay. He responded, "I knew it."

Roberto: Health and Sexuality

When working with Roberto in the context of HIV (Milton, 1997), I tried to resist the pull of being the "expert." This was due to a respect for the E-P notion of the self being co-constructed (and not something to be understood separately from the individual by the other). This was also due to a naiveté on my part as there were many areas of difference between us, such as age, country of origin, language and religion.

The differences between Roberto and I facilitated a stance of curiosity. This was manifest in the way I would often ask Roberto to elaborate on what he meant, on his story and on the dreams he would present. Encouragement to elaborate (and the discipline to adhere to the principle of horizontalisation as outlined above) does not have to be overly difficult. At times it meant trying to restrict my comments to, *"Tell me more,"* or *"What did that mean?"* or simply *"and?"* This would allow Roberto to reflect and add more detail to his story. I also think that it meant that we engaged together in a very different relationship–one in which I resisted being like so many others in his life who insisted he be different to the way he actually experienced himself.

The relationship between Roberto and I was sometimes difficult. Just because I could not tell him what to do, or resisted his invitations to "take over," did not mean that Roberto welcomed this. His history included growing up gay in a strictly Catholic village with pressure from family, church and community to deny his sexuality and to "change it" into something else that was more acceptable to others. This experience seemed to hold a meaning for Roberto about our own engagement–he seemed shy of me and wanted to ensure that I did not view him critically.

Roberto was concerned that his characteristic way of starting sessions–a review of the previous week–meant I would find him repetitive and uninteresting and this bothered him. Yet when I disclosed that my experience of him was quite different, he found it difficult to accept. This anxiety about trusting his sense of himself was also evident early in the therapy where Roberto had asked me my views on his needs and the work that he was doing. "What do you think of me?" he would ask. "Am I schizophrenic, paranoid, neurotic . . . ?"

These questions were illustrative of Roberto's struggle with authenticity. Roberto's way of being was to try to avoid the parts of himself that he thought were unacceptable.[14] Yet therapy was challenging this belief and he was engaging with some interest in himself as a whole– including his sexuality and his medical status issues that were "unspeakable" in his family and community. In Roberto's community, being HIV positive defined him as sinful or evil. This illustrates how the impressions of others can be a powerful invitation to view oneself negatively. This is often a factor in understanding low self-esteem or depression and anxiety in gay clients. This also shows the power of one's external world to generate sedimented beliefs and to ignore the plasticity of meaning.

At the end of his therapy, Roberto was able to engage in a more open way of relating; an openness to authenticity, rather than taking refuge in the inauthentic stance to the world that had been both protective at times but *also* inhibiting. Roberto was able to see therapy as enjoyable *and* difficult; his father as loving *and* demanding. However, he was also more able to consider his life more fully and with more enthusiasm.

Graham: Depression

The early stages of work with Graham (Milton, 1999) were characterised by a cautious and guarded stance to disclosure of his intimate experiences, feelings and ideas. Where clients have experienced prior attack or oppression, it is understandable that they will be anxious about further attack. I noted this in particular in relation to Graham's descriptions of intimate (or desired) others, as he tended to speak of the objects of his desire without referring to their genders. My asking if he was speaking about males or females allowed him to risk being open with me and led to reflections on his desire for intimacy.

This seemed to be an important turning point. While details of intimacy were forthcoming, a more important outcome was that Graham experienced a sense of security and curiosity about our therapeutic relationship. Once this level of trust had been developed between us, Graham engaged enthusiastically–albeit with a degree of anxiety–in the exploration of death, life, relationships and the impact suicide would have on others around him.

An E-P perspective was also useful in helping me consider the client holistically. I would attempt to include reflections on his comments, values, social interactions and embodied experiences. This turned out to be useful–whether thinking about the illnesses he had had as a child (that had left him feeling physical engagement with others was risky)– or by drawing attention to his bodily reactions in therapy. For example, I said, *"You've become more tearful in the last two sessions. This is somewhat different than earlier on in the therapy."* Observations such as this meant that he could think about his body and its responses that were indicative of his needs and desires in relation to others. This allowed him to begin to observe himself more and to reflect broadly on his bodily engagement with the world and with others.

CONCLUSION

This paper has outlined some core issues in existential-phenomenological psychotherapy and the way in which they avoid the pathologising inherent in some therapeutic models' views on the nature of sexuality, and on same-sex sexuality in particular. This stems from existential psychotherapy's ability to consider a holistic view of the person and the worlds in which they live, rather than a belief in the notion of self-contained individuals and notions of attainable uniformity.

While the material offered in this paper has primarily drawn on work with gay men, my experience of working with lesbian women has led me to think that E-P therapy has no less a contribution to offer. An existential approach can assist therapists in checking their pathologising stance to clients whether they are lesbian, gay or bisexual.

This paper does not address all the issues that sexuality raises for the practice of psychotherapy. For example, the practice of existential psychotherapy does not mean that the systems within which we work are necessarily challenged. Mental health services still struggle with understanding sexuality–and continue to perceive of mainstream sexuality as monogamous heterosexuality. Clients in the health services are still being refused therapy due to their sexuality; partners are still being treated as having no greater status than friends; and sexual reorientation therapy is still considered ethical in some services/contexts (Milton et al., 2003; Milton, in press).

While some may feel that psychotherapy has come a long way in the past few years, there remain many areas of conflict and difficulty that require attention. An existential-phenomenological approach to psychotherapy has much to offer in this debate. It can assist in keeping the experience of the individual in mind so that wider discussions and policies are considered in relation to those who are so often silenced but crucial to this debate–the lesbian, gay and bisexual clients who seek psychotherapeutic services.

NOTES

1. Much of my clinical work has taken place in services that have a high population of gay male users. This has allowed me to work with several clients in publishing accounts of our work. While I have worked with lesbian and bisexual clients, I am no longer in the services where this work was undertaken and cannot access those clients to secure permission to write about this work.

2. While it is commonplace to refer to the therapeutic process as "treatment" in the US context, this paper will not use this terminology as it runs counter to some of the core values and concepts upon which the existential-phenomenological approach is based. The term "therapy" will be used instead.

3. Editor's Note: In the US, authenticity is important in the work of Harry Stack Sullivan (1953). In the UK, it figures prominently in the work of D.W. Winnicott (1960). Understanding of this term varies between the existential and psychoanalytic paradigms.

4. This is a belief that challenges the power differentials that currently infuse public sector mental health systems; the latter frequently formulate (and offer the client a limited set of understandings of) the self as deviating from a rather rigid view of what is healthy and normal. By offering a more open view of the range of experience and meanings available to Dasein, the existential-phenomenological perspective offers clients possibilities of knowing themselves differently.

5. Editor's Note: American Interpersonalists refer to this as "problems in living" (Lionells et al., 1995).

6. Both authors allude to intentionality and inter-subjective relating as a central aspect of Being and, as Cohn has put it, in Being-in-the-World-Sexually (1997, p. 89).

7. It is not just psychoanalysis that has been criticised from within an existential paradigm. May (1983) notes that "when we talk of sexuality in terms of sexual objects, as Kinsey did, we may garner interesting and useful statistics, but we simply are not talking about human sexuality" (p. 30).

8. This is not a rejection of a political focus, but an attempt to capitalise on the experience of the individual as they experience it.

9. Cohn (1997) has suggested that in using the term "perversion," "Boss does not imply dismissal or condemnation, he sees the various sexual 'perversions' as attempts to achieve loving relationships in situations where the capacity to realise them fully is inhibited or crippled" (p. 95).

10. While many people experience no choice over their sexual attractions, it is evident that people respond to them in diverse ways. An E-P perspective recognises that where Dasein is preoccupied with one rigid identity at the expense of the full range of experiences available to them (often due to the need some gay men have to protect themselves from persecution by always being alert to the threat of rejection and abuse),

Dasein may respond with a deep depression, experience anxiety or adopt specific identities. These presentations can all be understood as limited aspects of existence which, if held to tenaciously, suggest bad faith. It is evident that other gay men use the awareness of their sexuality as a trigger for a reflective approach to life and state that it is a blessing to them due to the way it allows an open engagement with themselves, others and the world.

11. Conceptualisations like "arrest" and "cure" are based on an essentialist view of Dasein. To challenge these notions and take a different stance can mean that there is a clash of ideology in some of the public sector contexts in which therapists might work. This clash can be experienced in the therapist's own values or between the therapist and a conservative view of what sexuality "should" be. To understand these concepts as having any clear experiential meaning is absurd, because for a form of sexuality to be viewed in this way, essentialist interpretations of the "Truth" have to be accepted.

12. Contemporary oppression and attack take the form of denial of marriage and social rights in many countries, homophobic slurs, physical bullying (Rivers, 2003), the bomb in a gay pub in the Soho area of London and the murder of Mathew Shepherd in the US. We can also see a variant of this within sectors of the mental health establishment preoccupied with attempts to correct, cure and reorient gay clients.

13. In order to do this, three previously published (and anonymised) case studies are reviewed. While open-ended psychotherapy is undertaken in the British public sector, like most of the work, these case studies all utilise a once-weekly, time-limited approach of approximately 16 weeks.

14. Van Deurzen-Smith (1995) holds that psychological disturbance can be understood as an attempt to live life by evading parts of it.

REFERENCES

Bartolo, P. & Borg, M. eds. (2003), *Homosexuality: Challenging the Stigma*. Luqa, Malta: Agenda.
Bell, S., Kitzinger, C., Hodges, I., Coyle, A. & Rivers, I. (2002), Reflections on 'Science,' 'Objectivity' and personal investment in lesbian, gay and bisexual psychology. *Lesbian & Gay Psychology Review*, 3(3):91-95.
Bennett, C. & Coyle, A. (2001), A minority within a minority: Identity and well-being among gay men with learning disabilities. *Lesbian & Gay Psychology Review*, 2(1):9-15.
Binswanger, L. (1963), *Being-in-the-World: Selected Papers of Ludwig Binswanger*. New York: Harper Torchbooks.
Boss, M. (1966), *Sinn und Gehalt der Sexuellen Perversionen*. [Meaning and Content of Sexual Perversions] 3rd edition. Bern: Huber.
Burr, V. (1995), *An Introduction to Social Constructionism*. London: Routledge.
Clarke, V. (2001), Lesbian and gay parenting: Resistance and normalisation. *Lesbian & Gay Psychology Review*, 2(1):3-8.
Cohn, H. (1997), *Existential Thought and Therapeutic Practice: An Introduction to Existential Psychotherapy*. London: Sage.
Cooper, M. (2003), *Existential Therapies*. London: Sage.

Davies, D. & Neal, C., eds. (1996), *Pink Therapy: A Guide for Counsellors and Therapists Working with Lesbian, Gay and Bisexual Clients*. Buckingham: Open University Press.

Domenici, T. & Lesser, R.C., eds. (1995), *Disorienting Sexuality: Psychoanalytic Reappraisals of Sexual Identities*. New York: Routledge.

Drescher, J., D'Ercole, A. & Schoenberg, E., eds. (2003), *Psychotherapy with Gay Men and Lesbians: Contemporary Dynamic Approaches*. New York: Harrington Park Press.

du Plock, S. (1997), Sexual misconceptions: A critique of gay affirmative therapy and some thoughts on an existential-phenomenological theory of sexual orientation, *J. Society for Existential Analysis*, 8:56-71.

Ellis, M.L. (1997), Who speaks? Who listens? Different voices and different sexualities. *British J. Psychotherapy*, 13:369-383.

Ellis, S. (1999), Lesbian and gay issues are human rights issues: The need for a human rights approach to lesbian and gay psychology. *Newsletter of the BPS Lesbian & Gay Psychology Section*, 3:9-14.

Frankl, V. (1967), *Psychotherapy and Existentialism: Selected Papers on Logotherapy*. Harmondsworth: Penguin.

Heidegger, M. (1927), *Being and Time*. Trans. J. Macquarrie & E.S. Robinson. London: Harper and Row.

Herek, G. & Berrill, K., eds. (1992), *Hate Crimes: Confronting Violence Against Lesbians and Gay Men*. Thousand Oaks, CA: Sage.

Husserl, E. (1977), *Phenomenological Psychology*. The Hague: Nijhoff.

Isay, R. (1989), *Being Homosexual: Gay Men and Their Development*. London: Penguin Books.

Kruger, D. (1979), *An Introduction to Phenomenological Psychology*. Kenwyn: Juta and Co.

Laing, R.D. (1961), *Self and Others*. Harmondsworth: Penguin Books.

Lionells, M., Fiscalini, J., Mann, C. & Stern, D., eds. (1995), *Handbook of Interpersonal Psychoanalysis*. Hillsdale, NJ: The Analytic Press.

May, R. (1983), *The Discovery of Being: Writings in Existential Psychology*. New York: W.W. Norton and Company.

Merleau-Ponty, M. (1962), *Phenomenology of Perception*. London: Routledge & Kegan Paul.

Milton, M. (1996), Coming out in therapy. *Counselling Psychology Review*, 11(3): 26-32.

Milton, M. (1997), Roberto: Living with HIV–Issues of meaning and relationship in HIV related psychotherapy. In: *Case Studies in Existential Psychotherapy and Counselling*, ed. S. du Plock. Chichester: Wiley, pp. 42-58.

Milton, M. (1999), Depression and the uncertainty of identity: An existential-phenomenological exploration in just twelve sessions. *Changes: An International J. Psychology & Psychotherapy*, 17(4):265-277.

Milton, M. (in press), Political and ideological issues. In: *Existential Perspectives on Human Issues: A Handbook for Therapeutic Practice*, eds. E. Van Deurzen & C. Arnold-Baker. Basingstoke: Palgrave.

Milton, M., Abbot, K., Morland, T. & Walton, D. (2003), *Psychological and Psychotherapeutic Issues for Lesbians, Gay Men, Bisexuals and Trans-Gendered People: A NELMHT Survey.* Unpublished Study, North East London Mental Health Trust.

O'Connor, N. & Ryan, J. (1993), *Wild Desires and Mistaken Identities: Lesbianism and Psychoanalysis.* London: Virago.

Rivers, I. (2003), Building safer schools for lesbian and gay youth. In: *Homosexuality: Challenging the Stigma,* eds. P. Bartolo & M. Borg. Luqa, Malta: Agenda, pp. 29-48.

Sartre, J.P. (1943), *Being and Nothingness–An Essay on Phenomenological Ontology.* Trans. H. Barber. New York: Phil. Library.

Sartre, J.P. (1981), *Existential Psychoanalysis.* Washington, DC: Gateway Editions.

Spinelli, E. (1989), *The Interpreted World: An Introduction to Phenomenological Psychology.* London: Sage.

Spinelli, E. (1994), *Demystifying Therapy.* London: Constable.

Spinelli, E. (1996), The existential-phenomenological paradigm. In: *Handbook of Counselling Psychology,* eds. R. Woolfe & W. Dryden. London: Sage, pp. 180-200.

Spinelli, E. (1997), Some hurried notes expressing outline ideas that someone might someday utilise as signposts towards a sketch of an existential-phenomenological theory of sexuality. *J. Society for Existential Analysis,* 8:2-20.

Steffens, M. & Biechele, U. (2001), *Annual Review of Lesbian, Gay and Bisexual Issues in European Psychology,* Volume 1. Trier, Germany: ALGBP.

Strasser, F. (1999), *Emotions: Experiences in Existential Psychotherapy and Life.* London: Duckworth.

Strasser, F. & Strasser, A. (1997), *Existential Time-Limited Therapy: The Wheel of Existence.* Chichester: Wiley.

Sullivan, H.S. (1953), *The Interpersonal Theory of Psychiatry.* New York: W.W. Norton.

Van Deurzen, E. (2002), *Existential Counselling and Psychotherapy in Practice,* 2nd edition. London: Sage.

Van Deurzen-Smith, E. (1988), *Existential Counselling and Psychotherapy in Practice.* London: Sage.

Van Deurzen-Smith, E. (1995), *Existential Therapy.* London: Society for Existential Analysis.

Van Deurzen-Smith, E. (1997), *Everyday Mysteries: Existential Dimensions of Psychotherapy.* London: Routledge.

Winnicott, D.W. (1960), Ego Distortion in terms of true and false self. In: *The Maturational Processes and the Facilitating Environment.* New York: International Universities Press, 1965, pp. 140-152.

Yalom, I.D. (1980), *Existential Psychotherapy.* New York: Basic Books.

doi:10.1300/J236v11n01_04

Facilitating Gay Men's Coming Out:
An Existential-Phenomenological Exploration

Colin M. Clarke, MA, UKCP, UPCA, SEA

SUMMARY. This paper examines the core issues facing male clients in confronting their anxiety about whether or not to "come out" as gay. The author proposes that therapists can discover, through the process of working with the existential dimensions of the client and phenomenological description, the true essence of the client's sense of *being-in-the-world*. Therapists can also explore the client's need to identify as gay. These issues are discussed with reference to a specific case study, which explores a client's individual needs by confronting the problems experienced in his ongoing daily reality. doi:10.1300/J236v11n01_05 *[Article copies available for a fee from The Haworth Document Delivery Service: 1-800-HAWORTH. E-mail address: <docdelivery@haworthpress.com> Website: <http://www.HaworthPress.com> © 2007 by The Haworth Press, Inc. All rights reserved.]*

KEYWORDS. Authenticity, coming out, existential, gay men, givens, homophobia, homosexuality integration, isolation, phenomenology, psychotherapy

Colin M. Clarke is an existential psychotherapist and counsellor who works in private practice and specializes in sexual orientation and addictions (E-mail: colinmclarke@blueyonder.co.uk).

The author wishes to thank Colm Keegan, John Edwards and Emmy van Deurzen.

[Haworth co-indexing entry note]: "Facilitating Gay Men's Coming Out: An Existential-Phenomenological Exploration." Clarke, Colin M. Co-published simultaneously in *Journal of Gay & Lesbian Psychotherapy* (The Haworth Medical Press, an imprint of The Haworth Press, Inc.) Vol. 11, No. 1/2, 2007, pp. 61-73; and: *British Lesbian, Gay, and Bisexual Psychologies: Theory, Research, and Practice* (ed: Elizabeth Peel, Victoria Clarke, and Jack Drescher) The Haworth Medical Press, an imprint of The Haworth Press, Inc., 2007, pp. 61-73. Single or multiple copies of this article are available for a fee from The Haworth Document Delivery Service [1-800-HAWORTH, 9:00 a.m. - 5:00 p.m. (EST). E-mail address: docdelivery@haworthpress.com].

INTRODUCTION

Following the de-categorizing of homosexuality as a mental illness by the mental health authorities in the USA and in the UK, understanding the possible origins of homosexuality is no longer a priority for psychiatrists, psychologists, and therapists. It is now possible to explore coming out as one of the ways in which individuals attempt to experience themselves as fully functioning, integrated sexual human beings.[1]

This paper explores gay men's experiences of coming out, both to themselves, and to the outside world, and how–when working within an existential-phenomenological (E-P) framework–the therapist can facilitate the coming out process as one of self-affirmation. Issues examined in this process include (1) the need to deal with the values and beliefs both of the individual and of the society in which the individual exists and (2) the possible homophobic reactions that may be encountered when coming out. A third issue relates to the degree of internalised homophobia experienced by the client, which can support an undervalued perception of the self. A perception of being worthless can inhibit the ability of the client to function with any degree of authenticity in a relationship, both with themselves and others. The need to come out can be experienced by clients at any age–from youth to old age–with each individual case presenting its own unique problems. The act of coming out can be a natural development of a client's sexual self-discovery, or at the other extreme, a very difficult and painful experience, requiring professional facilitation.

The Existential-Phenomenological Approach: Background

In this section the philosophy supporting an existential-phenomenological (E-P) approach considers that in addressing the issue of facing up to our potential for being, individuals must accept that whatever meaning they arrive at, it is the result of their own choice, and not the result of outside influences. The ultimate aim of working in a phenomenological therapeutic way is to enable clients to "examine, confront, clarify and reassess their understanding of life, the problems encountered throughout their life, and the limits imposed upon the possibilities inherent in being-in-the-world" (Spinelli, 1989, p. 127). Existential therapy is understood and accepted "as a dialogic approach to therapy in which clients are encouraged to find their own answers to their own questions through an honest, empathic, challenging, supportive and individual relationship" (Cooper, 2004, p. 4). Rather than defining E-P practice as a technique, it is better understood as a working method. The E-P working method dispenses with any concerns about diagnostic frameworks. Instead, the therapist starts by considering the basic dimensions of human existence, and by attempting to clarify the client's personal worldview (Van Deurzen, 1988). May (1983) describes the three dimensions of the client's worldview:

> First, there is *Umwelt*, literally meaning "world around"; this is the biological world, generally called in our day the environment. There is, second, the *Mitwelt*, literally the "with world," the world of beings of one's own kind, the world of one's fellow men [sic]. The third [dimension] is *Eigenwelt*, the "own world," the world of relationship to oneself. (p. 126)

The Umwelt

The *Umwelt* is the natural, physical or "given" dimension, which encompasses the unchangeable biological and instinctual aspects of the person. Exploring this dimension can illuminate clients' ability to work within an environment in their own individual way, even though they have been "thrown" into this environment. Van Deurzen (1988) notes, "inhabiting the natural world requires the observation of certain rules and laws, but the home one builds in it can constitute an experience of utter individual interpretation of that given world" (p. 70).

The physical dimension is concerned with one's sense of one's body, and the interaction between the self and the physical environment. This interaction involves all the senses in one's connection with the earth from which all were created, with a genetic imprint containing the history of one's ancestors and the givens with which one is born. Exploring clients' way-of-being in the physical dimension can give an indication of their ability to chose a positive way of living in the natural world: their way of interacting with their environment; their physical sense of themselves as a person; and their way of relating to these givens. Jaspers (1970) identifies the struggle and suffering incurred when someone comes up against conflicting inner forces or goals which appear unable to be resolved. Jaspers feels that by studying how people cope with (or avoid) these situations, one can understand more about their spiritual way of being–embodied in their sense of selfhood. The existential perspective emphasizes the conflict that flows from the individual's confrontation with the givens of existence. If we feel that we have no meaning, no preordained design for living, we are forced to construct our own meanings in life (Yalom, 1998). As Cohn (1997) notes, "there is at the core of many (perhaps all) psychological disturbances a conflict between the 'givens' of existence and our response to them" (p. 125).

The existential view of the world, and of the self, suggests that there is never an end or a sense of completion. Returning to Jaspers (1970), he envisages a "handling" of oneself, in which "I retrieve myself from the I of consciousness at large, from the profusion of aspects in which I appear empirically to myself, and from my character as the given way I am" (p. 34). Jaspers also addresses the question of people having to seek meanings, and act meaningfully as part of their nature. Whatever choice they make about acting or not, it is impossible not to make (either actively or passively) a choice.

Because coming out is not a one-off event, but an ongoing experience for the whole of life (Johnson, 1997), some gay men consider suicide as an alternative to coming out. Certainly when fuelled by feelings of isolation, loneliness, and desperation, a significant number of young gay men in the UK choose suicide, rather than considering the possibility of having to live with a stigmatized, non-masculine identity (Davies, 1996). Badinter (1995) has explored male identity and masculinity generally, and makes the point that:

> Traditionally, masculinity is defined more often by the avoidance of something than by a desire for something. To be a man signifies *not* to be feminine, *not* to be homosexual; *not* to be effeminate in one's physical appearance or manners; *not* to have sexual or overtly intimate relations with other men . . . Homophobia is an integral part of heterosexual masculinity, so much so that it plays an essential psychological role: it signifies who is not homosexual and shows who is heterosexual. (p. 115)

The Mitwelt

The experience of a gay man growing up and existing in a predominately heterosexual society leads to consideration of the next existential dimension. The *Mitwelt* focuses on the relationship that is created between the individual and the "with-world" with which they are required to interact; it represents the public world–the interaction between the client and others who they frequently encounter. This dimension encompasses the client's existing cultural and social experience. The following case study demonstrates how theory can be linked to the client's actual experience.

Michael,[2] a young man, was referred to the Project for Advise Counselling and Education (PACE)–an organisation in London providing low-cost counselling for lesbian and gay clients on low incomes. He had come to London from a rural area, and had reached a crisis. He was unsure of how to continue with his life, and needed to address important issues about his sense of identity. Although he described himself as a creative person, he was experiencing the sensation of being imprisoned inside himself; identifying an extreme sense of "stuckness" or sedimentation. He acknowledged feeling very depressed, but said he had chosen not to let others see the very unhappy inner emotions that he was experiencing. He did not feel that he was allowed to communicate his real feelings of despair, loneliness, and low self-esteem "as this would be a burden to others," and would–he felt–result in them rejecting him. Before starting therapy, he had not talked to anyone about the inner turmoil of guilt and unexpressed grief he had been experiencing since his sibling had died some years before. He described his life over the previous three years as being a downward spiral into depression, marked by increasing anxiety about how he would ever be able to experience a change in his way-of-being.

In Michael's experience of dealing with daily encounters, he revealed confusion in many areas: his sense of self; his perception of feelings of not being accepted; not having an understanding of how "to fit in with others," or how to accept love from others. Further, his cultural background had led him to believe that he was unworthy to give or receive love.[3] Michael described the experience he felt daily as "being shut inside a dark room."

I learnt that Michael had grown up surrounded by a highly religious and bigoted family who were unable to express emotion towards each other and were mainly concerned with outward appearances. The only person who Michael had felt close to was his now deceased sibling. He had come to London hoping to find a way to understand how he could function as a gay man but had discovered that without outside help he was unable to achieve this goal.

If one is able to live creatively in meaningful ways, it affirms the self as engaging in those meanings, and there is an exchange of ideas that affirm the participation in life. It was this lack of perception in how to live creatively that concerned Michael. So our work focused on how he might insightfully allow light into his "darkened room" experience of being. His dilemma brings to mind the existential theologian and philosopher Paul Tillich (1952) who considers the anxiety of emptiness and meaninglessness as being embodied in the inability to experience a sense of self-affirmation:

> Spiritual self-affirmation occurs in every moment in which man [sic] lives creatively in the various spheres of meaning. Creative in this context, has the sense not of original creativity as performed by the genius but of living spontaneously, in action and reaction, with the contents of one's cultural life . . . Everyone who lives creatively in meanings affirms himself [sic] as a participant in these meanings. He [sic] affirms himself [sic] as receiving and transforming reality creatively. (p. 46)

Michael's need to engage with the concept of rediscovering how to be creative with his way of being-in-the-world focused on his need to establish his true essence as a gay man–by coming out both to himself and by "being-with-others-in-the-world." Facilitating this process was the core of our work together. It was through exploring this *Mitwelt* dimension of Michael's experience that we worked with his feelings of belonging and isolation, acceptance or rejection, and being admired or experiencing condemnation. Exploring this dimension exposed the anxiety Michael felt about choosing to come out, and the sense of responsibility that went with making that decision.

When looking at the *Mitwelt* dimension of coming out, therapists must seriously consider "that it depends only upon how far one's essential Being with Others has made itself transparent and has not disguised itself" (Heidegger, 1962, p. 162). Sartre (1943) argued that being authentic can only be discovered by acknowledging one's aloneness, otherwise one can only exist in bad faith, or through a sense of self-deception. This highlights a major part of the struggle towards accepting oneself and the need to identify how one can fit into society as a whole, or into any specific peer group with which one may wish to identify.

Also embodied in the issue of ontological anxiety is the question of "self-affirmation of the individual self as individual self without regard to its participation in the world" (Tillich, 1952, p. 113). This means having the courage to be authentically oneself, whether it is with family, friends, colleagues, when in a socially gay environment, or alone. It is in exploring this existential dimension, of being-with-the-other, that one encounters the social forces that impinge daily on the gay consciousness.

Eigenwelt

The third existential dimension is the *Eigenwelt*, or the inner psychological world. It is in this dimension that the client will have sense of identity, self-relatedness, and authentic self-awareness. Michael, it seemed, felt that he never had a real opportunity to look at who he was, or how he wanted to be. He felt bullied by his family and the world in which he existed. He felt that he had to conform to both his family and his Church's ideals, without considering his own needs and desires. Now, in therapy, he was faced with the possibility of the freedom to change the perspective of his inner world, and consider how that could present possibilities for discovering fulfillment.

My role as therapist was providing a safe place for this possibility to develop, and simultaneously challenging Michael to find his own values and beliefs. A factor contributing to Michael's experience of "stuckness" was his inability to imagine a future that would be any different from the past, even though his inner desire was to change that experience. This can be viewed as a sedimentation process, where values are so embedded in the client's character, that it is difficult to contemplate changing them (Strasser, 1999). It was this inner struggle that was contributing to Michael's anxiety and depression. As May (1983) puts it,

> Repression and other processes of the blocking off of awareness are in essence methods of ensuring that the usual relation of past to present will not obtain. Since it would be too painful or in other ways too threatening for the individual to retain certain aspects of his past in his present consciousness, he must carry the past along like a foreign body *in* him but not *of* him. (p. 138)

In Michael's case, he allowed the past to overwhelm his sense of being in the present. However, he then reached a moment in time when he felt that he had to make an attempt to challenge that feeling. He made a decision to seek a happier future by confronting the issues that appeared to be holding him back (see also Merleau-Ponty, 1962).

WORKING WITH THE INDIVIDUAL ELEMENTS OF COMING OUT

This section addresses the therapeutic process of facilitating self-awareness and confronting both external and internal homophobia.

Therapists using an existential-phenomenological perspective can explore and help clients to resolve feelings of isolation, alienation, and meaninglessness. These issues are particularly relevant when contemplating engaging with the coming-out process. For the gay man, it is the sense of non-being that threatens his whole perspective of living successfully in a predominately heterosexual society.

Two obvious aspects of coming out are those of both physical and emotional safety. Therapists must be conscious of the fact that "the growing openness of male homosexuality has been accompanied by an apparent rise in homophobic violence, sometimes performed by those who are themselves behaviourally homosexual" (Altman, 1982, p. 65). Physical safety is an element of the everyday experience in the thoughts of any gay person who is open about their sexuality. The absence of a sense of being safe–or a constant fear of physical attack–diminishes the foundation of any ongoing sense of emotional safety (Johnson, 1997). On the other hand,

> Severe anxiety, hostility and aggression are states and ways of relating to one's self and others which would curtail or destroy being. But to preserve one's existence by running away from situations which would produce anxiety or situations of potential hostility and aggression leaves one with the vapid, weak, unreal sense of being. (May, 1958, p. 49)

There is a paradox in the existential proposition that human beings are both existentially alone *and* related. From this perspective, ultimately we are alone; the sense of isolation or the experience of aloneness can give us strength when we accept that we cannot depend on anyone else to confirm who we are. In other words, we must, on our own, give a sense of meaning to life (Corey, 1996). The act of coming out can require tremendous courage. Moreover, it involves taking a calculated risk as it may result in "rejection and condemnation from significant others" (Shelley, 1998, p. 136).

In the face of these threats to physical and emotional safety it is worth considering why anyone should want to come out. Yet from an E-P perspective, the need for a sense of wholeness–and the existential anxieties created by not experiencing oneself as an authentically sexually integrated person–makes coming out a priority. The desire to seek a way of coming together with oneself and the world, and a need to live authentically (without hiding any parts of the self) is what prompts coming out. The conflict engendered by attempting to exist without being validated by others in an authentic way is what often brings gay men into therapy. This is what happened in Michael's case.

The E-P psychotherapeutic approach is concerned with examining the present situation of the client and exploring both the strengths and the limitations of that situation (Van Deurzen, 1988). Michael was coming from a background of experience leaving him feeling disillusioned with his life. He had felt isolated and unable to look beyond his current negative experience of his world. Coming to London marked, for him, the beginning of finding another way to feel part of a world that previously he experienced as rejecting. He had correctly identified London as containing a large community of gay men, among whom he thought he could discover a true way-of-being. However, his overriding existing sense of isolation and rejection was just too strong for him to cope with this issue of sexual self-development on his own.

Despair is not only about the courage *not* to be, but is also about guilt and condemnation. As Tillich (1952) notes, anxiety develops when a person experiences an awareness of "unresolved conflicts between structural elements of the personality—between different drives trying to dominate the centre of the personality, between imaginary worlds and the experience of the real world" (p. 64).

EXPRESSING THE FREEDOM IN COMING OUT

Working with a client who is considering coming out requires an examination of every aspect in the physical, psychological, public and spiritual dimensions of the client's way-of-being. It encompasses examining the values and belief system that the client works with, as well as the client's learned attitude towards homosexuality, obtained from parents, teachers, and society:

> Coming out is not an activity for which a gay person is likely to have built up, as a result of childhood learning, a secure and flexible procedural sequence. Consequently the psychopathological difficulties which centre on coming out often have the same form as adjustment reactions. (Denman and de Vries, 1998, p. 169)

The act of coming out involves a complicated developmental process which involves, at a psychological level, a person's awareness and acknowledgement of homosexual thoughts and feelings. By exploring the three major existential dimensions of Michael's life, in our weekly sessions, and working through a phenomenological description of his experience, Michael–for the first time–came to regard himself from a viewpoint that was not totally negative. He discovered that by choosing to take some risks, and allowing himself to work with the resulting experience, he became more open to himself and more accessible to others. His friends responded by being more open with him, and in the process found him to be more understandable and likeable–not less, as he had feared. Michael recognised that he needed to come to terms with the death of his sibling and to allow himself to grieve. He also had to explore his need to come out as a gay man so that he would be free to focus on living in the present. As our work together proceeded, and his trust in the therapeutic relationship grew, he was able to explore the confusion surrounding his sense of selfhood and the mistrust about interacting with a perceived hostile world.

A major step forward in Michael's therapy was his writing a letter to his mother explaining his inner feelings and coming out to her as a gay man. This took a lot of courage and it was quite a painful process for him. He felt very vulnerable at the time, but ultimately he felt psychologically strengthened by this action. He eventually received a response which was not the condemning one that he had expected, but instead was quite supportive and understanding. This reply boosted Michael's determination to work at his own personal need for self-understanding and encouraged him to engage with the process of proceeding into the world as an unashamed adult gay man.

DISCUSSION

Understanding clients' relationship "to the structure of their natural world is a crucial step in the full understanding of their way of being in the world" (Van Deurzen, 1988, p. 70). An overwhelming sense of *being* is established by the E-P therapeutic experience. The therapist cannot actually experience the client's experience and vice versa, but the relationship "is concerned with your behaviour and my behaviour *as I experience it*, and your and my behaviour *as you experience it* (Laing, 1967, p. 17). The existential viewpoint helps therapists to consider clients' uniqueness and their existential way of being-in-the-world, their capacity for self-awareness, their sense of freedom and responsibility, and their striving for an identity and relationship to others.

Therapists also need to acknowledge the ambivalence gay clients may encounter within the gay community once they have taken the step to come out which can create new tensions in the sense of freedom and identity that they have newly acquired. As Ratigan (1996) notes, "an aspect of isolation experienced by older gay men, can be the overvaluation of youth and good-looks, and although superficial in reality, [this] represents a powerful shaper of the internal realities of gay men–put simply, the older you are the less you exist" (p. 161).

Freedom in coming out means the freedom to choose, and with it all the concerns and questions that arise about lifestyle, sexuality and whether to disclose gay sexuality or not. This is a journey that a therapist and client can explore together using phenomenological description. Such a phenomenological stance gives therapists the core idea of standing back and allowing what is presented to be as it is. Any other considerations are bracketed off. Free of one's own ideas or needs one can be totally concerned with the reality as it occurs. As Heidegger (1962) puts it:

> Phenomenology is our way of access to be what is to be the theme of ontology, and it is our way of giving it demonstrative precision. In the phenomenological conception of "phenomenon" what one has in mind as that which shows itself is the Being of entities, its meaning, its modification and derivatives. And this showing-itself is not just any showing-itself, nor is it some such thing as appearing. (p. 60)

CONCLUSION

An existential-phenomenological exploration of coming out is concerned with looking at what might be called "the core essence" of an individual's sense of being, and how they describe their experience. From a phenomenological stance, therapists do not have to qualify the client's experience. Individual clients will have varying degrees of both ontological and ontic anxieties. Therefore, they will be experiencing different individual problems at negotiating the path to fully emerging, and in being able authentically to engage with life as a gay man. In working with the individual's unique experience of coming out and the need to achieve a sense of authentically being-in-the-world, therapists can begin to understand and clarify the gay client's worldview. This clarification, through description of the lived experience, can help the client and therapist learn more about the client's perceptions of successfully achieving a sense of autonomy.

Coming out for any gay client is the start of a process of discovering the individual potential to feel whole as a person, of experiencing relatedness to others, and new personal ideas and values. From this can develop a sense of communion or belonging, a consciousness of psychological freedom, and a feeling of goodness about who one is (Fromm, 1960). Coming out can be understood in an existential context as a constant renewal, and rediscovery of required coping tools and strategies to help in the daily task of living as a gay man. Being able to be open about one's sexual orientation can initiate a learning process of allowing experiences that are both rewarding and adverse.

NOTES

1. My own experience may be illustrative. I came out at the age of eighteen in a trauma free situation whilst at Art College. I discovered that my openness about identifying as a gay man acted as a catalyst to others (including college staff) to be open about their sexuality, rather than closing down possibilities for me. In fact, I created them. I felt very comfortable with who I was, and so others seemed to feel comfortable being with me.

2. Michael is a pseudonym.

3. In proceeding towards another in creating a relationship, the possibility of authentically negotiating this process has been suggested by Van Deurzen (1998) in the following way: "When I move towards the other, giving up my reserve in myself, I do away with the usual moulding and fabrication of attitude and appearance. I let go of a sense of superiority or inferiority: I stop comparing myself to the other or trying to create an impression–I allow myself to be a vessel for the meeting with the other and I move out of my shell into the open field, where I can meet the other and be ready for whatever is to come" (p. 49).

REFERENCES

Altman, D. (1982), *The Homosexualization of America*. Boston: Beacon Press.
Badinter, E. (1995), *X Y On Masculine Identity*. New York: Columbia University Press.
Cohn, H.W. (1997), *Existential Thought and Therapeutic Practice*. London: Sage.
Cooper, M. (2004), Viagra for the brain. *J. Society for Existential Analysis*, 15(1), 2-14.
Corey, G. (1996), *Theory and Practice of Counselling and Psychotherapy*. Pacific Grove: Brooks/Cole.
Davies, D. (1996), Working with people coming out. In: *Pink Therapy: A Guide for Counsellors and Therapists Working with Lesbian, Gay and Bisexual Clients*, eds. D. Davies & C. Neal. Buckingham: Open University Press, pp. 66-85.

Denman, C. & deVries, P. (1998), Cognitive analytic therapy and homosexual orientation. In: *Contemporary Perspectives on Psychotherapy and Homosexualities*, ed. C. Shelley. London: Free Association Books, pp. 156-189.

Fromm, E. (1960), *The Fear of Freedom*. London: Routledge & Kegan Paul.

Heidegger, M. (1962), *Being and Time*. Trans. J. Macquarrie & E. Robinson. Oxford: Blackwell.

Jaspers, K. (1970), *Philosophy 2*. Chicago: University of Chicago Press.

Johnson, B.K. (1997), *Coming Out Every Day*. Oakland: New Harbinger Publications.

Laing, R.D. (1967), *The Politics of Experience and the Bird of Paradise*. Harmondsworth: Penguin.

May, R. (1958), Contributions of existential psychotherapy. In: *Existence*, eds. E. Angel, R. May & H.F. Ellenberger. New York: Basic Books.

May, R. 1983), *The Discovery of Being*. New York: Norton.

Merleau-Ponty, M. (1962), *Phenomenology of Perception*. Trans. C. Smith. London: Routledge & Kegan Paul.

Ratigan, B. (1996), Psychoanalysis and male homosexuality: Queer bedfellows? In: *Contemporary Perspectives on Psychotherapy and Homosexualities*, ed. C. Shelley. London: Free Association Books, pp. 58-86.

Sartre, J.P. (1943), *Being & Nothingness*. Trans. H. Barnes. New York: Philosophical Library.

Shelley, C. (1998), Individual psychology and homosexualities. In: *Contemporary Perspectives on Psychotherapy and Homosexualities*, ed. C. Shelley. London: Free Association Books, pp. 117-155.

Spinelli, E. (1989), *The Interpreted World*. London: Sage.

Strasser, F. (1999), *Emotions*. London: Duckworth.

Tillich, P. (1952), *The Courage to Be*. New Haven: Yale University Press.

Van Deurzen, E. (1988), *Existential Counselling in Practice*. London: Sage.

Van Deurzen, E. 1998), *Paradox and Passion in Psychotherapy*. Chichester: Wiley.

Yalom, I.D. (1998), *The Yalom Reader*. New York: Basic Books.

doi:10.1300/J236v11n01_05

Gay Subjects Relating:
Object Relations Between Gay Therapist and Gay Client

Aaron Balick, MA, MSc, UCKP reg

SUMMARY. This paper discusses the development of object relations theory which, in Britain, was developed as an extension of Freudian psychoanalysis by such thinkers as Melanie Klein, Fairbairn, Winnicott and their followers and later supported by research from attachment theorists like Bowlby. Object relations theorists made a shift from the conception of a drive-based psyche to one that was primarily motivated towards relationships. Contemporary object relations theory acknowledges the primacy of relationships, which results in the close attention and utilisation of the constantly active system of transference, countertransference, and projective identification in the space between therapist and client. This paper examines object relations in the context of its unique challenges for gay male therapists working with gay male clients in the *gay therapeutic dyad*. This paper reviews the legacy of homo-negativity in the therapeutic process. It then explores how knowledge of object relations theory can be useful for therapists working within a gay therapeutic dyad. doi:10.1300/J236v11n01_06 *[Article copies available for a fee from The Haworth Document Delivery Service: 1-800-HAWORTH. E-mail address: <docdelivery@haworthpress.com> Website: <http://www.HaworthPress.com> © 2007 by The Haworth Press, Inc. All rights reserved.]*

Aaron Balick is a writer, lecturer, and psychotherapist in private practice, London.
Address correspondence to: Aaron Balick, 6a Elmore Street, London N1 3AL, UK (E-mail: aaron@n1psychotherapy.co.uk).

[Haworth co-indexing entry note]: "Gay Subjects Relating: Object Relations Between Gay Therapist and Gay Client." Balick, Aaron. Co-published simultaneously in *Journal of Gay & Lesbian Psychotherapy* (The Haworth Medical Press, an imprint of The Haworth Press, Inc.) Vol. 11, No. 1/2, 2007, pp. 75-91; and: *British Lesbian, Gay, and Bisexual Psychologies: Theory, Research, and Practice* (ed: Elizabeth Peel, Victoria Clarke, and Jack Drescher) The Haworth Medical Press, an imprint of The Haworth Press, Inc., 2007, pp. 75-91. Single or multiple copies of this article are available for a fee from The Haworth Document Delivery Service [1-800-HAWORTH, 9:00 a.m. - 5:00 p.m. (EST). E-mail address: docdelivery@haworthpress.com].

KEYWORDS. Attachment, countertransference, gay, gay therapeutic dyad, gay therapist, homosexuality, object relations, projective identification, psychoanalysis, psychotherapy, therapeutic relationship, transference

INTRODUCTION

The term "object relations" developed from Freud's (1917) work in which he describes the object as that towards which a libidinal drive strives (a person, or indeed, a thing). Contemporary object relations therapists, however, think of objects as either people or psychic representations of people. As Cashdan (1988) puts it, these relations can be "internal or external, fantasied or real, but they essentially center around interactions with other human beings" (p. 4). Object relations therapy, then, is most concerned with people (real or imagined) and the relationships between them. In fact, among many psychoanalysts, there has been a shift away from Freud's libidinal drive theory towards an alternative one that focuses on a human being's innate need to relate to another.

The shift in focus from drive to object has changed the psychoanalytic landscape and led to a contemporary rethinking of the analytic relationship. It has led to a corresponding shift from viewing the role of the analyst as a neutral, blank slate to that of the analyst using the analytic relationship as part of the therapeutic process. This paradigm shift has led to a rethinking not only of some core psychoanalytic concepts (most notably the therapeutic use of transference and countertransference), but also of the role of the analyst himself.[1] When transference is no longer conceptualized as a neurotic re-routing of old feelings and relationships on to the analyst, the analyst cannot avoid participating in the object relational arena of client. The traumas from the earliest relationships with primary caretakers are likely to be played out within the therapeutic context (Ferenczi, 1933). Consequently, the current relationship with the therapist is seen as an opportunity for these early, often unresolved and traumatic object relations to be modified (Scharff, 1995). It is within the patient's "here-and-now" relationship with the therapist that unresolved early relationships can be worked through.

Though each individual, regardless of sexual orientation, brings own unique relational experience to the therapeutic relationship, gay men as a client group are likely to bring such themes as fear of rejection and abandonment. These themes may arise from a previous lack of acceptance of their sexuality in both the family and wider social context (Isay, 1993a; 1989). Via unconscious communication established within the dyad, object relations of both the therapist and client are played out. Object representations can reverberate between therapist and client (e.g., the internalised father of the client may invoke the internalised father of the therapist), and themes such as a sense of rejection or abandonment may be repeated in the transference (e.g., the therapist becomes the rejecting father). It is the therapist's job to enable the client's awareness and integration of previously unconscious object relations while also playing a reparative role that enables the development of more stable and accepting internal objects within the client. Though awareness of such dynamics will prove crucial to all therapeutic dyads, exploring the clinical relevance of object relations in a gay dyad is a useful way to explore a gay subjectivity in the therapeutic encounter.[2]

HISTORICAL OVERVIEW

Freud fled Austria to England in 1938 (Jones, 1953). While psychoanalysis vanished under the Nazi occupation of Vienna, it was to be reborn in Hampstead, North London. After Freud's death in 1939, his daughter Anna Freud inherited the mantle of what came to be known as classical psychoanalysis and ego psychology in the US (Young-Bruehl, 1988). However, in the UK, Melanie Klein, through her clinical focus on the early experience of children, hypothesized a theoretical model that would lead to the development of contemporary object relations theory.

Object relations is seen by some as a logical development of Freud's later work. Hamilton (1998), for example, argues that the groundwork for what would later become object relations theory can be found in three of Freud's essays: *Mourning and Melancholia* (1917), *Group Psychology and the Analysis of the Ego* (1921), and *Inhibitions, Symptoms, and Anxiety* (1926). In these essays, Freud focuses his attention on the dynamics of identification, the projection of aspects of self onto others, and "the importance of attachment to the mother and fear of losing her over and above sexual aggressive drives" (Hamilton, 1998, p. 298). In addition, in Freud's *Outline of Psychoanalysis* (1939), he explicitly makes a connection between the nascence of the superego (the "new psychical agency") as resulting from internalising an aspect of the outside world:

A portion of the external world has, at least partially, been abandoned as an object and has instead, by identification, been taken
into the ego and thus become an integral part of the internal world.
This new psychical agency continues to carry on the functions
which have hitherto been performed by the people [the abandoned
objects] in the external world [. . .] exactly like the parents whose
place it has taken. (Freud, 1939, p. 205)

Here Freud is still focusing on objects developed primarily during the
oedipal period of development. Melanie Klein (1932) differs in her conception of the timing of such introjections by prioritising the earliest
years of development with reference to the internalisation of object relations. Klein believed that she was merely extending this late work of
Freud's, although Greenberg and Mitchell (1983) have argued that she
was moving entirely in another direction. Klein's pioneering psychoanalytic work with children focused on instinctual forcefulness and unconscious phantasy[3] in relation to the baby's relationships to its first
object, the breast. Klein altered the timeline in Freud's developmental
scheme by positing that the individual's world of object relating starts
from the baby's relation to the breast that feeds it. By the time the
Oedipus complex comes into play, the individual has already achieved
an intense level of object relating. In addition to shifting the timeline of
dynamic experience to the earliest moments of life, Klein also maintained that instincts are inherently connected to their objects, a position
contrary to Freud's conception that drives are objectless (St. Clair,
2000).

Klein's contribution to object relations theory falls into the following
four themes: (1) transferring the primacy of psychic development to the
very early years and months of a child's life; (2) acknowledging the existence and importance of unconscious phantasy; (3) distinguishing object relations in the early *paranoid/schizoid position*, where part-objects
are, by their nature, split between good and bad, nourishing and perse-
cuting, from object relations of the *depressive position*, wherein whole
objects are integrated, containing both good and bad elements; and (4) introducing the conception of projective identification where parts of the
self are projected into external objects (i.e., people) (Segal, 1964).

Melanie Klein subtly shifted the emphasis of psychoanalysis into another direction; Ronald Fairbairn (1952) unabashedly altered the focus
entirely:

> Whereas [Klein] pictured a primitive internal world, created by the infant's phantasmal transformation of external objects using its own instinctual palette, Fairbairn opted for the opposite–a transformation of the infant's instinctual world through impingement or neglect by external persons, the transformation being an accommodation of *necessity* in order to survive in the closed system of the family. (Grotstein and Rinsley, 1994, p. 7, italics in original)

In Fairbairn's paradigm, the focus shifts from a purely internal world to a psyche dependent upon external relationships. His break from the traditional analytic paradigm of his time would serve to sever British object relations both from classical psychoanalysis and from the developments in object relations theory in the US:

> Unlike early American object relations theorists who fit their ideas around ego-psychology, British object relations theories have challenged classical psychoanalytic assumptions . . . Klein advanced the Oedipus complex to the first year of life yet retained the Freudian concept of the instinctual basis for development, whereas Fairbairn replaced drive theory altogether with a purely object relations motivational perspective. (Scharff and Scharff, 1998, p. 97)

In a shift away from Freudian drive theory unlike that of the Kleinians– who continued to believe in the dominance of the drives–Fairbairn had positioned object relating as the central basis for human motivation:

> emphasis on the relational rather than the hedonic aspects of the object-seeking drives challenged the primacy of Freud's pleasure principle and substituted for it the primacy of the reality principle– a concept that has been affirmed by infant developmental research. (Grotstein, 1994, p. 319)

The research to which Grotstein refers to derives from the attachment theory of John Bowlby (1969) which was further developed by Mary Ainsworth et al. (1978). As object relations theorists were constructing a formal qualitative framework of the psyche, attachment theorists were measuring and testing attachment phenomena in the laboratory. Bowlby's work with children enabled him to qualitatively assess the effects of early parenting on later relationships by investigating how early attachment needs were met. Ainsworth would go on to de-

scribe how children's attachment strategies range between secure, am-
bivalent, and avoidant. The synergy between object relations theory and
the empirical work of attachment theorists (Marrone and Cortina, 2003)
would eventually be integrated into contemporary object relations practice.

Another important contributor to contemporary object relations theory is D.W. Winnicott (1982). Among his many important contributions are: (1) the holding environment (how an infant's feelings are
contained by its mother); (2) the "good enough mother" (the mother's
ability to contain these feelings within a margin of error); (3) transi-
tional objects (how the infant is gradually able to internalise the mother
through use of a physical object, such as a blanket, received from the
mother); and (4) object constancy (the importance of a reliable external
object). As will be shown in the following section, the necessity for a
therapist to model object constancy for his client will be a vital aspect of
a therapy dealing with issues of rejection and abandonment.

THE LEGACY OF HOMONEGATIVITY
IN THE THERAPEUTIC PROCESS

One need not look far to find confirmation of the harm that a homophobic and compulsorily heterosexual environment can have on gay
men (and other sexual minority individuals). The field of psychotherapy
has certainly played its part in pathologising gay men. Lewes (1995) argues that classical Freudian psychoanalysis appears benign in comparison to the psychoanalytic theories of homosexuality developed–most
notably in the US–after the Second World War.[4]

It should be noted that object relations theorists also played a part in
the pathologising of homosexuality. Drescher (1998, pp. 131-132)
notes that Bowlby "compares homosexuality to the military concept of
friendly fire":

> An example of a system or rather integrate of systems that is in
> working order but not in functionally effective working order is
> the integrate responsible for sexual behaviour in an adult who is a
> confirmed homosexual. In such a case all components of behav-
> iour may be performed efficiently but, because the object towards
> which they are directed is *inappropriate*, the functional conse-
> quence of reproduction cannot follow. The integrate not only has a
> predictable outcome, namely sexual orgasm with a partner of the

same sex, but is so organized that the outcome is achieved. What makes it functionally ineffective is that for some reason the system has developed in such a way that its predictable outcome is unrelated to function. Were a similar error to have crept into the design of a radar and predictor-controlled anti-aircraft gun, it might lead to the gun's firing efficiently but aiming so that it always destroyed a friendly plane and never an enemy one. (Bowlby, 1969, pp. 130-131, emphasis added)

In a similar vein, Domenici (1995) describes Fairbairn's less than sympathetic assessment of the gay condition:

Fairbairn maintained that the distress homosexuals feel is from their forfeiture of social and material advantages rather than from guilt or remorse and that typically they resent society's attitude towards them. Ultimately, the homosexual does not want "cure," but acceptance. Therefore, homosexuality is the naturally sexual expression of a psychopathic personality. (p. 42)

In Fairbairn's case, at least as Domenici presents it, homosexuality is considered psychopathic because of the "homosexual's" desire for public acceptance. Ironically, this claim highlights one of the core issues to be considered in relation to the gay therapeutic dyad: acceptance. The conscious awareness within the homosexual patient of a desire for acceptance comes from an *a priori* expectation, often based on past experience, of not being accepted (Isay, 1989). It is essential that these therapists maintain awareness of the dynamics inherent in the way a gay man has navigated his way through his early life. After all, there is an expectation placed on gay men from an early age by family and friends that they become heterosexual, and gay men "often recall childhood experiences that symbolised, to them, the cultural biases against their homoerotic longings" (Drescher, 1998, p. 13).

The therapeutic encounter is ripe for the activation of such internalisations. For it is within this encounter that the gay client makes himself vulnerable: he exposes himself and his sexual identity in the hope of being accepted. An innate representation of non-acceptance by others is likely to be an element of the gay client's personality, and this can be activated within the therapeutic arena. If the therapist himself is gay (and likely to have experienced rejection due to his own sexual identity), he will also have to address these issues of rejection and non-acceptance with relation to his client and himself. This is an occasion when the reverberation of similar dynamic constellations can be transformed through conscious-making awareness, or the potential to be repeated through the therapist's enactments.

Shame and internalised homophobia, however, are not the only shadows haunting the gay therapeutic dyad. This dyad must also contend with issues of difference and sameness, erotic demands, and aggressions:

> Difficulties for the male psychotherapist may lie in tolerating either the projection of intense feelings of homoerotic love, or aggressive and competitive Oedipally-derived feelings from their male patients. Successfully managing such countertransference reactions might involve the therapist facing any unresolved issues concerning his own male identity. These might include confronting his own feelings of love and attraction for other men, as well as acknowledging the potential arousal of his own aggression and envy. (Simon, 2003, p. 345)

Certainly, within every psychotherapeutic relationship, such elements exist and practitioners ought to be aware of them. In object relations practice in general, use is made of these transferential and projective phenomena. In the case of the gay therapeutic dyad, the explicit discussion of the gay-related objects can be a great healing element within the therapeutic process. In order for this to occur, the therapist himself must be conscious of his own conceptions and object weaknesses. Working in an object relations framework requires that the therapist actually operate within the environment of projective identifications of his client. Lack of awareness of the therapist's own psyche could, at best, render him ineffective and, at worst, render him harmful.

Cornett (1995) maintains that it is crucial that the therapist be conscious of his own "anti-homosexual prejudice" as this will inevitably exercise itself within the relationship. This expression would have an expectably adverse impact on the client; a situation that is exacerbated when, in the name of anonymity, real homonegativity is safely explained away as a projection of the patient. Cornett draws attention to the way in which there is a "real" relational matrix going on between therapist and client: not simply a transference reaction based upon past relationships. The unconscious object relating between therapist and patient is constantly activated and it is within this sphere of relating that the real psychological work is completed. The therapist, in allowing himself to be affected by both his own and his client's object worlds, is better able to attend to the deficits in the object world of his client.

CASE EXAMPLE

The case of "Tony" illustrates an event where failure as a therapist becomes a source of learning. The regrettable therapeutic error arose from a combination of inexperience (Tony was one of the author's first clients) and the failure of the author's then-supervisor to recognise some of the themes elucidated here.

Tony was referred through his General Practitioner for 13 weeks of short-term therapy in a clinical setting. For this reason, Tony would have no reason to assume that the author was gay. Tony was experiencing depression following the break-up of a relationship with his boyfriend.

During the therapy, Tony shared explicit content about his sexual life. Much of this included cruising for sex and auditioning for a pornographic film. Tony succeeded in his audition for the film and was introduced to the men with whom he would be required to have sex for the production. Tony felt these men were "down-and-outs" and he was not prepared to have sex with them. When he presented this information, he felt victorious in his sense of confidence and his ability to say "no" in these circumstances. I felt this was an especially positive assertion of Tony's independence, given his earlier demonstrated need for acceptance and validation–a need he felt was met by his acceptance on the production.

I related this content to my supervisor at the time. His response was, "I'm very concerned about the behaviour of your client. Aren't you concerned?" My sense of my supervisor's concern was that it was based solely on Tony's cruising and auditioning for a pornographic film, rather than on Tony's phenomenological experience of positive movement towards self-direction.

"No," I replied, "I'm not particularly concerned about that." To which the supervisor responded, "I'm concerned that you're not concerned." He went on to say, "Even if you take the position that homosexuality is non-pathological, certainly there are some issues here with regard to attachment and appropriate relating."

As a gay man, my sense of the situation was that this supervisor had no conception of the particular gay culture Tony inhabited, and further, that the supervisor's sense of "appropriate relating" was based on his limited conception of a heterosexual model. However, it was too early in my working life to challenge such statements. He was the supervisor, I was the trainee therapist; hence he was right. Sadly, I also took my supervisor's advice that I should not disclose my sexual identity to Tony.

As the sessions with Tony continued, I remained rather distant when he described his sexual life. He spoke as if I were heterosexual; he assumed I knew nothing of the gay world. In adopting this supervisor-encouraged position of not disclosing my sexuality, I failed to bring it into the therapeutic process as an accepted part of myself. In retrospect, I feel that my withholding in the name of analytic anonymity disabled the therapeutic relationship (Cornett, 1995). While I was not unconscious of our object relational position to each other (his need for unconditional acceptance with regard to his sexual practices along with my need to demonstrate acceptance and understanding), this awareness was suppressed out of an imposed adherence to psychoanalytic protocols. In addition, my supervisor's open disdain for Tony's lifestyle contained an implicit disdain for my own lifestyle, reflected in the statement, "Even if you take the view that homosexuality is non-pathological . . ." This cast a shadow on the therapeutic alliance between Tony and myself and myself and the supervisor. It certainly inhibited Tony and myself, ultimately relegating the most important aspects of the work into the realm of the unspoken and unacknowledged. Hence, perhaps it is no surprise that Tony did not show up for the final session. An essential part of myself had been shorn away in the interest of the protocol advocated by my supervisor. This resulted in the unwitting creation of a "no go" area with regard to the acceptability of my own (and hence Tony's) sexual identity. At the time, I speculated that Tony's absence from the last session testified to the unspoken lack of acceptance that had been a component of the therapy from the start.

Months after Tony left, I ran into him in a gay venue. When he saw me, there was a look of total surprise on his face. He came over to me and said, "Why didn't you tell me?" I did not have an appropriate response to his question and was ashamed for not having told him about my sexual identity. He had confided in me, relied on me to act as a positive psychological force in his life. In keeping my sexual identity out of the room, I had replaced positive acceptance of homosexuality with shame; the "real" relationship within the gay therapeutic dyad had been corrupted. When Tony reached out to me, I held back. My own learned bracketing of real experience and empathy tainted what could have been honest relating. The result was a reaction formation in which the withheld information became a source of something very much its opposite: shame.

Shame and non-acceptance are likely to be integral to many men's experience of growing up gay in a compulsory heterosexual world. Compounding this in the therapy room is a situation that should be avoided at all costs. Optimally, I would have brought my whole authentic self into the room. While I would not have disclosed the particulars of my own sex-life to Tony, I would have come out to him as gay. This could have opened up our relationship through my modelling the acceptance of my own sexuality, and hence, his. Further, it would have allowed (rather than disallowed) the exploration of the transference and countertransference reactions within the room. Finally, it would have been a more honest therapy.

OBJECT RELATIONS SCHEMA PARTICULAR TO GAY MEN

All individuals develop their own object relations schema in a unique way. The conditions for such a development are over-determined: they are based on a complex mix of heredity, family life, culture, sexuality, and other diverse and contingent elements. This being the case, it might be fair to ask, why focus on the rather specific phenomenon of the gay therapeutic dyad. My first response is a practical one: gay male therapists tend to attract gay male clients. Both the gay therapists and the clients will have been "brought up," to varying degrees, under broadly similar conditions.[5] This is stated with caution: there is a need to recognise potential themes across gay male experience without stigmatising, pathologising, or specifying gay experience. For this reason, object relations is to be used as a tool to access subjective experience, without attempting to enforce a rigid model on a wide variety of people.

Isay (1993b) notes, "Gay men and lesbians generally feel that there are specific developmental and social issues confronting them that most analysts and dynamically oriented therapists have little knowledge of" (pp. 179-180). The gay client is going to need his therapist to understand and accept him on a profound and unconditional level. Simply being gay does not guarantee that the therapist will approach his client in this way. In fact, as addressed above, it could potentially be a hindrance if the therapist has not worked out his own issues regarding his sexual identity. However, the meeting of two gay psyches in the therapy room can be, in itself, a source of enormous healing. However, this healing is not inevitable:

> Mutual recognition is concerned with knowing and being known by the other, whilst simultaneously accepting the other's independence and unknowability. The ideal resolution of its central paradox might be achieved via the maintenance of a constant ten-

sion between recognising the other and asserting the self. Whilst it may take place within a loving and harmonious relationship, its form of connection may also be oppressive or facilitating, controlling or liberating and can involve failure, destruction and aggression. (Simon, 2003, p. 342)

Simon recognises that gay therapist and gay client are not the same, but this does not prevent them from working out issues of difference together (see also Milton, in this collection). Further, he notes the danger of such a relationship in the absence of adequate self-awareness. For example, it is especially important to be mindful of the potential for rejection within the gay therapeutic dyad. Isay (1989) has highlighted this issue in the context of early withdrawal by the heterosexual father of his pre-gay son. "The withdrawal of the father, which is invariably experienced as a rejection, may be a cause of the poor self-esteem and of the sense of inadequacy felt by some gay men" (p. 34). From this perspective, Isay (1993b) further argues that self-disclosure of the therapist's sexual orientation can be one way to temper any potentialities of shame based on sexuality itself. Isay argues that refraining from disclosure automatically implies that the therapist is heterosexual and this alone could be damaging to the self-esteem of the client. Isay argues that so long as the aim of the patient's well-being is at the forefront of the work, disclosure by the therapist can be healing. Disclosure may occur when the client asks the therapist, "Are you gay?" While object relations therapists will certainly be sensitive and thoughtful regarding their responses to such explicit questions, they will also be keenly sensitive to unconscious questions and communications as well.

Object relation therapists see projective identifications as one of these forms of unconscious communication. Cashdan (1988) calls them "the residuals of early object relations that are expressed as disturbances in interpersonal relationships" (p. 81). As projective identifications are played out in the therapy room with the therapist, they can be made conscious, and therefore altered into manifestations that are more positive. Cashdan further describes four fundamental projective identifications: (1) dependency (demonstrated by signals of helplessness); (2) power (issues of dominance and control); (3) sexuality (use of eroticism in relationships); and (4) ingratiation (issues of martyrdom). The confrontation and challenge of such projective identification is encouraged "so that it can be dealt with therapeutically" (p. 102). These projective identifications are likely to be in play within the gay therapeutic dyad. The therapist is encouraged to recognise them by becoming aware of his own countertransferential reactions and to bring them into the awareness of the client.

From this perspective, it is the therapist's duty to be constantly aware of his own countertransference in order to help interpret to himself and to his client the relational dynamics of the situation. Bollas (1987) calls "not-knowing-but-experiencing" the most common countertransference. In this mode, the therapist loses himself within the object relational matrix of the patient in order for the patient to ultimately find himself. Feelings of uncertainty have to be tolerated and contained within the therapist until meaning(s) can be found for them. Within the gay therapeutic dyad, the reactions are likely to reverberate in a particular way. The unique interactions within the gay therapeutic dyad can serve to synergise and heal, whilst ignoring them can stunt progress, or worse, confirm feelings of abandonment and non-acceptance that were already a part of the object relational environment of the client.

The following vignette is an example of object relational reverberation through the use of the author's countertransference in relation to the feelings of rejection he encountered in once-weekly psychotherapy with a long-term client called "James." James came to the author's private practice through the referral of an "out" gay individual familiar with the author's work so James was aware of the author's sexuality from the start–it had been his stated intention to work with a gay psychotherapist. Hence, the problems that were encountered with Tony (see above) were not replicated.

James, who had been abandoned by his father at the age of eight, came to therapy with complaints about repetitive difficulties in his relationships with men, namely feelings of paranoia regarding the consistent potential of being rejected by his partners. After several years of therapy, this paranoia was largely mitigated, and a particular session was devoted to exploring the possibility of ending the psychotherapeutic relationship. Though this conversation appeared to be rational and considered, the author had an uncanny countertransferential reaction: a feeling that something simply was not right. Reminded of Bollas's (1987) conception of "not-knowing-but-experiencing" mentioned above, the author contained this experience until an answer emerged.

The sessions that followed consisted of James reporting anecdotal daily events resulting in the countertransferential feeling within the author that the work being accomplished was superficial. Attending to the countertransference alerted the author that these sessions felt rather empty of any *relational* element (i.e., he felt alone in the consulting room). This was an indication that the author was implicated in the object relational world of his client as a potentially rejecting object. The role, then, was to check if his intuition was correct and, if so, to make the phenomenon conscious to James, thereby revealing the unconscious communication:

> "I get the sense that in the last few sessions you've been reporting information to me–and I've felt as if my function here has been to listen to material that you've already processed–making my role redundant. What do you think?"

> James responded that it was true, and that the past few sessions had felt unproductive. When I pressed him as to why this might be, he was unable to find an answer.

> I responded, "I noticed that this seems to have occurred after our conversation about ending the therapy, and I'm wondering if this had an effect on you."

As it turned out, James told me that though he *knew* there was no implicit rejection in that session, it had *felt* like a rejection. He had been reticent to bring up the material again for fear of awakening these feelings that he had suppressed. By opening and exploring the phenomenon through the author's own countertransference, a sense of relief occurred, and the dyad began to work again on a deeper level. Furthermore, in a reparative effort (intended to counteract previous abandonments and rejections and provide a "good" object to introject), the author agreed that while an ending should be discussed and kept in sight, it would be James who would eventually set the date when he felt ready. This mutually negotiated intervention enabled both client and therapist to access the client's object relational world, and allow for more flexibility to emerge within it. The fact that the non-rejecting external object (the therapist) was an out gay man added a further dimension to the realignment of the client's rejection-tainted internal object world.

CONCLUSION

Object relations provides a rich resource with which to deconstruct, analyse, and reconstruct the way that gay male therapists work with gay male clients. Where affirmative therapy rightly encourages therapists to validate and affirm the (homo)sexuality of their clients, object relations requires that therapists unearth and examine the *unaffirmed* aspects that may be related to their own sexuality. It requires therapists to work deeply on their own internalised complexes and schemas; it compels them to be vulnerable to the client's unconscious communications; it asks them to open themselves to a true relating that fundamentally challenges their own ingrained issues, as well as those of their clients.

NOTES

1. The aim of this paper is to examine the use of object relations theory with special regard to the relationship between gay male therapists and their gay male clients. For this reason, I will be using masculine pronouns throughout.

2. I purposefully use the word "gay" to denote men who *identify* as such. While object relations theory and practice will be just as useful to those working with men who have sex with men, but do not identify as gay, my aim in this paper is to take into account how one's *identity* (self-conception) as a homosexual individual is processed through the therapeutic encounter with a therapist who also identifies as such.

3. In keeping with convention, the author uses two different spellings: *Fantasy* refers to an event taking place in consciousness (e.g., a daydream) whereas *phantasy* refers to events taking place in the unconscious (e.g., conceptions of the good and bad breast).

4. Theorists such as Bergler (1956), Bieber et al. (1962), and Socarides (1989) created aetiological models that pathologised homosexuality. "Homosexuals" were portrayed as either gynophobic, tragically regressed to the oral stage of development, or oedipal failures whose identifications with the mother disrupted their clear dissolution of their Oedipus complex.

5. See Drescher (1998) and Isay (1989).

REFERENCES

Ainsworth, M.D.S., Blehar, M.C., Waters, E. & Wall, S. (1978), *Patterns of Attachment: A Psychological Study of the Strange Situation.* Hillsdale, NJ: Erlbaum.

Bergler, E. (1956), *Homosexuality: Disease or Way of Life?* New York: Collier Books.

Bieber, I., Dain, H., Dince, P., Drellich, M., Grand, H., Gundlach, R., Kremer, M., Rifkin, A., Wilbur, C. & Bieber, T. (1962), *Homosexuality: A Psychoanalytic Study.* New York: Basic Books.

Bollas, C. (1987), *The Shadow of the Object: Psychoanalysis of the Unthought Known.* New York: Columbia University Press.

Bowlby, J. (1969), *Attachment and Loss: Volume 1: Attachment.* London: Pimlico.

Cashdan, S. (1988), *Object Relations Therapy: Using the Relationship.* New York: W.W. Norton and Company.

Cornett, C. (1995), *Reclaiming the Authentic Self: Dynamic Psychotherapy with Gay Men*. Northvale, NJ: Jason Aronson.

Domenici, T. (1995), Exploding the myth of sexual psychopathology. In: *Disorienting Sexuality: Psychoanalytic Reappraisals of Sexual Identities*, eds. T. Domenici & R.C. Lesser. London: Routledge, pp. 33-64.

Drescher, J. (1998), *Psychoanalytic Therapy and the Gay Man*. Hillsdale, NJ: The Analytic Press.

Fairbairn, W.R.D. (1952), *Psychoanalytic Studies of the Personality*. New York & London: Routledge.

Ferenczi, S. (1933), Confusion of tongues between the adult and the child. In: *Final Contributions to the Problems and Methods of Psychoanalysis*. New York: Brunner/Mazel, 1980, pp. 156-167.

Freud, S. (1917), Mourning and melancholia. *Standard Edition*, 14: 243-258. London: Hogarth Press, 1957.

Freud, S. (1921), Group psychology and the analysis of the ego. *Standard Edition*, 18: 65-145. London: Hogarth Press, 1953.

Freud, S. (1926), Inhibitions, symptoms and anxiety. *Standard Edition*, 20: 75-175. London: Hogarth Press, 1959.

Freud, S. (1939), An outline of psychoanalysis. *Standard Edition*, 23: 141-207. London: Hogarth Press, 1964.

Greenberg, J. & Mitchell, S. (1983), *Object Relations in Psychoanalytic Theory*. Cambridge, MA: Harvard University Press.

Grosskurth, P. (1986), *Melanie Klein: Her World and Her Work*. New York: Knopf.

Grotstein, J.S. & Rinsley, D.B. (1994), *Fairbairn and the Origins of Object Relations*. London: Free Association Books.

Hamilton, G.N. (1988), *Self and Others: Object Relations Theory in Practice*. Northvale, NJ: Jason Aronson.

Isay, R.A. (1989), *Being Homosexual: Gay Men and Their Development*. New York: Avon Books.

Isay, R.A. (1993a), The homosexual analyst: Clinical considerations. In: *Affirmative Dynamic Psychotherapy with Gay Men*, ed. C. Cornett. Northvale, NJ: Jason Aronson, pp. 178-198.

Isay, R.A. (1993b), On the analytic treatment of homosexual men. In: *Affirmative Dynamic Psychotherapy with Gay Men*, ed. C. Cornett. Northvale, NJ: Jason Aronson, pp. 23-44.

Jones, D. (2001), Shame, disgust, anger and revenge: Homosexuality and countertransference. *British J. Psychotherapy*, 17(4): 531-534.

Jones, E. (1953), *The Life and Work of Sigmund Freud*. New York: Basic Books.

Klein, M. (1932), *The Psychoanalysis of Children*. London: Vintage.

Lewes, K. (1995), *Psychoanalysis and Male Homosexuality*. Northvale, NJ: Jason Aronson.

Marrone, M. & Cortina, M. (2003), Introduction: Reclaiming Bowlby's contribution to psychoanalysis. In: *Attachment Theory and the Psychoanalytic Process*, eds. M. Cortina & M. Marrone. London: Whurr, pp. 1-24.

Rado, S. (1949), *Psychoanalysis of Behavior: The Collected Papers of Sandor Rado*. New York: Grune and Stratton.

Scharff, J. (1995), *The Primer of Object Relations*. Northvale, NJ: Jason Aronson.

Scharff, J. & Scharff, D.E. (1998), *Object Relations Individual Therapy*. London: Karnac Books.

Segal, H. (1964), *Introduction to the Work of Melanie Klein*. London: Heinemann.

Simon, T.D.R. (2003), Talking man to man: transference-countertransference difficulties in the male same-gender analytic dyad. *British J. Psychotherapy*, 19(3): 335-347.

Socarides, C.W. (1989), *Homosexuality: Psychoanalytic Therapy*. Northvale, NJ: Jason Aronson.

St. Clair, M. (2000), *Object Relations and Self Psychology: An Introduction*. London: Thompson Learning.

Winnicott, D.W. (1982), *Playing and Reality*. London: Routledge.

Young-Bruehl, E. (1988), *Anna Freud: A Biography*. New York: Summit Books.

doi:10.1300/J236v11n01_06

SECTION 3:
EXPLORING LGB IDENTITIES, AND NEEDS FOR SUPPORT AND COMMUNITY

"The Difference that Makes a Difference": What Matters to Lesbians and Gay Men in Psychotherapy

Maeve Malley, DPsychotherapy
Fiona Tasker, PhD

Maeve Malley is a systemic psychotherapist working in the National Health Service and the not-for-profit sector in London.

Fiona Tasker is Senior Lecturer in Psychology, Birkbeck College, University of London School of Psychology, Malet Street, London WC1E 7HX, UK. She is the co-author (with Susan Golombok) of *Growing up in a Lesbian Family: Effects on Child Development* (1997, Guilford).

Address correspondence to: Maeve Malley, DPsychotherapy, HSMT, 729 London Road, Hounslow TW3 1SE, UK (E-mail: maeve.malley@nhs.net).

[Haworth co-indexing entry note]: " 'The Difference that Makes a Difference': What Matters to Lesbians and Gay Men in Psychotherapy." Malley, Maeve, and Fiona Tasker. Co-published simultaneously in *Journal of Gay & Lesbian Psychotherapy* (The Haworth Medical Press, an imprint of The Haworth Press, Inc.) Vol. 11, No. 1/2, 2007, pp. 93-109; and: *British Lesbian, Gay, and Bisexual Psychologies: Theory, Research, and Practice* (ed: Elizabeth Peel, Victoria Clarke, and Jack Drescher) The Haworth Medical Press, an imprint of The Haworth Press, Inc., 2007, pp. 93-109. Single or multiple copies of this article are available for a fee from The Haworth Document Delivery Service [1-800-HAWORTH, 9:00 a.m. - 5:00 p.m. (EST). E-mail address: docdelivery@haworthpress.com].

SUMMARY. Lesbians and gay men are more likely to use psychotherapy services than are heterosexual men and women, yet little is known of the aspects of psychotherapy that lesbians and gay men find helpful. A postal survey with a community sample of lesbians and gay men in the UK who had used counselling or psychotherapy services examined this issue. Content analysis of the responses that lesbians and gay men (n = 365) gave to a series of open-ended questions on what was helpful or unhelpful in psychotherapy revealed that issues related to sexual identity were important in addition to generic qualities of the therapeutic relationship. Lesbians and gay men also listed friends, family of choice, and family of origin, and complementary or "alternative" therapies as important sources of support aside from psychotherapy. This study has implications for counselling and psychotherapy training, for counsellors and psychotherapists working with lesbians and gay men, and for lesbians and gay men who use psychotherapy. doi:10.1300/J236v11n01_07 *[Article copies available for a fee from The Haworth Document Delivery Service: 1-800-HAWORTH. E-mail address: <docdelivery@haworthpress.com> Website: <http://www.HaworthPress.com> © 2007 by The Haworth Press, Inc. All rights reserved.]*

KEYWORDS. Coming out, counselling, families of choice, families of origin, gay, homosexual, lesbian, psychotherapy

INTRODUCTION

Psychotherapy, like medicine and like other professions, is not a neutral activity, though it is often presented as such. The theory and practice of counselling and psychotherapy are pervaded by personal, societal and cultural bias and by beliefs presented as "fact" or "truth" (Geraghty and Meddings, 1999). These beliefs, necessarily, will tend to be those of the prevailing social orthodoxy (Shamai, 1999) which will, equally, tend to be both heterosexist and homophobic (Siegal and Walker, 1996). Given the marked historical connection in mental health services, between homosexuality and "sickness" or pathology, professional helpers from this field may not always be an entirely benign source of support for lesbians and gay men.

Use of Psychotherapy

Even given this history, however, there is a clear consensus in the literature, that lesbians and gay men are more likely than the population in general to use psychotherapy (or counselling) at some stage of their lives (Morgan, 1997; Herman, 1994; Hughes et al., 1997). The proportions of gay men using psychotherapy services seem to be lower than for lesbians, although the rates for gay men are still higher than the general population averages (Jones and Gabriel, 1999). Given the relatively high proportions of lesbians and gay men who use psychotherapy services, surprisingly little is known about what aspects of therapy are experienced as helpful or unhelpful. The factors that a sample of 365 lesbians and gay men in the UK see as helpful or unhelpful are explored in the current study.

Therapist Characteristics

The question of how therapy might be helpful to lesbians and gay men has yet to be addressed. Previous studies have concentrated on describing various characteristics of the therapist that seem to be associated with client satisfaction as reported by lesbians and gay men. The gender of the therapist was seen as the most important characteristic for women, but important also for men (Liddle, 1997; Spier, 1998). The sexuality of the therapist was also regarded as important by lesbian and gay male clients (Jones and Gabriel, 1999; Milton and Coyle, 1999).

Reasons for Using Therapy

The reasons why lesbians and gay men use psychotherapy services more than heterosexuals have yet to be empirically investigated, so explanations are necessarily speculative. Reviewing the available literature, lesbians and gay men are no more characterized by psychopathology than the population in general (Hooker, 1957; Coleman, 1982; Gonsiorek, 1982 and 1991), but there may still be specific difficulties associated with various aspects of lesbian and gay identities that are unique to this population (Sayce, 1995). These may be associated with specific life-stages or more generally to do with defining identity and achieving a desirable level of self-acceptance (Dunkle, 1994).

Some life issues arising for lesbians and gay men are common to the population at large. Existential experiences are inherent in negotiating between self and family, self and friends, self and lover(s), self and society, and self and the environment. Even these experiences, however, are mediated through the context into which one is born and one's innate attributes. For example, there may be differences of age, race, culture and gender in how lesbian and gay male clients express distress or unhappiness and indeed in how they deal with distress or unhappiness. These will make a great deal of difference in the way common life events are experienced.

Psychotherapy and Other Sources of Support

Another consideration is: how well does psychotherapy help lesbians and gay men link with other non-professional sources of emotional, social, practical and financial support (Annesley and Coyle, 1998)? There are particular factors pertaining to the experience of many lesbian and gay men that may preclude their families of origin from being close and supportive links. Whereas children from other minority cultures can be taught by their families how best to combat and protect themselves from the consequences of minority status, this is rarely the case for lesbians and gay men (Blumenfeld and Raymond, 1988; Ross et al., 1996). The trauma of coming out and of the reactions of family members to this disclosure often leads to adverse consequences, at least in the short-term, and not atypically may lead to long-term family schisms. Lesbians and gay men will select to whom they come out–and in what order; typically, a best friend first, then a sibling(s) or a mother, and lastly father (Savin-Williams, 1998). Some choose never to be out to certain family members.

Families of choice may be the "chosen family" of lesbians and gay men. Family of choice may include lovers, ex-lovers, friends, the families of lovers or ex-lovers and children, along with chosen family of origin members (Weston, 1991). Thus it may include ties of blood and ties of friendship (and sometimes of marriage) in a fluid structure. Family of choice may interconnect with friends or provide entry into a wider community of lesbians and gay men (Nardi and Sherrod, 1994). Family of choice and friends can give ongoing support, reinforcement, emotional intimacy and a context in which lesbians and gay men can be "out" and can discuss their social, emotional and sexual lives. A felt connection and involvement with the lesbian and gay communities has been identified as a protective factor for the psychological well-being of lesbians and gay men and a support in dealing with issues of isolation, marginalisation, conflicts of identity and alienation (Greene, 1994; DiPlacido, 1998; Green, 2000).

THE STUDY

To investigate the helpfulness or unhelpfulness of psychotherapy as experienced by lesbians and gay men, an anonymous community survey was conducted during 1999 and 2000 within the United Kingdom. Survey questionnaires asked lesbians and gay men a series of questions about use of, experience within, and feelings about psychotherapy. This paper discusses the responses to four open-ended questions that asked respondents to express their own views on the helpfulness or unhelpfulness of psychotherapy. These questions provided suitable data for content analyses to identify factors that lesbians and gay men experienced as helpful or unhelpful in psychotherapy.

The Hypotheses

It was predicted that:

- The ability of the therapist to discuss/address sexual identity specific issues in the therapy will be important to respondents.
- There might have been sexuality-related issues, or discussions as part of the therapy that had proved particularly helpful or unhelpful to lesbian and gay male clients.
- Other sources of emotional support to psychotherapy would include family (both of choice and origin), friends, and the lesbian and gay community.
- In terms of selecting a therapist in future, issues of sexuality and of gender would be prominent.

Method

Sample

Two thousand questionnaires entitled "What do lesbians and gay men think about counselling/therapy?" were distributed during 1999-2000 across the United Kingdom. A total of 646 questionnaires were returned anonymously of which 637 were complete and statistically analysed. Slightly more gay men than lesbians returned surveys: 336 men, as compared with 291 women. Ten respondents identified as transgendered. Respondents ranged from 20 to over 60 years old with 28% of respondents aged between 20-29 years, 40% of respondents aged between

30-39 years and 21% of respondents aged between 40-49 years. The majority of respondents (92%) reported that they were White (British, European, Irish or of other white ethnicity) while the remaining respondents recorded a variety of ethnicities including Bangladeshi, Black British, Black African, Black Caribbean, Chinese, Indian, Pakistani, and of mixed race. Most respondents lived in London (63%), with a further 9.6% living in the southeast of England and the rest resided in different regions across the UK. Perhaps because of the larger numbers of lesbians and gay men in the London area, London residents tend to be overrepresented in many studies of lesbians and gay men. The large majority of respondents were in paid employment (79.6%) with only 6% and 7% respectively receiving either job-seekers' allowances/unemployment benefit or invalidity benefits (all state benefits provided to people who have been unable to find work, or who are unable by reason of illness or disability to sustain paid work). Just over 30% of respondents (31.3%) earned less than £15,000 [$25,000 approx.]. Nearly 40% of respondents (38.2%) were earning between £16-25,000 per annum [$26,000-$41,000], 13.1% earned between £26-40,000 [$43,000-$66,000], and 5% earned over £41,000 [$68,000]. Just over a third of the sample (34%) reported having an undergraduate degree and 21% reported having a postgraduate degree, 19.6% had left school at 18 years old or held OND/HND (vocational, rather than academic qualifications) or apprenticeship level qualifications and 21.4% had left school at the minimum school leaving age (16 years old).

Procedure

Respondents were recruited via stalls at lesbian and gay community festivals (for example, Gay Pride/Mardi Gras and Winter/Summer Rights festivals in London) and throughout Britain via lesbian and gay male organisations (helplines, lesbian and gay centres, advice services, special interest groups, HIV and other health support groups, and lesbian and gay Black and minority ethnic, Jewish, men's, and women's organizations, and disability groups). Questionnaires were returned either in person (via stalls at festival events) or by pre-paid post (see Malley [2001] for full details). Clearly, this distribution network necessarily favoured the inclusion of respondents who were happy (at least in some contexts) to identify openly as lesbians or as gay men.

Measures

There is no clear division or definition–even among counsellors and psychotherapists–of what constitutes counselling and what constitutes psychotherapy. Consequently, it is even less likely that users of services would be entirely clear about the precise definition of the kind of service that they currently use or have used. Therefore, the portmanteau term "counselling/therapy" is used throughout this study and throughout the questionnaires.

Respondents were invited to write in answers or thoughts in response to the four open questions. The space left for the answers will, of course, have played a part in determining the length of the response, as will the placing of the questions at the end of the questionnaire, when respondents might be expected to be running out of time and energy. The questions were:

- "What did the counsellor/therapist do that was particularly helpful?"
- "What did the counsellor/therapist do which was particularly unhelpful?"
- "What would you do differently now (if anything) in choosing a counsellor/therapist?"
- "What other sources of support do you use as well as, or instead of, counselling/therapy?"

Content Analysis

Respondents were invited to write in answers to, or thoughts in response to, the four open questions. Participants' written responses were analysed using content analysis techniques (Weber, 1990; Berger, 2000), where categories were created from direct quotations from respondents' answers to the open-ended questions. Where there was different wording but similar content in responses, they were assessed by two independent raters before being assigned to categories. There was extremely good agreement on categories and allocation of items between raters (95.4%). As respondents could give answers that fell into more than one category, the categories are not mutually exclusive (e.g., "listened and was empathetic" contributes to more than one category. Listening constituted a discrete category of response, as did respondents feeling that the therapist's response was empathic). Therefore, adding up the total number of responses in each category may exceed the number of respondents to a particular question.

RESULTS

"What Did the Counsellor/Therapist Do Which Was Particularly Helpful?"

The 365 respondents who answered this section made a total of 424 comments giving insights into what they experienced as helpful in therapy (see Table 1). The majority of answers to this question focused on the traditional elements of counselling/therapy rather than referred to sexuality specific issues.

The most valued attribute was when respondents felt that their therapist had "listened" to them (n = 102, 28%). Similarly appreciated generic therapist skills were "understanding" (n = 38, 10.4%), "reflected back to me" (n = 29, 7.9%), "was empathetic" (n = 21, 5.7%) and "helped me get in touch with my feelings" (n = 10, 2.6%). This use of language suggested a familiarity with counselling terminology from some respondents.

Intriguingly, some "generic" elements may have had a specific meaning for this client group, although they were not flagged as such by respondents. For example, categories such as "gave information, support or advocacy" (n = 38, 10.4%), "gave me faith in myself" (n = 32, 8.7%) and "didn't judge me" (n = 20, 5.4%), may have a specific meaning for

TABLE 1. Summary of Main Findings from Content Analysis of Survey Responses

- therapists with knowledge of, and the confidence to discuss, issues of sexual identity were valued by respondents
- therapist negativity about clients' sexuality was seen as a major negative factor by respondents
- the most common change that respondents would make in future therapy, was in seeking out lesbian or gay male therapists
- generic factors such as "understanding" and "listening" were highly valued by respondents
- friends were highly valued as a source of support by respondents
- a wide range of complementary therapies was seen as valuable by respondents

lesbians and gay men in considering their life experience or the impact of their sexual identity.

The most sexual identity specific category mentioned was "talked about my sexuality" (n = 15, 4.1%); whether this was an issue raised first by therapist or client, is not defined, but its inclusion in this category defines it as a conversation that was experienced as positive.

"What Did the Counsellor/Therapist Do Which Was Particularly Unhelpful?"

Fewer comments were made about unhelpfulness of therapists or counsellors (n = 254, 70%) in contrast to the 400 plus comments made in response to the previous question on what was helpful. There were two categories very specifically related to sexual identity: the therapist "was negative about my sexuality" (n = 18, 4.9%) and, separately, "had a lack of understanding about sexual identity issues" (n = 11, 3.0%). The former was the single factor that accounted for the greatest number of dissatisfied feelings about the counselling/therapy experience as cited by respondents. Furthermore, there were a number of responses that could have had a particular sexuality specific meaning for lesbian or gay respondents: "was judgmental" (n = 15, 4.1%), "patronised me" (n = 9, 2.4%), "I had no choice about attending" (n = 5, 1.3%), "made assumptions" (n = 3, .8%), although respondents did not necessarily flag sexuality when writing these comments.

Finally, in response to this question, there were a number of answers that related to general dissatisfaction with therapy and seemed to have no apparent link to the respondent's lesbian or gay identity. General dissatisfactions included "didn't talk" (n = 18, 4.9%), "was too directive" (n = 18, 4.9%), "talked too much" (n = 18, 4.9%), and "didn't challenge me" (n = 12, 3.2%). Only a couple of therapy approaches or techniques were named as unhelpful including "too detached/analytical" (n = 18, 4.9%) and a Gestalt technique using two chairs ("did Gestalt 'chair' work"–n = 6, 1.6%). There is also the profoundly disturbing finding that at least one therapist had had sex with a respondent.

"What Would You Do Differently Now (if Anything) in Choosing a Counsellor/Therapist?"

Some responses to the above question could apply to any population group. The most cited answer was, "look around more" (n = 38, 10.4%).

There were also respondents who said that they would "go to therapy sooner" (n = 3, .8%), "would go to longer-term therapy" (n = 6, 1.6%) or "would be more assertive" (n = 5, 1.3%). There were also a few respondents who would seek out specific qualities in a therapist, for example, "a Black therapist" (n = 4, 1.2%) and "an older therapist" (n = 4, 1%). Some respondents said they would either not return to therapy (n = 14, 3.8%), would do nothing differently (n = 14, 3.8%), or would return to the same therapist (n = 9, 2.4%).

Other written reflections on what respondents would do differently were definitively linked to sexual identity, so 6.3% (n = 23) of responses mentioned "would seek a lesbian counsellor" and 5.4% (n = 20) of responses mentioned "would seek a gay male counsellor," and 2.4% (n = 9) indicated that they "would ask more about the therapist's approach to lesbian or gay issues." There were further responses given by both male and female respondents who said that they "would choose a woman therapist" (n = 5, 1.4%) and female respondents who said they would "choose a feminist therapist" (n = 5, 1.4%). Some other areas that might be linked with sexual identity specific concerns for lesbians and gay men were cited by respondents who said that they would "ask more about training/ethics/models of working" (n = 32, 8.7%), "would see someone privately" (n = 14, 3.8%), "would look for, or would avoid, a specific model of working" (n = 12, 3.2%) or "would not be forced to go" (n = 3, .8%).

"What Other Sources of Support Do You Use as well as, or Instead of, Counselling/Therapy?"

There was a high degree of consensus among respondents as to the most used sources of support: over 60% of respondents indicated that they looked to their friends for support (n = 222, 60.8%); 12.3% (n = 45) of responses indicated that respondents looked to "family" for support, however, many written answers did not indicate whether this was family of choice and/or family of origin. Of the family of origin members specifically named, "sister" (n = 109, 30% of those named) and "mother" (n = 219, 60% of those named) were easily the most often cited–fathers, brothers or more distant relations were much less frequently mentioned. Partners or lovers were specifically named as a source of support by 11.8% (n = 43) of respondents.

More than 10% of respondents indicated that they looked to the lesbian and gay community, to groups, centres or drop-ins for support. Among the other sources of support given by respondents, many complementary therapies or activities were mentioned. These were an eclectic selection of yoga/tai chi/other bodywork/relaxation/meditation, shiatsu, acupuncture, Chinese medicine, cranial osteopathy, herbs, hypnotherapy, dance therapy, diet, reiki, massage and homeopathy. Respondents more often used these categories, combined, than any other source of support apart from "friends."

Other sources of support listed were self-help groups, colleagues, spirituality/religion, and groups such as Alcoholics Anonymous, Narcotics Anonymous and Al-Anon (a support group for relatives of drinkers). Activities or resources such as exercise, reading and writing were also regularly cited. Just over 1% of respondents cited their general practitioner (family doctor) as a source of support. Only one respondent mentioned "prescribed drugs" whereas four people mentioned "alcohol or recreational drugs" as a source of support.

DISCUSSION

Lesbians and gay men as clients in psychotherapy find the same things useful as general populations, but may find it particularly helpful if the therapist is able to discuss sexual identity issues, or acknowledge the importance of a lesbian or gay male identity. They also find some therapeutic work unhelpful in ways similar to the general population, but lesbians and gay men also may have specific additional concerns. These will vary, but will often focus around the therapist's knowledge of potential issues connected with sexual identity and/or an anxiety about negative attitudes towards lesbian or gay male sexual identity. Thus the results support the predictions made that sexual identity specific issues are very important but also indicate that these are in addition to generic concerns about psychotherapy. The main findings of the survey are summarized in Table 1.

Findings

There were several aspects of the experience of psychotherapy identified in the content analysis of written survey responses that seem to be specific to lesbians and gay men. These were issues having to do with the therapist's perception of the client's sexual identity, those addressing or validating this identity, and the varied sources of socioemotional support used by lesbians and gay men outside therapy. "Had a lack of understanding about sexual identity issues" and "Was negative about my sexuality" were both cited by respondents. "Was negative about my sexuality" was the single factor that accounted for the greatest number of negative feelings about the counselling/therapy experience in the content analysis. This accords with the finding of the British "Count Me In" study (CMI, 2001) where 14.8% of respondents felt that their "problems" were inappropriately attributed by their therapists, to their lesbian or gay male sexual identity.

Respondents had some clear ideas about the things that they might do differently in the future, both in terms of selecting a therapist and in the questions they might ask of the therapist. It seems that the experience of therapy that they discussed may have made them feel both clearer about whom they wanted as their therapist and what they wanted from this therapist. In terms of selecting a therapist in the future some respondents suggested sexual identity specific concerns as predicted, but many also indicated possible generic issues. For example, 10% of respondents indicated that they would look around more before signing up with a therapist.

This study focussed not just on the use of psychotherapy by lesbians and gay men, but also on their use of other sources of support, and some particularly interesting–and unexpected–findings emerged in these responses. One source of support that emerged clearly within this survey was the use of a wide range of complementary or alternative therapies by the lesbian and gay male respondents. There have been suggestions that the stigmatized position of lesbians and gay men may be damaging not just to their emotional and psychological health, but also to their physical health (Wilton, 1997; Bailey et al., 2000). Since the relationship between the statutory medical and mental health services and lesbians and gay men has traditionally been somewhat conflicted, this population may be particularly open to the use of complementary medicine, for support with both physical and psychological health (Saphira and Glover, 2000).

In terms of the people known to respondents that may be viewed as sources of emotional/psychic support as well as, or instead of, counselling or therapy, it is clear that the lesbians and gay men in this survey accord with previous lesbian and gay male samples in terms of valuing their friends as their most important sources of support (Weeks et al., 1996) thus supporting the prediction made. Lovers or partners and family members were also mentioned as sources of support (Laird, 1996). For respondents naming family of origin members as sources of support, mothers and sisters were more often mentioned than were fathers and brothers. This accords both with reports that women may be identified as less homophobic than men (Herek, 1988; Smith and Gordon, 1998) and with research indicating that lesbians and gay men tend to come out to siblings and mothers before fathers (Savin-Williams, 1998).

Limitations of the Study

Respondents to the current study may not be representative of the wider lesbian and gay community; given that it is impossible to know what a representative sample of this community would be, this limitation is inevitable (Rothblum, 1994; Wellings et al., 1994). With a sample that was less London-based, middle-class, white and youthful, different responses may have been given to the survey questions, and distribution in other contexts could have generated answers from respondents who were less "visible" as lesbians or gay men.

The questions could have been framed to differentiate between "generically" helpful, or unhelpful, therapist/therapy factors, though this might well have excluded factors that were seen as contextually important to lesbians and gay men. The questions could also have specifically asked respondents to differentiate between factors that they felt were specific to their sexual identity, as opposed to those linked to other variables. The delivery context of therapy (private sector, public sector or charitable sector) may also have affected respondents' feelings about the therapy, as may factors such as whether or not they were given choices about the therapist they saw (in terms of model of working, or variables such as gender, sexual identity, "race" or culture) or the kind of therapy offered. This was clearly an issue for respondents who said they had "no choice about attending."

Finally, respondents could have been asked if the issue that they sought to address in therapy was one that they felt was directly or indirectly connected to their sexual identity, or to other aspects of their lives.

IMPLICATIONS

There are implications arising from the findings of the present study for therapists, for therapist training institutions and for lesbian and gay male clients. Based on responses from this study, it appears that respondents want their therapists to have the confidence to raise or to respond to issues concerned with sexual identity in the same way therapists consider or question other contextual identities, such as age, culture, family status, dis/ability. This implies that the ability to work with lesbian or gay male clients requires that therapists should be secure enough in their practice to acknowledge that there may be issues that are specific to lesbian or gay identities, rather than subscribe to a liberal agenda for therapy equating "acceptance" with no difference between heterosexual and lesbian or gay clients (Malley and Tasker, 1999).

In terms of therapist practice, if a client does not raise the issue of sexual identity during therapy, should the therapist do so? Admittedly, this can be seen as a Catch-22 situation for therapists. On the one hand, a therapist raising the issue may imply to the client that the therapist is assuming that sexual identity is connected with every life issue, even when the client does not feel this to be the case. On the other hand, if the therapist does not put sexual identity in the therapeutic foreground, both identity and context issues are obscured and neglected (Hellman, 1996). This is a discussion therapists have engaged in while working with clients who may be different or similar to their own groups, or to dominant, societal groups, in the areas of culture, "race," class, age or disability (Siegal and Walker, 1996). There is no single answer as to how this should best be addressed, but there is an increasing acceptance that these "differences" need to be contextualized and not ignored or dismissed as irrelevant.

Therapists would do well to acknowledge that their own personal contexts and histories will influence these processes and allow themselves to be "curious" (Cecchin, 1987) about these differences without feeling, or being, voyeuristic or judgmental about them. The challenge to counselling and psychotherapeutic training institutions is firstly to recognise the need for such skills acquisition in their trainees, and secondly, to help them learn these skills. Whatever the orientation of a therapeutic modality (and respondents had experienced a range of therapeutic orientations), the issue of sexual identity is relevant to the experience in therapy of many of these respondents.

Many of these clients valued their experience of therapy, but many of them also indicated that they had learnt from their experience of therapy to seek out specifics from their therapists and from the therapy in future. The desire for therapists to be transparent both about their training, ethics and models of working and about their approach to lesbian and gay issues is evident. Evident also is the possible choice to see a private therapist (possibly on the basis of greater client control and choice) and to look for a therapist who may resemble her/his client in some key variables (gender, sexual identity, "race" or age) or simply to look around more, possibly to compare therapists.

AUTHORS NOTE

The authors wish to thank the anonymous respondents for sharing their experiences of psychotherapy and counselling in this survey. Thanks to Monica Max West for inter-rater reliability ratings contributing to the content analyses of written responses.
This title draws on Gregory Bateson's (2000, p. 459) notion that "a difference is a very peculiar and obscure concept. It is certainly not a thing or an event. This piece of paper is different than the wood of this lectern. There are many differences between them–of colour, texture, shape, etc. . . . Of this infinitude, one selects a very limited number which become information. In fact, what is meant by information–the elementary unit of information–is a difference which makes a difference."

REFERENCES

Annesley, P. & Coyle, A. (1998), Dykes and Psychs: Lesbian women's experiences of clinical psychology services. *Changes: An International J. of Psychology & Psychotherapy*, 16(4):247-258.
Bailey, J.V., Kavanagh, J., Owen, C., McLean, K.A. & Skinner, C.J. (2000), Lesbians and cervical screening. *British J. General Practice*, June, 50(455): 481-482.
Bateson, G. (2000), *Steps to an Ecology of Mind: Collected Essays in Anthropology, Psychiatry, Evolution, and Epistemology.* Chicago: University of Chicago Press.
Berger, A.A. (2000), *Media and Communication Research Methods: An Introduction to Qualitative and Quantitative Approaches.* Thousand Oaks, CA: Sage.
Blumenfeld, W.J. & Raymond, D. (1993), *Looking at Gay and Lesbian Life.* Boston: Beacon Press.
Cecchin, G. (1987), Hypothesizing, circularity and neutrality revisited: An invitation to curiosity. *Family Process*, 26:405-413.
Coleman, E. (1982), Changing approaches to the treatment of homosexuality: A review. *American Behavioral Scientist*, 25:397-405.
Count Me In (CMI) (2001), Survey undertaken by East Sussex Health Authority and Brighton and Hove Regeneration Partnership's Social Inclusion Programme. *Unpublished report.*
DiPlacido, J. (1998), Minority stress among lesbians, gay men, and bisexuals: A consequence of heterosexism, homophobia, and stigmatization. In: *Stigma and Sexual Orientation: Understanding Prejudice Against Lesbians, Gay Men, and Bisexuals,* ed. G.M. Herek. Thousand Oaks, CA: Sage.
Dunkle, J.H. (1994), Counseling gay male clients: A review of treatment efficacy research: 1975-present. *J. Gay & Lesbian Psychotherapy*, 2(2):1-19.
Geraghty, W. & Meddings, S. (1999), Lesbian, gay and bisexual issues in systemic therapy: Reflections on the wider context. *Context*, 45:11-13.

Gonsiorek, J. (1982), Results of psychological testing on homosexual populations. *American Behavioral Scientist*, 25(4):385-396.

Gonsiorek, J.C. (1991), The empirical basis for the demise of the illness model of homosexuality. In: *Homosexuality: Research Implications for Public Policy*, eds. J.C. Gonsiorek & J.D. Weinrich. Newbury Park, CA: Sage, pp. 115-136.

Green, R.J. (2000), Lesbians, gay men and their parents: A critique of LaSala and the prevailing clinical "wisdom." *Family Process*, 39:257-266.

Greene, B. (1994), Ethnic-minority lesbians and gay men: Mental health and treatment issues. *J. Consulting & Clinical Psychology*, 62(2):243-251.

Hellman, R.E. (1996), Issues in the treatment of lesbian women and gay men with chronic mental illness. *Psychiatric Services*, 47(10):1093-1098.

Herek, G.M. (1988), Heterosexuals' attitudes toward lesbians and gay men. *J. Sex Research*, 25(4): 451-477.

Herman, E. (1994), *Psychiatry, Psychology, and Homosexuality*. New York: Chelsea House Publishers.

Hooker, E. (1957), The adjustment of the male overt homosexual. *J. Projective Techniques*, 21:18-31.

Hughes, T.L., Haas, A.P. & Avery, L. (1997), Lesbians and mental health: Preliminary results from the Chicago Women's Health survey. *J. Gay & Lesbian Medical Association*, 1(3):137-148.

Jones, M.A. & Gabriel, M.A. (1999), Utilization of psychotherapy by lesbians, gay men, and bisexuals: Findings from a nationwide survey. *American J. Orthopsychiatry*, 69(2):209-219.

Laird, J. (1996), Invisible ties: Lesbians and their families of origin. In: *Lesbians and Gays in Couples and Families*, eds., J. Laird & R.J. Green. San Francisco: Jossey-Bass Publishers.

Liddle, B.J. (1997), Gay and lesbian clients' selection of therapists and utilization of therapy. *Psychotherapy*, 34(1):11-18.

Malley, M. & Tasker, F. (1999), Lesbians, gay men and family therapy: A contradiction in terms? *J. Family Therapy*, 21:3-29.

Malley, M. (2001), *Straight Talking? Lesbians, Gay Men and Psychotherapists*. Unpublished Doctoral dissertation. Birkbeck College, University of London, UK.

Milton, M. & Coyle, A. (1999), Lesbian and gay affirmative psychotherapy: Issues in theory and practice. *British Association for Sexual & Marital Therapy*, 14(1):43-59.

Morgan, K.S. (1997), Why lesbians choose therapy: Presenting problems, attitudes, and political concerns. *J. Gay & Lesbian Social Services*, 6(3):57-75.

Nardi, P.M. & Sherrod, D. (1994), Friendship in the lives of gay men and lesbians. *J. Social & Personal Relationships*, 11:185-199.

Ross, M.W., Fernandez-Esquer, M.E. & Seibt, A. (1996), Understanding across the sexual orientation gap: Sexuality as culture. In: *Handbook of Intercultural Training*, eds. D. Landis & R.S. Bhagat. Thousand Oaks, CA: Sage, pp. 414-430.

Rothblum, E.D. (1994), Introduction to the special section: Mental health of lesbians and gay men. *J. of Consulting & Clinical Psychology*, 62(2):211-220.

Saphira, M. & Glover, M. (2000), New Zealand lesbian health survey. *J. Gay & Lesbian Medical Association*, 4:49-56.

Savin-Williams, R.C. (1998), " . . . *And Then I Became Gay": Young Men's Stories.* New York: Routledge.

Sayce, L. (1995), *Breaking the Link Between Homosexuality and Mental Illness: An Unfinished History.* Unpublished MIND discussion document.

Shamai, M. (1999), Beyond neutrality: A politically orientated systemic intervention. *J. Family Therapy,* 21:217-229.

Siegal, S. & Walker, G.J. (1996), Connections: Conversations between a gay therapist and a straight therapist. In: *Lesbians and Gays in Couples and Families,* eds. J. Laird & R.J. Green. San Francisco: Jossey-Bass Publishers.

Smith, M.R. & Gordon, R.A. (1998), Personal need for structure and attitudes toward homosexuality. *J. Social Psychology,* 138(1):83-87.

Spier, T. (1998), *The Search for Congruence: Lesbian Clients' Perceptions of Their Lesbian Feminist Therapists.* Paper presented at American Psychological Association Convention, San Francisco, August 14.

Weber, R.P. (1990), *Basic Content Analysis* (2nd edition). London: Sage.

Weeks, J., Donovan, C. & Heaphy, B. (1996), *Families of Choice: Patterns of Non-Heterosexual Relationships. A Literature Review.* Social Science Research Papers, No. 2. London: South Bank University.

Wellings, K. & Wadsworth, J. (1994), *Sexual Attitudes and Lifestyles.* Oxford: Blackwell.

Weston, K. (1991), *Families We Choose: Lesbians, Gays, Kinship.* New York: Columbia University Press.

Wilton, T. (1997), *Good for You: A Handbook on Lesbian Health and Wellbeing.* London: Cassell.

doi:10.1300/J236v11n01_07

Community in the 21st Century: Issues Arising from a Study of British Lesbians and Gay Men

Sonja J. Ellis, PhD, AFBPsS

SUMMARY. Historically, lesbians and gay men (sometimes together; sometimes separately) have created "communities" because their oppressed status has often rendered them invisible from one another. At the height of second-wave feminism, lesbian communities in the UK comprised a wide range of organised social activities and venues, including Women's Centres (although not exclusively lesbian) in most major cities. Likewise, the HIV/AIDS crisis of the 1980s proliferated a range of health-based organisations and groups available (again not exclusively) to gay men. However, with a few notable exceptions, the mainstreaming of lesbian and gay culture, together with the ever-increasing commercialisation of lesbian and gay venues, appear to have resulted in the marginalisation and in many cases disappearance of non-scene venues

Sonja J. Ellis is Social Scientist and Senior Lecturer in Psychology, Sheffield Hallam University, UK.

Address correpondence to: Dr. Sonja J. Ellis, Applied Social Studies Division, Faculty of Development and Society, Sheffield Hallam University, Collegiate Crescent Campus, Sheffield S10 2BP, UK (E-mail: S.J.Ellis@shu.ac.uk).

The author offers thanks to her colleagues Damien Fitzgerald and Matthew Waites, and two anonymous reviewers for their helpful feedback on earlier drafts of this paper.

A preliminary version of this paper was presented at the British Psychological Society West Midlands Branch Conference on Sexuality and Identity in November 2003.

[Haworth co-indexing entry note]: "Community in the 21st Century: Issues Arising from a Study of British Lesbians and Gay Men." Ellis, Sonja J. Co-published simultaneously in *Journal of Gay & Lesbian Psychotherapy* (The Haworth Medical Press, an imprint of The Haworth Press, Inc.) Vol. 11, No. 1/2, 2007, pp. 111-126; and: *British Lesbian, Gay, and Bisexual Psychologies: Theory, Research, and Practice* (ed: Elizabeth Peel, Victoria Clarke, and Jack Drescher) The Haworth Medical Press, an imprint of The Haworth Press, Inc., 2007, pp. 111-126. Single or multiple copies of this article are available for a fee from The Haworth Document Delivery Service [1-800-HAWORTH, 9:00 a.m. - 5:00 p.m. (EST). E-mail address: docdelivery@haworthpress.com].

and organised social activities for lesbians and gay men. Drawing on data from a current (and ongoing) interview-based study with UK lesbians and gay men, this paper highlights the ways in which these changes have affected the lives and lifestyles of lesbians and gay men, resulting in the social exclusion of certain individuals and groups. The implications of these findings for psychotherapy–in particular the need for support based in the LG community–are discussed. doi:10.1300/J236v11n01_08

[Article copies available for a fee from The Haworth Document Delivery Service: 1-800-HAWORTH. E-mail address: <docdelivery@haworthpress.com> Website: <http://www.HaworthPress.com> © 2007 by The Haworth Press, Inc. All rights reserved.]

KEYWORDS. Community, community-based support, gay, homosexual, isolation, lesbian, psychotherapy, social exclusion, social networks, social support, social identity

INTRODUCTION

Internationally, lesbians and gay men (sometimes together; sometimes separately) have historically organised socially because their marginalised status within society has often rendered them invisible to both society and each other (D'Augelli and Garnets, 1995; Green, 1997). The existence of UK and US lesbian and/or gay male communities prior to the New York Stonewall riots in 1969 are well documented (Berube, 1990; Hamer, 1995; Porter and Weeks, 1998; Robb, 2003). Whilst contemporary writers and historians have undertaken considerable groundwork to reclaim lesbian and gay (L/G) histories, making them visible, from the late Victorian period to the mid 1900s, L/G communities in the UK comprised largely underground networks of social connection. This may be attributable, at least in part, to the illegal status of (male) homosexual acts in the UK from 1885-1967.[1] Nevertheless, community–both the literal environments (e.g., gay spaces) and the affiliative links that individuals have with each other (D'Augelli and Garnets, 1995)–has for L/G (to a greater or lesser extent) been very important in developing both social and political networks with one another.

Although lesbians in the UK have always organised socially and (sometimes) politically, the 1970s and early 1980s represent–as two interviewees put it–a "golden era" in terms of lesbian social life. Largely due to women-centred political organisation around a feminist agenda, many lesbians internationally aligned themselves with women and in most cities in the UK there were women's groups, organisations and centres that attracted large followings of lesbian women. Whilst these spaces served as places where lesbians could temporarily be free of heterosexist oppression (Green, 1997; Kitzinger and Perkins, 1993), it was also through these that (middle-class) lesbians connected with one another primarily on a social, rather than a sexual basis.

Gay men in the UK, on the other hand, have tended not to organise politically, developing visible communities primarily based on sexual ties. Nevertheless, they also had well-established social networks, although typically on a more invisible level. The gay press, notably the *Gay Times*,[2] provided a rich support network for men to gradually come out and to connect socially with others, serving a dual role as both a means for meeting potential sexual partners as well as a source of social support, community and companionship. In addition, the UK L/G Switchboard network[3] played a consistent and powerful role in putting gay men in touch with appropriate support networks and social events.[4] In the mid-1980s, gay men (often with support from lesbians) organised politically around the AIDS/HIV crisis, which in some UK cities (e.g., Sheffield) resulted in the emergence of sexual health centres. The crisis fuelled a heightened need for social support within the gay male community, resulting in many of these centres becoming a focal point for support and social connection.[5]

Although communities have clearly provided a basis for organising politically around L/G issues, they have also served other important roles (Esterberg, 1996). Despite knowledge of their existence and accessibility being primarily limited to those who are already relatively confident about their homosexual identity (cf. D'Augelli and Garnets, 1995), a number of UK (Holt and Griffin, 2003; Markowe, 2002) and US (McCarthy, 2000) studies have highlighted the way in which L/G communities have historically served an important function as a reference point from which to develop and reaffirm a positive identity as L/G. In this respect they have been an essential focal point for services, resources and information as well as (often) a source of social support.

In the UK over the last twenty years, there has been a significant shift in L/G community and social culture. The mid 1980s marked the decline of second-wave feminism and the gradual assimilation of the lesbian community into an "integrated" L/G community. This shift also saw the depoliticisation of lesbian identity and community, resulting in the gradual demise of the thriving support and social networks that existed at the height of second-wave feminism. Whilst the decline in provision may be attributed at least in part to a lack of interest/involvement by L/G themselves, in many cases lack of financial resources has also been a problem.

More recently, "L/G culture" has become increasingly assimilated into the mainstream heterosexual pub-club culture with social provision for L/G predominantly comprising commercialised venues in which people (L/G and "straight") are consumers of primarily white, middle-class, gay male social culture (cf. Visser, 2003). As a result, the focus of L/G social life became much more organised around *sexual*, rather than *social*, identity (Esterberg, 1996). Furthermore, with L/G lifestyles being viewed as trendy and chic (especially among young people), gay spaces have become increasingly frequented by heterosexuals and therefore often not the spaces where L/G can escape the "heterosexual gaze" or heterocentric society (Binnie and Skeggs, 2004; Holt and Griffin, 2003). Whilst some non-scene L/G-centred provisions (e.g., cafes; women's/LGBT centres) still exist in a few places in the UK (e.g., Nottingham; Manchester; Edinburgh), this is almost exclusively youth focused. In most places outside London and the South East of England, with the exception of a handful of places (e.g., Manchester, Edinburgh, Glasgow) provisions of spaces and opportunities to connect socially with other L/G people (for support or to establish networks) are extremely limited.

Whilst the broader social science literature in the UK and elsewhere has explored lesbians' and gay men's use of and relationship to L/G space (Binnie and Skeggs, 2004; Holt and Griffin, 2003; Valentine and Skelton, 2003; Visser, 2003), there is a dearth of psychological work internationally, empirically investigating issues around L/G community(ies). Whilst there has been some limited discussion of changes in the structure of L/G community from a US perspective (e.g., D'Augelli and Garnets, 1995; Esterberg, 1996), the impact of contextual changes in community structure and provision on the lives and lifestyles of L/G remains largely unexplored. To date, only two recent (US) studies (McCarthy, 2000; Oswald and Culton, 2003) have specifically explored L/G lives in relationship to community and social support. Whilst these particular studies raise many issues about access to social and support networks, they specifically focus on rural L/G, with the underlying assumption (explicitly stated in both cases) that access to social and support networks is considerably better in, or close to, urban areas. Drawing on preliminary research, the purpose of the present paper is to highlight the ways in which changes in L/G social space and community have had an impact upon the lives and lifestyles of urban L/G in the UK, with a view to identifying ways to better provide social support to the contemporary L/G community.

THE STUDY

Participants and Recruitment

This paper draws upon data from a current (and ongoing) interview-based study with UK lesbians and gay men. A total of 32 interviews (19 women and 13 men) have been run to date. Whilst a small number are students (either at secondary [high] school or university), most are in full- or part-time employment, predominantly in socially-oriented occupations (e.g., health care; youth work).

Participants for the study were initially recruited through an online network for professionals working in the area of L/G psychology, through which the request reached other related networks. Further participants were recruited through letters to community-based organisations (e.g., youth organisations; student LGBT groups); community spaces likely to be frequented by L/G (e.g., Women's Centres; LGB Centres); and gay-centred organisations (e.g., The Metropolitan Community Church). Recruitment was undertaken across a wide geographical area predominantly comprising the Midlands and North of England, with most interviewees (N = 17) residing in the Sheffield-Rotherham metropolitan areas of South Yorkshire. The balance of participants comprised those resident in or around seven other large metropolitan areas (Leeds, Leicester, Coventry, Manchester, Liverpool, Newcastle and Edinburgh: N = 11), and some in smaller towns/cities in semi-rural areas (Lincolnshire, West Yorkshire, Derbyshire, Lancashire: N = 4).

Although the study was set up as a study of "lesbians and gay men," it was not a requirement that potential participants define themselves in this way. However, whilst most defined themselves as "lesbian" (or sometimes "gay") for women, and as "gay" for men, some participants defined themselves as "bisexual" because this seemed a more accurate representation of their sexual history or because they are still exploring/questioning their sexuality. Others indicated a preference not to label their sexual identity or provided alternative descriptions (e.g., "My sexuality is called Penny"; "sexually ambiguous").[6] In all cases, participants' current sexual orientations and experiences are directed towards members of the same sex as themselves.

Similarly, the past and present life experiences of interviewees varied considerably. For example, some participants are currently single or in relatively new same-sex relationships whilst others are in well-established, committed same-sex relationships; some have been heterosexually married in the past and have children, whilst others have not. Two participants self-identified as "Irish," one as "Indian," whilst all others self-identified as "white." Although the sample to date is not representative of the mix of racial and ethnic groups which comprise the L/G community in the UK, it is diverse in terms of the age, social background, life experiences, and geographical location. A summary of participants can be found in Table 1, however, because some information collected on participants (e.g., occupation, background, family composition, and geographical location) could potentially identify them, the information reported in the table has been restricted to pseudonym, age and ethnic origin only.

TABLE 1. Breakdown of Participants

Female Participants			Male Participants		
Pseudonym	Age	Ethnic origin	Pseudonym	Age	Ethnic origin
Clare	42	white	Alec	16	white
Donna	28	white	Brian	32	white
Emily	38	white	Francis	49	white
Helen	16	white	Glen	16	white
Karen	52	white	James	35	Irish
Leanne	39	white	Rajit	27	Indian
Maria	23	white	Wayne	21	white
Naomi	43	Irish	Zane	34	white
Penny	56	white	Chris	23	white
Steph	28	white	David	30	white
Tina	53	white	Eddie	28	white
Vanessa	43	white	Frank	35	white
Abby	19	white	Howard	37	white
Brenda	25	white			
Gina	43	white			
Josie	50	white			
Kate	35	white			
Lillian	58	white			
Mary	56	white			

Carrying Out the Study

Interviews were carried out to explore the social aspects of the lives and lifestyles of lesbians and gay men in the UK. Semi-structured interviews were chosen to enable participants to talk about their lives and experiences in their own words and therefore to prioritise the issues and concerns that were important to them, rather than to the author. In order to afford individuals the opportunity for their "story" to be heard, one-to-one interviews (rather than focus groups) were employed although in a small number of cases (n = 6) participants requested to be interviewed as a couple and this request was respected.

Questions covered a range of aspects of gay lives and lifestyles including work/study, identity and coming out, relationships, family, L/G community, and growing older. Participants were asked a range of questions in relation to community such as "how important is it to you to connect socially with other L/G?," "have you ever been part of an L/G support group or social network?," "what opportunities are there locally to connect socially with other L/G? Do you use them? Why/why not?" Although the data presented here primarily relates to this particular section of the interviews, issues about community and social life often came up under other topics and therefore the analysis has not been restricted simply to this section. Depending on the age and life experiences of participants, interviews ranged between 40 and 90 minutes and were undertaken at a mutually convenient time and place. The venue used for the interviews varied; some were carried out in interviewees' workplaces or their own homes, some in university settings, and others in public spaces.

Following interviewing, tapes were transcribed verbatim, and participants' narratives analysed using thematic analysis. As the topic being explored here formed only a part of the interviews, data pertaining to community and social life was first identified from across the transcripts. Then using the approach used by other feminist researchers (Gilligan, 1982; Ristock, 2003) relevant sections of the transcripts were reviewed placing the voices of participants at the centre of the analysis. Hence, participants were regarded as informants, and the emphasis of the analysis therefore focused on *what* was being said. The data was then read and reread to identify key issues or "themes" around L/G community and barriers to connecting socially with other L/G persons emerging from participants' narratives.

KEY ISSUES

The Importance of Connecting Socially with Other Lesbians and Gay Men

To suggest that there is a need for community-based social and support networks presupposes that L/G *want* to connect socially with other L/G. Whilst many interviewees expressed a desire for social integration (i.e., to be able to socialise as L/G people in majority heterosexual settings), there was considerable support for opportunities to connect socially with other L/G outside of mainstream settings.

The majority of those interviewed stated that they thought it "very important" to connect socially with other L/G. As one participant so eloquently put it, "it's incredibly important, it's like life-blood" (James, 35).

The most frequently cited reason for connecting specifically with other L/G persons was the notion of having (collectively) shared understandings, values and experiences:

> We share a perspective and an understanding and a kind of vocabulary, an emotional vocabulary, that however much our heterosexual friends love us they don't understand. It's just a *different* experience of being in the world. (Penny, 56)

> Sometimes it's nice to talk about things like girly sex stuff that you couldn't necessarily talk about with your heterosexual friends. (Maria, 23)

Others highlighted the importance of being able to be yourself without having to first educate heterosexuals about L/G life to provide a basis from which to have meaningful discussions about one's own life and lifestyle:

> It's quite nice to go somewhere where I don't have to start off explaining the basics. The gay thing's kind of out of the way and I can relate to somebody on a much more political level knowing that they know I know about them and how it works and stuff I suppose. I don't have to re-explain things or stop and explain references or say whatever's not the case and stuff. (David, 30)

There was, however, considerable variation in the extent to which participants felt that socialising with other L/G should be a part of their social life. Although some participants stated that ordinarily they didn't have a great need to connect socially with other L/G, certain life events had meant that at particular times they had felt a need to access specifically L/G networks:

> I've got a fantastic network of friends that I've known for a long time that are not lesbian or gay and they've just been absolutely wonderful . . . but . . . I'm finding more so now as a lesbian parent and a mother and being a partner as opposed to being the birth mother . . . [it's] become much more important to meet up with like-minded people to talk about those sorts of issues as well and to be in a group of people where you don't have to explain anything. It's a very comfortable feeling. (Leanne, 39)

> When the realisation and dealing with the rape and everything . . . I phoned [the] rape crisis [helpline] because I wanted to, not be with other men who had been through something similar, but I needed to know that there was help, that there were other people I could lean on. I phoned rape crisis to see, and they said well you're a man, why are you phoning rape crisis? I said because I've been raped. "There's no services available for you" . . . So that's when I physically looked for a community. (Zane, 34)

Consequently, although most L/G do not ordinarily need a L/G community around which to organize their social lives, there are times when having a point of contact through which one can access the community would be most advantageous: When one has just moved to the area; when one's circumstances have changed (e.g., the death of a partner; dissolution of relationship; meeting new partners; becoming a L/G parent); and in times of crisis (e.g., bereavement; abuse).

The Difficulty of Connecting Socially with Other Lesbians and Gay Men

Despite the importance placed on connecting socially with other L/G, the interview data highlights a number of difficulties of doing so. It provides evidence that for most of those interviewed, provision and availability of L/G-centred activities or spaces for socialising, seeking support, or simply connecting with others is somewhat limited. Often this limitation was attributed to geography. For example, some interviewees reported a lack of provision of activities/spaces in their local area, and that accessing community-based venues (e.g., LGBT Centre; gay pubs/clubs) often meant having to travel considerable distances:

> I would be interested in things like a gay choir but there isn't one locally . . . the non-commercial and non-drinking scene community things interest me a lot and it's an area I'd like to help build up in this area . . . There aren't any gay pubs within [the North-West England areas of] Chorley or South Ribble. You'd have to go about 10 miles in any direction to a bigger town like Preston or Blackburn. In Preston I think one of the pubs is open till 2 a.m. in morning Thursday, Friday, and Saturday, so it's effectively a nightclub . . . I don't like the clubbing environment . . . [so I would] have to go further afield to [the cities of] Blackpool or Manchester . . . It's feasible to get into Manchester but it's a bit hard; it's 25 miles or so and I don't like driving in the evening too much, and the last train out is 11.15 p.m. It's awkward really. If I actually lived in Manchester, there would be other things I could do. It's a bit of a desert here really. (Francis, 49)

> If you live outside the city of Edinburgh it's virtually a wasteland. As far as LGBT groups go, there's very little, if anything. (David, 30)

However, even participants living in large metropolitan areas reported that provision of non-scene spaces and networking opportunities was often patchy. In some large cities (e.g., Sheffield, England's fourth-largest city) there is currently no LGBT or Women's Centre and no other non-scene social spaces. Although some (notably men) attempted to overcome issues of location and/or lack of provision by connecting with others via the internet, a common complaint was that "chat rooms" (e.g., Gaydar *http://www.gaydar.org.uk/*) tended to be dominated by people seeking sexual partners, and therefore were less than ideal for establishing friendships and simply connecting with others on a social level.

Likewise, the predominantly scene-based (i.e., pub/club) focus of L/G space and community was heavily criticised by participants. For many, the noise and highly sexualised nature of these spaces made them difficult spaces to connect socially (in non-sexualised ways) with others:

> I've just found the scene . . . not a very sociable place and I've found it not a very friendly place . . . the music's too loud, it's all

geared around getting drunk and having one night stands, and I'm older. I'm not as attractive as I used to be. (James, 35)

I find it [connecting with other lesbians and gay men] hard to do on the scene with the noise and the atmosphere . . . If I go to a gay pub in Preston, I would almost always be going on my own and there wouldn't be anybody there that I knew. I don't like that because everybody else is in groups . . . I just feel a bit strange and I don't feel that in a straight pub if I go in to read the paper and have a pint at lunchtime occasionally on Saturday. (Francis, 49)

Often such places were located in places that were seen as "unsafe" and the venues themselves described as "seedy" or "dives" (i.e., dirty, dingy, disreputable) and therefore undesirable.

Unlike the types of local suburban or rural (and predominantly heterosexual) pubs in the UK, where it is often possible to connect socially with other people (even in a detached way), the sexualised environment of "gay" pubs appears to preclude simply having a drink in a relaxed and casual environment in the company of other L/G persons. Conversely, whilst some indicated that ideally they would like to be able to "be themselves" in regular pub settings, this was often not possible because the heterocentric nature of generic social spaces means that expressions of homosexual identity are deemed or perceived to be inappropriate (Holt and Griffin, 2003; Visser, 2003). Consequently, gay people in this study report constantly finding themselves managing their identities and monitoring their behaviours in ways that heterosexuals do not, so as not to disrupt the taken-for-granted norms of heterosexual space.

In attempting to connect with other L/G, those interviewed often mentioned attempts to access non-scene venues (i.e., not pubs/clubs). Several participants highlighted the way in which these types of social groups and spaces could sometimes be unfriendly or unwelcoming– e.g., "I found that [The Women's Centre] really an oppressive place to be . . . it didn't feel very welcoming" (Tina, 53); "I find people in the Centre a little cliquey, a little bit hard, and you're either 'in' or 'out' " (Naomi, 43); " . . . the groups are quite cliquey, the community is quite cliquey generally" (David, 30).

Many participants also highlighted the way in which age can sometimes be a major barrier to connecting socially with other L/G, in particular, the way in which most organised activities within the L/G community are youth-focused. This youth-centredness is particularly problematic for L/G who do not fit the (psychologically) "normative" pattern of identifying as L/G in youth. As one participant, who herself had only recently identified as lesbian remarks:

> If you've already got a network of friends then it's not going to be such a problem; but if you're an older woman coming out in your 40s and 50s, I think it would be bloody hard to try and meet other people because usually by then as well you've got your own interests and things and your social life revolves around your interests . . . when you're younger there's more activity to organise around being lesbian or gay. (Leanne, 39)

Age appeared to be particularly pertinent when talking with women about their social networks. For example, although they rarely accessed organised social activities, most women over the age of 40 had extensive informal networks for social support, typically friends they had established in the heyday of second-wave feminism. Predominantly these women had remained in largely the same geographical area, thus their social lives centred on regularly meeting up with those friends for dinner, going on holiday together, or staying over at each other's houses. For many women and men, however, leaving university and beginning a career often meant taking up employment in new places, or not being settled in one location long enough to establish friendships. For these individuals, the lack of non-scene spaces or organised activities made connecting with other lesbians and/or gay men difficult.

Although age appears to be a salient factor in limiting opportunities for access to formal sources of connecting socially with other lesbians and/or gay men, it is often the way in which age interacts with other socio-demographic factors (e.g., class, economic status, political orientation, etc.) which has a much greater impact on the extent to which it is possible for any given person to connect socially with others. The following excerpt highlights the way in which for some these factors combine to exclude certain people:

> Our entire socialising is to do with [clubs and pubs]–I mean the sort of organisations . . . I could go to the lesbian choir group, but I don't; I'm not old enough to go to the over 40s; I've also found that sometimes my politics don't sit very well with radical lesbian feminists, so I've never had that kind of, the access to the middle-class lesbian community . . . I can't afford a house in Hebden Bridge[7] at the moment . . . I've found that if I go out on the scene they're all

much younger than me now . . . [so] you're looking in the free ads, you're looking in *DIVA*,[8] how do you meet eligible middle-class lesbians that are non-scene oriented? (Steph, 28)

Although most of those interviewed "got by," it would appear that accessing lesbian and gay social networks and resources is still problematic for many L/G. If anything, the mainstreaming of the L/G culture has increased the difficulty of accessing the L/G community, even for those within it.

ESTABLISHING LINKS: CONNECTING LESBIANS AND GAY MEN WITH ONE ANOTHER

Despite predominantly living in or near large urban areas, the views of those interviewed in the present study resonated with those of McCarthy's (2000) and Oswald and Culton's (2003) rural US L/G. Although most believed that it was important to connect socially with other L/G, their collective experiences suggest a lack of (non-sexualised) L/G spaces where L/G can meet socially and when necessary seek information and support. In most cases, participants highlighted a lack of provision of such spaces, or where provision existed, there were barriers (e.g., age; environment; location) to accessing networks and support.

In the past, the UK L/G community was seen as a "safe" space (cf. Green, 1997; Holt and Griffin, 2003; Kitzinger and Perkins, 1993) for L/G to seek refuge from a hostile society. Whilst the need for "safe" space is perhaps less salient today than in previous generations, the data presented here suggests that there is still very much a need for specifically L/G-focused provision separate from mainstream provision. Many participants highlight the need for places where they can access the L/G community. Ideally, such spaces might act as a focal point and have multiple roles as a public meeting space (e.g., for L/G-centred support/social groups), an access point for information (e.g., appropriate health information; information about support groups and social events), a support centre (e.g., a base for L/G-centred counselling/therapy or self-help groups), and at the same time be a social space (e.g., a café or drop-in centre). Such a space would play a vital role as an access point for a wide range of L/G to establish networks and access L/G community groups and resources. This, of course, is not a new idea but rather a call to reinstate and expand the network of social spaces that have gradually disappeared. Ideally, such "Centres" should be funded as an essential service to the L/G community in the same way that community centres are centrally provided to other groups within UK society. A reliance solely on voluntary services and donations for resources and support services to any minority group is likely to result in provision disappearing.

However, this issue is more long-term and complex than is possible for individuals or the psychotherapeutic profession to single-handedly resolve. It is therefore important to explore how therapists might best be able to bridge this gap in provision. In the first instance, it is useful for therapists to have an awareness of the broader social contexts that result in the social exclusion and isolation of their clients. An increased awareness of the way in which the L/G community (in terms of space and provision) has changed might help the gay-affirmative therapist to better understand the factors contributing to a (lesbian, gay, bisexual or questioning) client's issues. However, it is not enough to simply assume that being informed once is enough. Clients would benefit if their therapists continually update their awareness and actively review what provision is available, in order to be able to offer informed and current advice.

Those interviewed in this study did not seem to be particularly vulnerable as a result of the current lack of provision of social spaces and formal support networks. Many of the participants have well-established informal support systems, and others "get by" with their immediate social circles. However, the lack of community-based points of contact or organised social and support networks is problematic in that it is these which provide the infrastructure for initially establishing informal networks of social support and for strengthening the notion of L/G as a "community" within broader society (an important goal for securing human rights). Also, in times of crisis, the availability of mainstream support networks that are able to meet the needs of L/G clients cannot be taken for granted as they more readily can be for heterosexual clients (cf. Warwick and Aggleton, 2002). Community-based resources are therefore an important "safety net for people to turn to when their more informal relationships break down or are unable to address their needs" (Oswald and Culton, 2003, p. 78), particularly for more "vulnerable" L/G persons (e.g., the mentally ill; the aged; the socially/geographically isolated; those coming out post-youth).

It is this latter group with which therapists are most likely to come into contact. The key issue for the psychotherapist, therefore, is how to provide appropriate support to those who need it, in a climate where L/G may be excluded from both generic societal networks (because they are

L/G) and from L/G networks (because they are old or mentally ill, etc.). It would seem, then, that a priority for psychotherapy is to provide specifically L/G services, including services separate from mainstream provision. Whilst psychotherapy has often been seen as the antithesis to community-centred support for L/G (cf. Kitzinger and Perkins, 1993), if focused in a much more L/G-centred way, it could be an integral part of the L/G community and a vehicle for integrating the most excluded and isolated of L/G (and bisexual and questioning) persons into the community. Psychotherapists can therefore provide a crucial link for these individuals by identifying appropriate sources of community-based support for L/G, and being a source of information for L/G trying to integrate themselves into the L/G community.

NOTES

1. The UK's 1885 Sexual Offences Act (repealed in 1967) made "gross indecency" between men (in both private and public) a criminal offence, punishable by two years imprisonment.

2. *Gay Times* is a UK-based mainstream magazine for gay men.

3. The UK Lesbian and Gay Switchboard is a phone network staffed by volunteers and based in most cities and large towns across the UK. It operates primarily to provide information, and in some centres support, to lesbians and gay men.

4. Personal communication, name withheld on request.

5. For a US-based overview of the social history of the lesbian and gay communities see D'Augelli and Garnets, 1995.

6. In recruiting and briefing participants, I made my own identity as "lesbian" explicit.

7. Hebden Bridge is a small town in the Pennine Hills, West Yorkshire, England alleged to have the highest number of lesbians per head of population in the UK (Bindel, 2004). It has historical associations with lesbian separatism.

8. DIVA is a UK-based mainstream commercial magazine for lesbians.

REFERENCES

Berube, A. (1990), *Coming Out Under Fire: The History of Gay Men and Women in World War Two*. New York: Free Press.

Bindel, J. (2004), Location, location, orientation. *The Guardian*, March 27.

Binnie, J. & Skeggs, B. (2004), Cosmopolitan knowledge and the production and consumption of sexualised space: Manchester's gay village. *The Sociological Review*, 52:39-61.

D'Augelli, A.R. & Garnets, L.D. (1995), Lesbian, gay, and bisexual communities. In: *Lesbian, Gay and Bisexual Identities over the Lifespan: Psychological Perspec-*

tives, eds. A.R. D'Augelli & C.J. Patterson. New York: Oxford University Press, pp. 293-320.

Esterberg, K.G. (1996), Gay cultures, gay communities: The social organisation of lesbians, gay men and bisexuals. In: *The Lives of Lesbians, Gays and Bisexuals*, eds. R.C. Savin-Williams & K.M. Cohen. Fort Worth, TX: Harcourt Brace, pp. 377-392.

Gilligan, C. (1982), *In a Different Voice: Psychological Theory and Women's Development*. Cambridge, MA: Harvard University Press.

Green, S.F. (1997), *Urban Amazons: Lesbian Feminism and Beyond in the Gender, Sexuality and Identity Battles of London*. Basingstoke: Macmillan.

Hamer, E. (1995), *Britannia's Glory: History of Twentieth Century Lesbians*. London: Continuum.

Holt, M. & Griffin, C. (2003), Being gay, being straight and being yourself: Local and global reflections on identity, authenticity and the lesbian and gay scene. *European J. Cultural Studies*, 6:404-425.

Kitzinger, C. & Perkins, R. (1993), *Changing Our Minds: Lesbian Feminism and Psychology*. London: Onlywomen Press.

Markowe, L. (2002), Coming out as lesbian. In: *Lesbian and Gay Psychology: New Perspectives*, eds. A. Coyle & C. Kitzinger. Leicester: BPS/Blackwell, pp. 63-80.

McCarthy, L. (2000), Poppies in a wheat field: Exploring the lives of rural lesbians. *J. Homosexuality*, 39:75-94.

Oswald, R.F. & Culton, L.S. (2003), Under the rainbow: Rural gay life and its relevance for family providers. *Family Relations*, 52:72-81.

Porter, K. & Weeks, J. (1998), *Between the Acts: Lives of Homosexual Men 1885-1967*. London: Rivers Oram Press.

Ristock, J.L. (2003), Exploring dynamics of abusive lesbian relationships: Preliminary analysis of a multisite, qualitative study. *American J. Community Psychology*, 31:329-341.

Robb, G. (2003), *Strangers: Homosexual Love in the 19th Century*. London: Picador.

Valentine, G. & Skelton, T. (2003), Finding oneself, losing oneself: The lesbian and gay 'scene' as a paradoxical space. *International J. Urban & Regional Research*, 27:849-66.

Visser, G. (2003), Gay men, leisure space and South African cities: The case of Cape Town. *Geoforum*, 34:123-137.

Warwick, I. & Aggleton, P. (2002), Gay men's physical and emotional well-being: Re-orienting research and health promotion. In: *Lesbian and Gay Psychology: New Perspectives*, eds. A. Coyle & C. Kitzinger. Leicester: BPS/Blackwell, pp. 135-153.

doi:10.1300/J236v11n01_08

Safe Spaces and Sense of Identity: Views and Experiences of Lesbian, Gay and Bisexual Young People

Colm Crowley, MA, MSc
Rom Harré, BPhil, DLitt
Ingrid Lunt, PhD

SUMMARY. Empirical data on the life experiences of contemporary school-age lesbian, gay and bisexual (LGB) young people in Britain remains somewhat sparse. This paper reports the preliminary findings of a study conducted at a recently-initiated LGB youth Summer School. To further an appreciation of issues of concern to today's LGB teenagers, in-depth interviews were conducted with 10 Summer School participants (five female and five male, aged 15-18 years). The aim was to elicit their views and experiences relating to their need for support such as that offered by the Summer School. Themes drawn from participants' interviews are presented. Key issues included: being positioned as dif-

Colm Crowley is Senior Lecturer in Psychology, University of Greenwich.
Rom Harré is Distinguished Research Professor at Georgetown University Department of Psychology, and Emeritus Fellow of Linacre College, University of Oxford.
Ingrid Lunt is Professional Senior Research Fellow and Director of Graduate Studies at the Department of Educational Studies, University of Oxford.
Address correspondence to: Colm Crowley, Youth and Identity Project, School of Culture Language and Communications, Institute of Education, University of London, 20 Bedford Way, London WC1H 0AL, UK (E-mail: ccrowley@ioe.ac.uk).

[Haworth co-indexing entry note]: "Safe Spaces and Sense of Identity: Views and Experiences of Lesbian, Gay and Bisexual Young People." Crowley, Colm, Rom Harré, and Ingrid Lunt. Co-published simultaneously in *Journal of Gay & Lesbian Psychotherapy* (The Haworth Medical Press, an imprint of The Haworth Press, Inc.) Vol. 11, No. 1/2, 2007, pp. 127-143; and: *British Lesbian, Gay, and Bisexual Psychologies: Theory, Research, and Practice* (ed: Elizabeth Peel, Victoria Clarke, and Jack Drescher) The Haworth Medical Press, an imprint of The Haworth Press, Inc., 2007, pp. 127-143. Single or multiple copies of this article are available for a fee from The Haworth Document Delivery Service [1-800-HAWORTH, 9:00 a.m. - 5:00 p.m. (EST). E-mail address: docdelivery@haworthpress.com].

ferent by their majority heterosexual peers; feelings of isolation and loneliness in their peer groups and families; difficulties in finding others like themselves for companionship; and the importance of meeting more LGB people of their own age. doi:10.1300/J236v11n01_09 *[Article copies available for a fee from The Haworth Document Delivery Service: 1-800-HAWORTH. E-mail address: <docdelivery@haworthpress.com> Website: <http://www.HaworthPress.com> © 2007 by The Haworth Press, Inc. All rights reserved.]*

KEYWORDS. Adolescence, gay, homosexuality, identity, lesbian, safe space, same-sex, youth work

This paper reports the views and experiences of ten 15-18 year old lesbian, gay and bisexual (LGB) teenagers on two matters of considerable consequence to them: the difficulties they face as they progress through adolescence while forming an LGB identity, and their experiences of attending a special Summer School for young LGB people in August 2003. This represents a further exploratory phase of a more wide-ranging study of identity formation in adolescents with same-sex sexuality commenced in the north of England (Crowley, Harré and Lunt, 2001). With the assistance of the Project for Advice, Counselling and Education (PACE) Youth Work Service–which had initiated the Summer Freedom Summer School in London one year before in 2002–the inquiry was continued in the south of England with the teenage LGB population. The overall purpose of this phase of the research is to gain an appreciation of issues and themes of concern to today's British LGB teenagers. The research questions explore: what happens from their perspectives; how it feels to be them; and their perceptions of the attitudes they encounter.

BACKGROUND

Having undertaken substantial psychological research on LGB adolescents in the United States, D'Augelli (1999) notes that current research finds that LGB teenagers of today are coming to terms with their sexual orientation much younger than earlier generations. However, there remains a dearth of research on present-day British LGB adolescents, and recently published studies have tended to focus specifically on issues of hostility and harassment (see Bridget, 2003).

A Climate of Hostility Still Exists

That the prevailing climate in Britain remains hostile to young LGB people is evident from their life narratives (Crowley, Hallam, Harré and Lunt, 2001). Attempts to legislate for equality in the age of consent for male same-sex relationships repeatedly foundered until 2000, following emotive debate in which the dominant views reflected a legacy of prejudicial views emanating from British psychiatry and psychology (Rivers and Hardcastle, 2000). In a critique of psychiatrists' attitudes and practices to date, King and Bartlett (1999) argue that the pathologisation of same-sex sexuality over the past century has been underpinned by social and religious opposition, together with the (poorly supported) assumption that sexuality could be altered. It is only very recently that the first large-scale systematic study of the mental health and well-being of LGB people in Britain has been undertaken (King and McKeown, 2003). Although the research was conducted with participants over 16, based on the findings, noteworthy recommendations of the report are that:

> Professionals working with children and young people, including teachers, youth workers and health and social services professionals, should receive specific training in: how developing sexuality and related issues around "coming out" affect psychological development and mental well-being; [and] strategies to support the prevention of self-harm and suicide in LGB people and that agencies working with children and young people (including schools, youth services and health and social services) should develop policies around bullying and victimization related to sexuality. (King and McKeown, 2003, p. 54)

Hassles and Harassment in Daily Life

A generation ago, Trenchard and Warren (1984) conducted a landmark questionnaire-based study about the lives and needs of 400 LGB youth under the age of 21 living in London (20% of the respondents were under 18). They reported that one in five had attempted suicide and almost 40% said they had problems at school related to their sexuality (Warren, 1984). Little appears to have improved for school-age LGB youth since then, and most schools lack anti-gay bullying policies (Douglas et al., 1997). Two decades after Trenchard and Warren's survey, Ellis and High (2004) set out to replicate it. They offer some comparisons indicating that any changes that have occurred are not necessarily for the better. For example, whilst homosexuality is now *mentioned* more in schools than it was in 1984, most of their respondents shared the view of their 1984 counterparts that same-sex sexuality was *unhelpfully* mentioned in secondary (high) school. Furthermore, Ellis and High note significant increases in LGB young people's reports of problems at school (e.g., verbal abuse, physical assault and feelings of isolation).

Rivers's (1995) study of the bullying experienced by lesbians and gay men in their school years (and its impact on later life) found that homophobic bullying was more severe than general bullying. The Office for Standards in Education (OFSTED), the UK Government's schools inspectorate, notes that "in too many secondary schools homophobic attitudes among pupils often go unchallenged" (2002, p. 14). Resources to help schools in addressing these problems are now available. For example, the practical handbook, *Talking About Homosexuality in the Secondary School* (Forrest, Biddle and Clift, 1997) is aimed at a range of people working in schools (and those supporting them, such as school governors and parents) to help them to tackle the issues related to insufficient and unhelpful talk about homosexuality in schools. An action plan to prevent homophobic bullying in secondary schools is provided by *Safe for All* (Warwick and Douglas, 2001). It is now widely acknowledged that nothing less that a *whole-school approach* is likely to make a decisive difference in these matters. This means a comprehensive effort involving, for example, the school's policies, procedures, curriculum and training opportunities for staff (see National Union of Teachers, 2004a and 2004b).

A recently completed review commissioned by the UK Government's Department for Education and Skills (Warwick, Chase and Aggleton, 2004) addresses questions regarding: the extent and impact of homophobic bullying on pupils; how homophobia and sexual orientation are addressed as curriculum issues within classrooms and as part of whole school approaches; and how issues of equity and diversity regarding sexual orientation also affect school staff. Based on a combination of literature review and interviews with key informants, the report provides a valuable update on the current state of play regarding these aspects of life (and related policy) in the UK. Nevertheless, it concludes that "based on the available evidence, only partial answers to these questions exist" (Warwick, Chase and Aggleton, 2004, p. 25).

The Response of Counselling and Therapy

According to Fontaine and Hammond (1996), formation of sexual identity is facilitated by environments such as school, family and neighbourhood. They observe that for LGB adolescents, however, such resources are often unavailable or are very likely to be negative and stigmatising. Fontaine and Hammond propose a role of advocacy for school counsellors, not least because of the "invisibility" of many LGB students that makes it difficult to provide direct services to them. Improving awareness of, information and quality of life for LGB students in general are identified as salient goals.

Davies (1996), in a review of therapeutic issues of relevance to LGB young people, asserts that therapists working with this population need to be affirmative of their emergent sexual identities (while recognising also that many adolescents who are homosexually active do not identify as LGB). Davies suggests a further role for therapists is that of advocate and consultant in bringing about "a safer environment in which the young can develop identities without being harmed" (p. 148).

Safe Spaces for Identity Formation

Coyle (1998) concluded that although many young lesbians and gay men succeed in resourcefully creating a workable and satisfying sexual identity, the formation and negotiation of a lesbian or gay identity is nevertheless difficult for young people in the face of generally negative social attitudes. It seems, then, that the numerous LGB youth groups in today's Britain provide useful opportunities for young people wanting to "be themselves" among equals (Keogh, 1999).

Whilst the prime interest of the present research lies in how, from a psychological perspective, young people are getting on with living their lives, it seems inevitable that much of the business of exploring an LGB identity as a young person centres on negotiating and coping with the persisting climate of negativity about same-sex sexuality (see Rivers, 2002). Central to the ethos underpinning the Summer Freedom Summer School is the notion that it should represent a *safe space* where young LGB people "can really be themselves" (Hind, 2004, p. 27) away from the pressures that typically constrain them in the other arenas of their lives. This notion, derived from youth work, in Winnicottian (1965) terms would be called a "facilitating environment." In particular, it is this aspect of the Summer School that led (in view of the paucity of research with this focus) to the authors' interest in gathering the accounts of the LGB young people attending. It was hoped to further an under-standing of their sense of who they are or *personhood* (see Harré, 1998), and the social psychological significance for them of the safe space.

THE SUMMER SCHOOL CONTEXT

The Summer Freedom Summer School (henceforth referred to as the Summer School) is run once a year and is open, free of charge, to all LGB young people under 25. Approximately 100 attended in 2003. It lasts for one week in August and is non-residential, taking place from 10 a.m.-4 p.m., followed by a movie (on site) and other social activities. Participants are free to attend as and when they can if it does not suit them to come for the full week's programme. All tutors and other workers are LGB people (the majority) or "LGB friendly." The programme content includes personal, social and health education (e.g., workshops on coming out, depression, assertiveness, relationships and sexual health) and enjoyable, creative activities (e.g., self-defence, creative writing, drama, relaxation, yoga, massage, acupuncture, aerobics and dance). In addition to the daily late-afternoon movie, the social activities include an end-of-school disco party where friends (of any sexuality) are also welcome.

METHOD

There is a strong tradition of qualitative research within UK lesbian and gay psychology (see Coyle and Kitzinger, 2002). Qualitative research is valued for placing a strong emphasis on the personal meanings of participants (Coyle, 2000). Qualitative research as is undertaken in the present study does not impose researcher-derived categories on the experiences of participants, but rather allows participants to speak for themselves, in their own words. The authors adopted a thematic approach to analysing the data. Thematic analysis (like qualitative content analysis) is concerned with identifying themes and patterns in participants' talk, and presenting an analysis that is grounded in the phenomenological world of the participants (Boyatzis, 1998).

The participants were ten young people with same-sex sexuality aged 15-18 (five female and five male). Volunteers for interview were selected by the Summer School organizers on the basis of achieving a distribution of ages up to 18 and a balance of genders. Anonymity (via using pseudonyms and removing any identifying information) and confidentiality were assured.

In-depth individual unstructured interviews (mean duration one hour) were tape-recorded at the Summer School. Verbatim transcripts were imported into qualitative data analysis software (QSR NVivo) to facilitate analysis (Richards, 1999; Gibbs, 2002), and enable the establishment of a clear "audit trail" (Miles and Huberman, 1994). Supplementary data included field notes and documentation on the PACE project's overall youth provision (e.g., Hind, 2004).

There are three possible designs within which to frame a research programme: idiographic, intensive and extensive (see Smith, Harré and Van Langenhove, 1995). The results of an idiographic study, looking at individuals one by one in depth, can be recruited as the foundations of the intensive design (DeWaele, 1983). The present study is framed within the intensive design, recruiting idiographic studies of each of the informants to reach a tentative specification of the character of the life of any young person in the situation of these studies. The case of Rosie provides the idiographical linchpin on which the intensive design of the study is based (McRunyan, 1986).

FINDINGS AND DISCUSSION

In examining the young people's interviews, the authors identified two overarching themes. The first focuses on the phenomenological dimension, and the second on the connections between individual realities and the broader social context. The authors explore here four sub-themes: Theme 1 (*a sense of being different*) and theme 2 (*feelings of isolation and loneliness*) are connected to the phenomenological aspect; and theme 3 (*difficulty of contact*) and theme 4 (*importance of own age group*) are more closely tied to the broader social context.

Theme 1: A Sense of Being Different

For young LGB people at school, being positioned as different by their majority "straight" peers can be a harsh experience as Rosie (16) describes:

> You're sitting in the classroom, no one wants to sit next to you, and there's like "oh is this why you came to a girls' school, so you can perv over all of us" and stuff.

While Sam's (16) positioning as different has not been hostile, he nevertheless notices that his difference from other boys is being brought to his attention by his friends:

> My close friends, they're aware that I'm not particularly interested in girls, but I think they see that maybe more as a nervousness, or too much of a concentration around academic stuff or something like that. Obviously, they say things like "oh I think Sam's gay" even when they're around me, but I think . . . that's more of a kind of joke, just kind of making the point again, the fact that I'm so kind of . . . seem so disinterested in things. [. . .] It wasn't when I started secondary school, cos I was only 11, so that wasn't kind of expected–but in the last couple of years maybe, and there was nothing particularly wrong at school, it's just that I wasn't fitting in.

Rosie (16) describes how, as she has begun to display a positive attitude about her difference from her peers, their hostility in positioning her as different has lessened and has even given way to curiosity:

> You're growing up and you're becoming, I suppose, a young adult. Here was someone standing up and saying "no, I'm going to be different, I don't want to be what you want to be" and then they start questioning themselves. [. . .] When I started going to the [LGB] youth club I would tell people that I went to a youth club, and tell people that I even met other gay people and it became more interesting to them. They wanted to talk about it and a lot of people, instead of giving me a hard time about it, would actually ask me questions [such as] "What's it like?," "Who'd you meet?," "Are there lots of other young gay people?" I think now it's got to the point, because I'm probably still the only openly gay person at my school and although people still have their prejudices, they don't discriminate [against] me because of it. And, if anything, people are quite interested about the fact that I go to a gay bar and I know lots of gay people and it's just a different lifestyle. I think they find that quite interesting now.

Rosie is now re-positioned as authoritative with respect to a certain mode of life. The sense of being different can, then, have positive as well as negative aspects. However, in the daily lives of these young people the negative consequences of being different mostly predominated.

Theme 2: Feelings of Isolation and Loneliness

Another phenomenological theme expressed by the participants concerns feelings of isolation and loneliness. For example, Steven (15) tells how solitary activities enabled him to affirm his long-felt position of being different, while nonetheless maintaining some important friendships:

> I've always been quite different from other people. I've always felt different. I've often tried to isolate myself [from] other people, and tried to get on with things on my own–although I do always have friends around. I mean my close friends.

Rosie (16) eloquently describes the extent of the isolation she has felt in most areas of her life. At school, her peers' positioning of her as different from them gave them the right to socially exclude her and hence the associated duty to avoid her:

> Well, in the changing rooms no one would want to stand next to me. "Turn around girls" they'd say to my face . . . shameless. In the classrooms they'd throw paper at me and they wouldn't want to sit with me. And you just think that, you know, it's silly, but it's just the feeling that you're completely isolated. Cos I went through a lot of groups of friends, you know. Some people say "oh come with us, it's not a problem." Then people start talking about them and saying "oh they're dykes too" so they wouldn't hang around with you. And I went through quite a lot of friends in a few years, really, cos no one wants to put themselves in the firing line you know–fair enough, they might not have a problem with you, but their friends do and they don't want to have to put themselves up for that. It's a childish attitude to have, but it just made me feel very isolated at the time.

Even when Rosie actively set out to find other young lesbian teenagers, the landscape seemed rather empty:

> Basically I felt [quite isolated] cos you know there are gay people out there but where are they? How do I get to know them? And even when I first started going to [LGB] youth clubs, I was one of the youngest and at the time there were quite a lot of guys, not a lot of girls [. . .] I was thinking "God, am I the only lesbian teenager out here?" Cos you do know there's gay people out there, but there's no

talk of teenagers, gay teenagers, in the media or even in society. I think as far as a lot of people are concerned gay teenagers don't exist.

A sense of companionship is what Ben (17) really wanted, and he ruled out the possibility of talking to a heterosexual parent about his isolation and feelings, in spite of indications that his mother feels positive about gay people:

> I was looking to find other people who've been through the same things–who I could talk to–just someone to speak to about stuff because obviously you're not exactly going to go "Mum I had a really bad day 'cos, you know, I like boys . . . tell me about your lesbian experiences" because obviously that's not going to work.

Kate (17) found the management of her public and private selves:

> Hard, and you feel kind of lonely as well–just like you have to live, but not a life. You have to live the heterosexuals' life as well. You have to be two people cos when I got home, I would be myself. When I'd go to school, I'd be someone else. I'd have to act in a certain way.

Theme 3: Difficulty of Contact

Finding others like themselves has not been an easy process for any of the young participants. In their interviews, all declared themselves to have been hindered in their quest for contact by the prevailing culture, and consequently having to struggle to achieve the sort of social contact that is taken for granted by their heterosexual peers. Ben (17) reports:

> It took me a long time, because through the Internet is how I met the first people who I ever knew who were gay. I mean the thing is that I made sure that I spoke to the person for something like six months, on the phone and things as well, and all this kind of thing–made sure that someone knew where I was going . . . I think we went to McDonald's [. . .] It was worth it . . . However, later I was like, okay, I'm not going to go find people on the Internet because, in the end, it's nice to meet people in a normal way.

Sam (16) explains how the lack of anyone openly LGB at his school means he has not yet identified anybody else like him there. He believes that meeting another LGB person through his network of friends outside school is a fairly fruitless prospect:

> I know there are differences between schools, but in my school, at least, there is no one I know of who is openly gay. It's kind of, if one person doesn't do it no one else does it. Obviously, school isn't the atmosphere where I would meet any gay or lesbian people. And then outside of school I do know some people, mainly through one particular friend, and from him I've met some more people outside school. But again, it's ultimately straight people. I don't know gay people very much at all. So again, I'm pretty sure no one there's either gay or lesbian either, outside of school. I mean I only know a certain number of people, it's not a massive network.

For Sam, the interests of his heterosexual peers diverge from those of their gay counterparts, making it less likely that they would want to mix socially in any case:

> In terms of the outside of school people, it's the boys from our school and girls from outside of school. At my age at least, straight people just wouldn't choose to mix with gay people for whatever reason, whether it's kind of deep homophobia or just lack of interest . . . or whatever.

Although Sam does not lack contact with friends, he resigns himself to withholding knowledge of his sexual identity from them until he has left school. Rosie finds that the expectation among heterosexual schoolgirls that they show affection to each other as a matter of course makes it difficult to gain any recognition of a potential sexual attraction: "It's like the attraction and the intimacy and the closeness would be just explained [away] by someone to themselves as "oh well, this is normal because women are close to each other."

Kate (17) alludes to the notion of "internalised homophobia" being a further barrier to meeting any lesbian or bisexual girls at her school. She reflects on how she used LGB-negative comments partly as a defensive ploy when she was younger, and she expects that, in turn, others who might be LGB are likely to be putting up a similar smokescreen:

> It was hard. I didn't know where to go to find them. I didn't have a way to recognize someone who was. Well I tried to, but it was

really hard, cos sometimes people that are gay themselves are homophobic–there's a special word for it, I used to be like that actually when I was about 13. People would talk about it and I would be like "oh that's disgusting." But deep down I knew I was, cos I thought maybe they were catching on.

As the usual opportunities for meeting others for school-age romance (at mixed schools and through networks of friends outside of school) are typically missing for young LGB people, it might seem that biting the bullet and venturing out on the "gay scene" could provide a solution for some. However, although Ben (17) remarked that "it's nice to meet people in a normal way," rather than meeting via the Internet, his exploration of bars and nightclubs for LGB people left him unimpressed:

My experience of the gay scene is that it's very superficial, that you can meet someone and it'll be–speak for two hours, an hour, or whatever, about how crap the music is or how great the music is and oh, how someone's making an ass of themselves trying to dance in the middle of–you know, all that kind of thing. External impersonal things. You can talk for two hours or whatever and then . . . you come away having nothing almost. Unless they sort of start being really pervy, in which case you have, like, a headache when you leave. [. . .] The gay scene was generally just this meat market where the whole thing was hit and miss, where people's expectation was: if I sleep with enough people, then one morning I'll wake up next to someone and we'll be able to have a conversation–wohoo!

Theme 4: Importance of Own Age Group

Most (but not all) of the participants emphatically located themselves within the micro-culture of their "own age." A key concern, then, of most of the participants is having contact with other LGB people their own age–above and beyond the difficulty of contact with other LGB people *per se*. This does not happen very easily for them in other LGB settings, and even where it does (for example, at some LGB youth groups) there may not be many other people in their immediate age range. Rosie (16) has been quite enterprising in going out to meet other LGB people, but, as she explains, there are major shortcomings for a girl of her age:

Even though I'm out on the gay scene quite a lot, and I go to pubs and clubs, but I always know that any time I go out there, I'm always going to meet people who are older than me. Because there aren't that many gay things aimed at people my age or younger–that's why I thought this would be a brilliant opportunity to meet people about my own age . . . talk about circumstances that we both might have gone through. I think that's probably the main reason really and you know you have fun as well with people your own age.

Sam (16), too, is in no doubt about the main thing he wants from the LGB youth group he recently started attending; however, one thing was unexpected:

It's just the idea of meeting a few people roughly my own age. So it's not the advice I get, I think, or even the support, but it's just meeting and talking to some people in a similar situation to myself. But I've been kind of surprised by how few people my age there are, which is a shame for people who are out there.

For the others who also go to youth groups, the Summer School has a key benefit, as Beth (15) makes clear: "First, there are more people." Jamie (17) declares that his incentive for making what is quite a journey across the city to the Summer School is "just to meet more friends" and he adds "because we live in a straight world, it's just nice to be among other gay people." Ben (17) agrees that meeting more of his peers is central to the experience because: "you need to meet more young people and then in the end you're likely to meet someone you actually connect with rather than, you know, just empty things."

Rosie (16) outlines the difficulties typically faced by a lesbian teenager wanting some age-appropriate companionship, but tells of a happy outcome:

Unless you go to a youth club, it's quite difficult to meet people your own age and again, you have that feeling of isolation that everyone is older, everyone else has been through it before, everyone else has had girlfriends and everyone else has done this and that, and you kind of feel left behind. Whereas if you meet people your age [or] a bit younger, you realise that you're working your way through . . . doing what everyone else is doing and you'll have a girlfriend soon. In a place like this I can meet people and know that they're interested in talking to me and we're going to have things in common and they're not going to freak out as soon as I tell them my age.

Rosie elucidates the further benefits of being in a place where, for a change, everyone is congruent both in terms of their sexualities *and* their ages: "I think that's what's cool about a place like this, you can have a bit of flirting . . . and it's okay, you know it's in a safe environment for you to do so."

When he was 15, the first youth group Jamie (17) contacted had nobody even close to his age, so he did not go to it:

A lot of boys aren't really out and at that time I didn't want to hang out with old people. I wanted to hang out with someone around my age. I mean, 22 is quite a lot–that was the youngest member in the group I called–it was too old.

Jamie later found a youth group with some boys closer to his age, and was keen to make more friends of his own age at the Summer School. But for Beth (15), in contrast, her friendships of choice are not with her immediate age group at all, as she says with conviction, "I just click with older people."

By coming to the Summer School the young participants extended their network of social contacts. As Amy (18) put it: "We're all like quite close now, we've all made friends, we're all happy with each other and it's kind of like a family type thing . . . we're all the same age–we're having fun."

The participants typically emphasised their determination to remain in contact with their newly-made friends, despite, in some cases, living significant distances apart. The enthusiasm expressed by the young participants throughout the week is encapsulated by Ben (17), who concludes "it's given me much more faith in gay people in general."

Key to transcripts

. . .	short pause, speaker trails off, hesitation
[. . .]	material edited out
[word]	editorial clarification

CONCLUSIONS

Four key issues emerged in the participants' narratives. First, for these young people, being in a place where they are in the majority is very important. It puts them on an equal footing with each other, rather than lacking the usual repertoire of rights to speak and act freely. Second, the Summer School increases the possibility of interpersonal contact with others like them of similar age. Due to their age, there are obstacles to achieving a rich enough network of social contacts in the bars and clubs that constitute the adult "gay scene." Even in LGB youth groups, opportunities for age-appropriate companionship may be limited due to the small numbers of younger people attending. Third, the safe space that the Summer School provides is vital in many respects. For example, knowing that it is acceptable to publicly flirt provides them with a key part of adolescent interaction not otherwise experienced by many LGB teenagers. Dedicated youth work settings are safer spaces for young LGB people than the bars and clubs of the commercial gay scene: they are less daunting, there are fewer pressures, and they aim to protect the interests of the young people. Moreover, they provide an arena in which personal resources that will help in coping with the challenges of the adult commercial scene can be developed. Fourth, one feature of the Summer School in particular, its focus on the body and possibilities of non-sexual touch and contact, provides a much-needed antidote to a typical daily situation where these young people may, at the extreme, be physically shunned by their peers. In other words, providing a suitable safe space can lead to better social integration for young LGB people.

REFERENCES

Boyatzis, R.E. (1998), *Transforming Qualitative Information: Thematic Analysis and Code Development.* Thousand Oaks, CA: Sage.

Bridget, J. (2003), *Preventing Homophobic Bullying in Calderdale Schools.* Calderdale, West Yorkshire: GALYIC. Retrieved April 15, 2004 from *http://www.lesbianinformationservice.org/bullying.rtf*

Coyle, A. (1998), Developing lesbian and gay identity in adolescence. In: *Teenage Sexuality: Health, Risk and Education*, eds. J. Coleman & D. Roker. Amsterdam: Harwood Academic Press, pp. 163-187.

Coyle, A. (2000), Qualitative research and lesbian and gay psychology in Britain. *British Psychological Society Lesbian & Gay Psychology Section Newsletter.* 4(2):2-5.

Coyle, A. & Kitzinger, C., eds. (2002), *Lesbian and Gay Psychology: New Perspectives.* Oxford: BPS Blackwell.

Crowley, C., Hallam, S., Harré, R. & Lunt, I. (2001), Study support for young people with same-sex attraction–Views and experiences from a pioneering peer support initiative in the north of England. *Educational & Child Psychology*, 18(1):108-124.

D'Augelli, A.R. (1999), The queering of adolescence: Implications for psychological researchers and practitioners. *British Psychological Society Lesbian & Gay Psychology Section Newsletter*, 3:3-5.

Davies, D. (1996), Working with young people. In: *Pink Therapy*, eds. D. Davies & C. Neal. Buckingham: Open University Press, pp. 131-148.

DeWaele, J.P. (1983), Individual psychology: methodology. In: *The Encyclopedic Dictionary of Psychology*, eds. R. Harré & R. Lamb. Oxford: Blackwell, pp. 302-304.

Douglas, N., Warwick, I., Kemp, S. & Whitty, G. (1997), *Playing It Safe: Responses of Secondary School Teachers to Lesbian, Gay and Bisexual Pupils, Bullying, HIV and AIDS Education and Section 28*. London: Health and Education Research Unit, Institute of Education, University of London.

Ellis, V. & High, S. (2004), Something more to tell you: Gay, lesbian or bisexual young people's experiences of secondary schooling. *British Educational Research J.*, 30(2):213-225.

Fontaine, J.H. & Hammond, N.L. (1996), Counselling issues with gay and lesbian adolescents. *Adolescence*, 31(124):817-830.

Forrest, S., Biddle, G. & Clift, S. (1997), *Talking About Homosexuality in the Secondary School*. Horsham: AVERT.

Gibbs, G.R. (2002), *Qualitative Data Analysis: Explorations with NVivo*. Buckingham: Open University Press.

Harré, R. (1998), *The Singular Self: An Introduction to the Psychology of Personhood*. London: Sage.

Hind, T. (2004), *Being Real: Promoting the Emotional Health and Mental Well-Being of Lesbian, Gay and Bisexual Young People Accessing PACE Youth Work Services*. London: Project for Advice Counselling and Education.

Keogh, P. (1999), *Group Outings: Young Gay Men's Experiences of Coming Out at Outzone*. London: Enfield and Haringey Health Authority.

King, M. & Bartlett, A. (1999), British psychiatry and homosexuality. *British J. Psychiatry*, 175:106-113.

King, M. & McKeown, E. (2003), *Mental Health and Wellbeing of Gay Men, Lesbians and Bisexuals in England and Wales*. London: National Association for Mental Health.

McRunyan, W. (1986), The place of the study of individuals within personality psychology. In: *Individual Persons and Their Actions*, eds. L. Van Langenhove, J.M. DeWaele, R. Harré & J.P. DeWaele. Brussels: Vrije Universiteit Brussel, pp. 135-152.

Miles, M.B. & Huberman, A.M. (1994), *Qualitative Data Analysis: An Expanded Sourcebook (2nd Edition)*. London: Sage.

National Union of Teachers (2004a), *Supporting Lesbian, Gay, Bisexual and Transgender Students: An Issue for Every Teacher*. London: Author.

National Union of Teachers (2004b), *Tackling Homophobic Bullying: An Issue for Every Teacher.* London: Author Teachers.
Office for Standards in Education (2002), *Report into Sex and Relationships in Schools.* London: Author.
Richards, L. (1999), *Using NVivo in Qualitative Research.* London: Sage.
Rivers, I. (1995), Mental health issues among young lesbians and gay men bullied at school. *Health & Social Care in the Community,* 3(6):380-383.
Rivers, I. (2002), Developmental issues for lesbian and gay youth. In: *Lesbian and Gay Psychology: New Perspectives,* eds. A. Coyle & C. Kitzinger. Oxford: BPS Blackwell, pp. 30-44.
Rivers, I. & Hardcastle, H. (2000), *The Representation and Misrepresentation of Research: Homosexuality and the House of Lords Debates 1998-2000.* Paper presented at the Inaugural Conference of the Lesbian and Gay Psychology Section of the British Psychological Society, University of Surrey, 18th July.
Smith, J.A., Harré, R. & Van Langenhove, L. (1995), Idiography and the case study. In: *Rethinking Psychology,* eds. J.A. Smith, R. Harré & L. Van Langenhove. London: Sage, pp. 59-69.
Trenchard, L. & Warren, H. (1984), *Something to Tell You.* London: London Gay Teenage Group.
Warren, H. (1984), *Talking About School.* London: London Gay Teenage Group.
Warwick, I., Chase, E. & Aggleton, P. (2004), *Homophobia, Sexual Orientation and Schools: A Review and Implications for Action. Department for Education and Skills Research Report 594.* London: DfES Publications.
Warwick, I. & Douglas, N. (2001), *Safe for All: A Best Practice Guide to Prevent Homophobic Bullying in Schools.* London: Citizenship 21.
Winnicott, D.W. (1965), *The Maturational Processes and the Facilitating Environment: Studies in the Theory of Emotional Development.* London: Hogarth.

doi:10.1300/J236v11n01_09

Gay Men with Learning Disabilities: UK Service Provision

Sören Stauffer-Kruse, MSc, Post MSc, CPsychol

SUMMARY. Whilst the UK's National Health Service (NHS) offers a solid structure of service provision for people with learning disabilities, sexuality issues are often overlooked. This paper offers an examination of how it may be possible that gay men with learning disabilities (GMLD) experience a complex set of increased difficulties in forming a functioning identity. A clinical case example is presented which allows the implications of below average functioning and stereotyping by the majority group to be explored. To conclude, suggestions are made regarding how practitioners could offer the best psychological service to gay men with learning disabilities. It is hoped practitioners will be more proactive and creative in helping gay men with learning disabilities explore their sexuality. doi:10.1300/J236v11n01_10 *[Article copies available for a fee from The Haworth Document Delivery Service: 1-800-HAWORTH. E-mail address: <docdelivery@haworthpress.com> Website: <http://www. HaworthPress.com> © 2007 by The Haworth Press, Inc. All rights reserved.]*

Sören Stauffer-Kruse is Chartered Counselling Psychologist, North East London Mental Health NHS Trust. He is also a specialist counselling psychologist in gay mens sexual health for the Terrence Higgins Trust, London.

Address correspondence to: Sören Stauffer-Kruse, Apartment 112, 1 Prescot Street, London E1 8RL, UK (E-mail: sorenkruse@counsellingpractice.co.uk).

The author thanks the South London and Maudsley NHS Trust Learning Disabilities Service for an invaluable learning opportunity. Thanks to Dr. Jacqui Farrants of City University for her guidance in academic matters.

[Haworth co-indexing entry note]: "Gay Men with Learning Disabilities: UK Service Provision." Stauffer-Kruse, Sören. Co-published simultaneously in *Journal of Gay & Lesbian Psychotherapy* (The Haworth Medical Press, an imprint of The Haworth Press, Inc.) Vol. 11, No. 1/2, 2007, pp. 145-152; and: *British Lesbian, Gay, and Bisexual Psychologies: Theory, Research, and Practice* (ed: Elizabeth Peel, Victoria Clarke, and Jack Drescher) The Haworth Medical Press, an imprint of The Haworth Press, Inc., 2007, pp. 145-152. Single or multiple copies of this article are available for a fee from The Haworth Document Delivery Service [1-800-HAWORTH, 9:00 a.m. - 5:00 p.m. (EST). E-mail address: docdelivery@haworthpress.com].

Available online at http://jglp.haworthpress.com

doi:10.1300/J236v11n01_10

KEYWORDS. Counselling, gay men, homosexuality, identity process theory, learning difficulties, mental health, National Health Service, psychological therapy, sexual identity, sexuality

INTRODUCTION

Sexuality is an integral part of people's lives. Everyone must pass through different stages of relating to others in their lifetime, and it is widely acknowledged that relating to others by combining love and sex can be complicated. However, people with learning disabilities[1]–approximately 1% of the general population (Bouras, 1999)–are often discouraged from establishing sexual relationships with others by anxious parents or carers (Craft, 1987). Gay men with learning disabilities[2] (GMLD) are particularly vulnerable to being restricted by parents or carers in expressing their sexual identities, or may even be encouraged to repress their homosexuality. As a result, they often do not explore their sexuality or sexual identities, which can result in what is termed "challenging behaviour." One way to improving the overall levels of well-being of GMLD may lie in helping them to explore their sexuality whilst being aware of the particular challenges they may face in so doing (Craft, 1996).

In the UK, the National Health Service (NHS) offers people with learning disabilities a wide range of services. Recently, many of these services have recognised the need to think specifically about the mental health problems encountered by GMLD and offer suitable psychological interventions. Most "Mental Health Trusts" have specialist learning disabilities teams that help service users (and their carers/families) to improve their overall levels of psychological well-being. In contrast to the US, the existing public service structure in the UK offers a network of valuable services to this vulnerable and often neglected group, but the specific needs of GMLD can be overlooked as no specific services currently exist.

SEXUALITY IN THE LEARNING DISABLED

Craft (1996) outlines the six rights of people with learning disabilities: (1) the right to grow up, that is, to be treated with the respect and dignity accorded to adults; (2) the right to know, that is, to have access to as much information about themselves and their bodies and those of other people, their emotions and sexual behaviours, as they can assimilate; (3) the right to be a sexual being and make and break relationships; (4) the right not to be at the mercy of individual sexual attitudes of different caregivers; (5) the right not to be sexually abused; and (6) the right to humane and dignified environments. While four of these six rights deal with issues of sexuality, their achievability may be influenced by numerous factors.

For example, people with learning disabilities may have more negative internalised values about sexuality and relationships than the general public (Brantlinger, 1985). They may lack the intellectual capacity to reflect on the attitudes of others and might find identifying support networks difficult. Those with learning disabilities may have difficulties establishing sexual relationships, coping with emotions in relationships, and negotiating relationship conflict (Craft, 1996). Lack of information and lack of assertiveness skills may have an adverse influence on the learning-disabled individual's sexual health (McCarthy and Thompson, 1991). Further, people with learning disabilities are vulnerable and open to exploitation from others (Craft, 1996). Sexual abuse has been highlighted as affecting people with learning disabilities (Turk and Brown, 1992), causing emotional distress and withdrawal (Sobsey and Varnhagen, 1990). All of these factors may cause people with learning disabilities to refrain from exploring their sexuality or even encourage the development of "difficult" sexual behaviours (Craft, 1996). In summary, the barriers for the learning disabled to achieve a fully developed and satisfying sexual identity and life are numerous.

As distressing as the situation may be for heterosexuals with learning disability, the situation for GMLD may be more dire. Whilst there are established literatures addressing mental health problems in gay men *per se* and people with learning disabilities *per se*, these two areas of study remain distinct from one another. For example, in the literature cited in the above paragraph, most authors only occasionally mention lesbian and gay sexualities–and then only in passing. GMLD are practically invisible in the current literature addressing sexuality in learning disabilities (A notable exception is Bennett and Coyle, 2001, 2007).

MENTAL HEALTH PROBLEMS IN GAY MEN WITH LEARNING DISABILITIES

Being a member of a minority group may have adverse implications for the mental health of an individual and GMLD may be doubly disadvantaged. Prevalence rates of depressive disorders indicate a greater risk for (non-learning disabled) gay men, with rates in the general population of 2% (Meltzer et al., 1995) compared to a rate of almost 4% in gay men (Gilman et al., 2001). Gay men appear to suffer from more generalised anxiety disorders (Cochran and Mays, 2000) than the general population (Raghavan, 1997), although the difference is less marked than in depressive disorders. It is probable that increased anxiety and depression are the results of being a member of a stigmatised minority.

Research on those with learning disabilities also suggests higher prevalence rates for common mental health problems (Bouras and Drummond, 1992). Prevalence studies overall show that 20-40% of people with learning disabilities have some form of a mental disorder (Bouras, 1999; Russell, 1997). For instance, the prevalence of schizophrenia in the general population has been found to be 0.4% (Meltzer et al., 1995), whereas it is 3% in people with learning disabilities (Deb, 2001). People with learning disabilities have higher rates of depression and anxiety than the general population (Collacott, Cooper and Lewis, 1992; Deb, 2001; Patel, Goldberg and Moss, 1993; Raghavan, 1997; Vitiello, Spreat and Behar, 1989).

Previous research has examined the stressors that are faced by gay men (DiPlacido, 1998) and by people with learning disabilities (Jahoda, Markova and Cattermole, 1988) separately. However, it would not be unreasonable to presume that a gay man with a learning disability may be at a higher risk of developing a mental health problem.

CASE EXAMPLE

This case example aims to highlight the difficulties encountered by a GMLD struggling to come to terms with his sexual identity.

B[3] is a 21-year-old white man with a diagnosis of a mild learning disability. He has been referred to an NHS psychiatric inpatient assessment and treatment unit after deterioration in his mental state and behaviour. B is admitted under a Section 3 of the Mental Health Act 1983 (Section 3 is a compulsory admission to hospital for assessment and treatment– initially for up to six months). The Community Learning Disabilities Team (CLDT)–a multi-disciplinary team looking after the needs of clients diagnosed with a learning disability within the community–felt that his unstable mental state put him at risk. B has been frequenting public sex environments and having anonymous sexual contact with men. The CLDT defined "risk" as the potentially adverse implications of B's behaviour, such as exploitation from others and the potential for his actions cause physical and/or psychological harm to himself and/or to others. B is discharged showing no signs of a psychotic illness and he is started on antidepressant medication. Upon discharge it is felt by the CLDT that he continues to be at risk from his "inappropriate sexual behaviour towards others." However, at no stage during B's admission has his sexual behaviour, sexuality or sexual identity been formally addressed.

IMPLICATIONS FOR TREATMENT AND INTERVENTION

A large part of the author's work has taken place in NHS-based mental health services with people with learning disabilities. These services have been quite reluctant to tackle the issues outlined in the case of individuals like B. For example, rather than treating B's cruising as merely a "symptom," issues around his homosexuality merited further exploration. Sexual behaviour seen by others as challenging and "risky" may need to be better understood against the backdrop of a GMLD's struggle to come to terms with his homosexuality and to acquire a gay sexual identity. Individuals like B are usually quite dependent on their families and these family environments often do not allow for any open discussions of (hetero)sexuality, let alone exploration of gay sexuality. The family, as well as the professionals involved in B's care, may feel that B would be at risk if given an opportunity to explore his sexuality, especially since he has taken risks in the past. However, it is often the lack of open conversation about sexuality–either from family or professionals–that may increase risky sexual behaviours. Consequently, individuals like B may be drawn to having sex with other men without having the skills or understanding to negotiate safer sex. They may lack assertiveness skills, or an understanding of sexually transmitted diseases. They may also lack the ability to distinguish a potential sex partner from a potential gay-basher.

Further, people with learning disabilities may hold negative internalised values about sexuality and relationships (Brantlinger, 1985). B himself may have particularly critical views of gay relationships; or he may be unaware of the existence of stable gay relationships. Someone like B (who may already have an awareness of being stereotyped for having a learning disability) may not feel good about identifying as a gay man (Cain, 1991). Moreover, it is unclear what support the gay community could offer people like B, who may have difficulties accessing and fitting into the mainstream gay community (Bennett and Coyle, 2001, 2007).

A WAY FORWARD IN CLINICAL PRACTICE

Helping service users, their families and caregivers understand that there are gay men with learning disabilities may seem obvious, but achieving this is often difficult in practice. Having professionals agree on the need to help educate these men about sexuality and to explore their sexual identity is important. However, this is often difficult as service users themselves hold negative attitudes on sexuality that reflect the environment around them. Helping GMLD to explore how they feel in psychological counseling and therapy is often an essential prerequisite to tackling issues with families and carers. The author has found that combining individual and family work can encourage an initial exploration of both client and family anxieties about sexuality. Art therapies can be a good way to explore issues that people struggle to verbalise; working collaboratively with an occupational therapist can be helpful.

The gay community may harbor negative stereotypes about individuals with learning disabilities that reflect those of the society at large. However, in my experience, lesbian and gay community projects have always been open to exploring collaborative ways of working in helping clients identify parts of the gay community that they may be able to access.

Important ethical concerns arise when considering the potential vulnerability of GMLD who struggle with their sexuality. There may be a perceived danger–among families and professionals–that assisting people like B in explorations of their sexual identity can increase their vulnerability. However, the beliefs and attitudes of caretakers need to be weighed against the adult needs of the GMLD, particularly if he shows a level of functioning that may permit many aspects of adult sexuality to be negotiated.

It is reasonable for therapists, counselors, families and caretakers to consider whether a person like B should have the right to take the risk of exploring what it means for him to be an adult, gay man. Undoubtedly, he may need some support in understanding the implications of taking this risk. Psychological services in the United Kingdom need to be available to offer this support.

NOTES

1. A learning disability is characterised by below average intellectual functioning and onset before adulthood. It reduces the individual's ability to cope independently, and is mostly accompanied by an impaired social functioning due to the person's reduced ability to understand new information and learn new skills (Bouras, 1999).

2. The phrase "gay men with learning disabilities" is used to describe men with learning disabilities who have sex with men. It is important to note, however, that some of these men would resist describing themselves as gay, and for these individuals the term "men who have sex with men" (MSM) may be more appropriate.

3. For the purposes of this discussion, a composite case example is used that is based upon a collection of NHS clients' experiences.

REFERENCES

Bennett, C.J. & Coyle, A. (2001), A minority within a minority: Identity and well-being among gay men with learning disabilities. *Lesbian & Gay Psychology Review*, 2(1):9-15.

Bennett, C. & Coyle, A. (2007), A minority within a minority: Experiences of gay men with intellectual disabilities. In: *Out in Psychology: Lesbian, gay, bisexual, trans and queer perspectives*, eds. V. Clarke & E. Peel. Chicester: Wiley, pp. 125-146.

Bouras, N., ed. (1999), *Psychiatric and Behavioural Disorders in Developmental Disabilities and Mental Retardation*. Cambridge & New York: Cambridge University Press.

Bouras, N. & Drummond, C. (1992), Behavioural and psychiatric disorders of people with mental handicaps living in the community. *J. Intellectual Disability Research*, 36(4):349-357.

Brantlinger, E. (1985), Mildly mentally retarded secondary students' information about and attitudes toward sexuality and sexual education. *Education & Training of the Mentally Retarded*, June: 99-108.

Cain, R. (1991), Stigma management and gay identity development. *Social Work*, 36:67-73.

Cochran, S.D. & Mays, V.M. (2000), Lifetime prevalence of suicidal symptoms and affective disorders among men reporting same-sex sexual partners: Results from the NHANIS III. *American J. Public Health*, 90:573-578.

Collacott, R.A., Cooper, S.A. & Lewis, K.R. (1992), Differential rates of psychiatric disorders in adults with Down's Syndrome compared with other mentally handicapped adults. *British J. Psychiatry*, 161:671-674.

Craft, A. (1987), Mental handicap and sexuality: Issues for individuals with a mental handicap, their parents and professionals. In: *Mental Handicap and Sexuality: Issues and Perspectives*, ed. A. Craft. Tunbridge Wells: Costello, pp. 1-22.

Craft, A., ed. (1996), *Practice Issues in Sexuality and Learning Disabilities*. London & New York: Routledge.

Deb, S. (2001), Epidemiology of psychiatric illness in adults with intellectual disability. In: *Health Evidence Bulletins–Learning Disabilities (Intellectual Disability)*, eds. L. Hamilton-Kirkwood, Z. Ahmed, S. Deb, W. Fraser, W. Lindsay, K. McKenzie, E. Penny & J. Scotland. Cardiff: National Assembly for Wales, pp. 14-17.

DiPlacido, J. (1998), Minority stress among lesbians, gay men, and bisexuals: A consequence of heterosexism, homophobia, and stigmatization. In: *Stigma and Sexual Orientation: Understanding Prejudice Against Lesbians, Gay Men, and Bisexuals*, ed. G.M. Herek. Thousand Oaks, CA: Sage, pp. 138-159.

Gilman, S.E., Cochran, S.D., Mays, V.M., Hughes, M., Ostrow, D. & Kessler, R.C. (2001), Risk of psychiatric disorders among individuals reporting same-sex sexual partners in the National Comorbidity Survey. *American J. Public Health*, 91: 591-598.

Jahoda, A., Markova, I. & Cattermole, C. (1988), Stigma and the self concept of people with a mild mental handicap. *J. Mental Deficiency Research*, 32:103-115.

McCarthy, M. & Thompson, D. (1991), The politics of sex education. *Community Care*, 21 November.

Meltzer, H., Gill, B., Petticrew, M. & Hinds, K. (1995), *The Prevalence of Psychiatric Morbidity Among Adults Living in Private Households: OPCS Survey of Psychiatric Morbidity in Great Britain, Report 1*. London: HMSO.

Patel, P., Goldberg, D. & Moss, S. (1993), Psychiatric morbidity in older people with moderate and severe learning disability II: The Prevalence Study. *British J. Psychiatry*, 163:481-491.

Raghavan, R., (1997), Anxiety disorders in people with learning disabilities: A review of the literature. *J. Learning Disabilities for Nursing, Health & Social Care*, 2(1):3-9.

Russell, O., ed. (1997), *Psychiatry of Learning Disabilities*. London: Gaskell.

Sobsey, D. & Varnhagen, C. (1990), Sexual abuse, assault and exploitation of individuals with disabilities. In: *Practice Issues in Sexuality and Learning Disabilities*, ed. A. Craft. London & New York: Routledge, 1996, pp. 93-115.

Turk, V. & Brown, H. (1992), Sexual abuse and adults with learning disabilities. *Mental Handicap*, 20(2):56-58.

Vitiello, B., Spreat, S. & Behar, D. (1989), Obsessive-compulsive disorder in mentally retarded patients. *J. Nervous & Mental Disease*, 177(4):232-236.

doi:10.1300/J236v11n01_10

Coming Out in the Heterosexist World of Sport: A Qualitative Analysis of Web Postings by Gay Athletes

Brendan Gough, PhD

SUMMARY. The literature on coming out typically concerns experiences with family and friends, but apart from a few (auto)biographies by elite gay athletes, there is very little published on how gay athletes come out to their sporting peers. Since most sports are infused with ideals and practices associated with hegemonic masculinity and heterosexuality, coming out is likely to present some unique challenges for gay athletes. This paper reports on a preliminary study based on an analysis of online accounts (N = 8) provided by North American gay athletes for a web-based newsletter. Techniques from qualitative research methods, popular with and informed by various feminist, critical, and lesbian and gay psychologists in the UK, are used to make sense of these accounts. A clear pattern emerged across all accounts, incorporating the following

Brendan Gough is affiliated with the University of Leeds where he works in Psychology and is Deputy Director for the Centre for Interdisciplinary Gender Studies. He co-edits the journal *Qualitative Research in Psychology*.

Address correspondence to: Brendan Gough, PhD, School of Psychology, University of Leeds, Leeds, LS2 9JT, UK (E-mail: b.gough@leeds.ac.uk).

The author would like to thank Eric Andersen for his constructive feedback on earlier drafts of this paper.

[Haworth co-indexing entry note]: "Coming Out in the Heterosexist World of Sport: A Qualitative Analysis of Web Postings by Gay Athletes." Gough, Brendan. Co-published simultaneously in *Journal of Gay & Lesbian Psychotherapy* (The Haworth Medical Press, an imprint of The Haworth Press, Inc.) Vol. 11, No. 1/2, 2007, pp. 153-174; and: *British Lesbian, Gay, and Bisexual Psychologies: Theory, Research, and Practice* (ed: Elizabeth Peel, Victoria Clarke, and Jack Drescher) The Haworth Medical Press, an imprint of The Haworth Press, Inc., 2007, pp. 153-174. Single or multiple copies of this article are available for a fee from The Haworth Document Delivery Service [1-800-HAWORTH, 9:00 a.m. - 5:00 p.m. (EST). E-mail address: docdelivery@haworthpress.com].

key themes: (1) Sport as distraction from sexuality; (2) Invisibility and isolation within sport; (3) Coming out to the team: difficult but rewarding; and (4) Becoming politicised: challenging heterosexism within sport. Discussion centres on the challenges and opportunities facing gay men within sporting contexts and the implications of the analysis for possible psychological interventions with gay athletes. The need for further qualitative research in this area is also underlined. doi:10.1300/J236v11n01_11 *[Article copies available for a fee from The Haworth Document Delivery Service: 1-800-HAWORTH. E-mail address: <docdelivery@haworthpress.com> Website: <http://www.HaworthPress.com> © 2007 by The Haworth Press, Inc. All rights reserved.]*

KEYWORDS. Athletics, coming out, gay, heterosexism, homophobia, homosexuality, invisibility, masculinity, online accounts, qualitative analysis, (self-)acceptance, sport

INTRODUCTION

The literature on coming out covers home, school and work environments, and although there is some illuminating research on coming out within sports contexts (Griffin, 1998; Pronger, 1990), there is much scope for further work in this area. There are some important sporting biographies, autobiographies and journalistic writing exploring issues in relation to coming out as a gay athlete (Louganis and Marcus, 1995; Woog, 1998); however, the social scientific literature to date tends to focus on the culture of androcentrism and heterosexism within sport, and its impact on specific groups and individuals, including gay athletes yet to come out to their peers (Hekma, 1998; Bryant, 2001). As more gay men come out in sporting environments, it becomes important to document their stories so that contemporary issues facing gay athletes can be addressed. This paper, then, reports on some exploratory qualitative research, which analyses the accounts provided by gay male athletes about coming out to their sports peers.

This paper's focus on gay men is not intended to detract from the issues facing heterosexual and lesbian women in sport, of which several prominent authors have written (Griffin, 1998; Krane et al., 2004). The interest in gay male athletes can be situated within the growing body of work on men and masculinities (Connell, 1995; Kimmel, 1987), and more specifically, on masculinities and sport (Messner, 1992; McKay, Sabo and Messner, 1999). It is also worth noting that while there is evidence of initiatives by government agencies to involve more minority groups in sport, there is little or no reference to gay men. For example, the UK organisation "Sport England," which is responsible for developing and funding sport-related projects, currently prioritises increasing the sport participation of four groups: ethnic communities, people with disabilities, women and girls, and people on low incomes (see www. sportengland.org). While these and similar initiatives are laudable, what is striking is the absence of any dedicated or explicit policy on gay men (or lesbian women) within sport. Moreover, there is no attempt to use sport as a means of educating "straight" men about forms of masculinity, which conventionally lie outside the sporting environment. In part, this can be related to the relative invisibility of gay men in sport, and prevailing stereotypes about homosexuality.

Apart from some prominent autobiographies, there is a dearth of publicly available textual data, which bears on coming out issues for gay athletes, especially in the UK. Hence the use of online accounts posted on a popular North American website: outsports.com. The use of qualitative data and analytic techniques in this study can be situated within an emerging field of lesbian and gay psychology in the UK, which features a range of innovative theoretical and methodological approaches to issues of importance for lesbian and gay individuals and groups (Coyle and Kitzinger, 2002; Clarke and Peel, 2007). The study presented here seeks to highlight common themes in the stories presented by gay athletes, and in so doing to discuss opportunities and challenges for gay men interested in sports participation. More broadly, the paper seeks to raise awareness of gay experiences within sport with a view to promoting discussion about potential psychological and social interventions.

COMING OUT

Coming out is generally portrayed as a fraught process, and it is well known that gay adolescents are vulnerable to a range of problems, including social isolation, family rejection, low self-esteem, school failure and substance abuse (Radkowsky and Siegel, 1997). A distinction has been made between coming out to self (individuation) and coming out to others (disclosure) (Greene and Herek, 1994), although the two are clearly interrelated (Davies, 1992). Coming out to self is depicted as a struggle between personal experiences relating to feeling "different" and the social devaluation of homosexuality, which will be internalised to some extent. As a result, there is denial of a gay identity, and distraction tactics may be deployed, such as heterosexual dating or immersion in intellectual or work activities (Cohen and Savin-Williams, 1996). If and when there is some self-acceptance, coming out to others might prove too daunting for various reasons, such as uncertainty about consequences, fear of rejection by significant others and/or dread of hurting loved ones (Wells and Kline, 1987).

To date, most research on the coming out process has concentrated on the home environment. The development of gay sexuality is typically linked to adolescence, and as most adolescents tend to live in the parental home, this domestic focus is hardly surprising. Coming out to parents is usually depicted as a problematic process for all parties, but one that is crucial for many gay youths. Relationships with parents are permanent and irreplaceable, and family support is greatly desired and is important for self-acceptance (Borhek, 1993). Conversely, a hostile family environment is associated with personal and social difficulties (MacDonald, 1984). Gay males prefer to come out to their mothers, and there is evidence that mothers tend to be more accepting than fathers (D'Augelli, 1994). However, some research suggests that rather than truly accepting their child's sexual orientation, many parents simply learn to acknowledge it (Ben-Ari, 1995).

Yet, it cannot be assumed that coming out is problematic for all gay people–there will always be examples of positive coming out experiences. Nor should it be assumed that coming out itself is easily definable or discrete–one may have disclosed to some friends but not others, some family members but not others, and so on. The complexities and subtleties of coming out for different individuals and groups are best grasped by qualitative research methods, where participants are encouraged to provide detailed accounts to a sympathetic researcher, accounts which can subsequently be analysed in-depth using established techniques. The use of quantitative methods, such as questionnaires, do not offer the participant sufficient opportunity to elaborate on their tick-box responses to a series of closed questions preconceived by the investigator (see Savin-Williams, 2001, for a full critique of quantitative methods used to investigate coming out and minority stress). To date, most research on the coming out process has used quantitative methods, but some qualitative research has been produced which sheds light on the complexity of coming out for different individuals and groups.

For example, Markowe (2002) interviewed 40 lesbians from London about their coming out experiences and found that they had to negotiate various difficulties such as invisibility, stereotyping, and background rumour and gossip. Coming out was fraught with ambiguity and uncertainty where a sense of authenticity and a need for affiliation were deemed crucial. Similarly, Flowers and Buston's (2001) interview study with working-class gay men in the North of England highlighted both overt and covert forms of heterosexism and homophobia encountered across home, school and work environments. In a sociocultural context structured by ideals of hegemonic masculinity (such as strength, self-discipline, endurance and competitiveness–see Connell, 1995) and compulsory heterosexuality, the impact of prejudice on interviewees ranged from a sense of isolation to "living a lie." This interplay between social forces and individual experiences needs to be explored further, and in relation to a range of social and institutional contexts, such as sport.

SPORT, HETEROSEXISM AND HOMOPHOBIA

Resistance to homosexuality within sport, especially mainstream sports, is well-known. Indeed, for males to be disinterested or perform poorly in sport is to risk ridicule in the form of homophobic terminology such as "poof" and "queer," especially in the context of youth sports, whether taking place at school or in the community (Swain, 2000). Since gay men are popularly associated with softness and effeminacy, they, too, are either excluded or devalued within the heteronormative world of sport. Wendel, Toma and Morphew (2001) found that heterosexual athletes were "unwilling to confront and accept homosexuality" (p. 470). Indeed, a man who is both gay and athletic transgresses pervasive understandings of homosexuality and sport and may well provoke negative press as a result. Various examples over the years reinforce this point. There is the tragic story of Justin Fashinu, a talented British football (soccer) player who ended up committing suicide in 1998 after a troubled career, while the gifted Australian rugby player Ian Roberts experienced much animosity after coming out in 1991. There is also the celebrated case of Greg Louganis, the US Olympic high diver who only came out late in his career at the 1994 Gay Games in New York. These and other stories are recounted in published biographies and autobiographies, and provide rich insights into being gay within sport.

As for the scholarly research on gay athletes, there is a small but growing body of work that documents and theorises instances of homophobia and heterosexism in a variety of sporting arenas. For lesbian athletes, there are pressures associated with "hegemonic femininity" whereby resistance–for example, in the form of muscularity–is pathologised, while conformity–for example, presenting a "feminine" appearance–risks trivialisation (see Krane, 2001). In an interview study with closeted gay male athletes, Hekma (1998) interviewed and illustrated the persistence of homophobic language and "hyper-heterosexuality" within sport. Clearly, such a discursive climate works to oppress and exclude gay sexualities from sport and makes it very difficult for gay athletes to come out.

A media analysis conducted by Dworkin and Wachs (1998) reinforces the policing of sexuality within sport. They review coverage of three HIV-positive athletes, two who are heterosexual and one homosexual (Greg Louganis). They found that the media made a concerted effort to locate the causes of HIV-AIDS concerning the heterosexual athletes only, whereas no inquiries were made into how Louganis contracted the disease. They found this phenomenon "consistent with the historically automatic conflation of HIV/AIDS with gay identity" (p. 20).

Apart from singular cases like Louganis, gay men in sport, especially team sports requiring "masculine" attributes of toughness, aggression and endurance, are conspicuous by their apparent absence (see also Pronger, 1990). A notable UK exception is Price's (2000) ethnographic study of a gay men's rugby team, which found that opposing heterosexual teams revised their homophobic attitudes when the gay rugby men came out of the closet. In the USA, there is some evidence of gay men coming in to sport–and coming out. This phenomenon is indicated by the emergence of various websites and listservs in recent years tailored to gay men with a passion for sport, as spectators, players or both (see, for example, outsports.com).

Research by Eric Andersen (2002), a highly respected coach and activist who has now become an academic working in California, highlights the increasing popularity of sport for gay men. Whereas previous research examined the reproduction of heterosexism by considering straight and closeted athletes, he recruited and interviewed some 42 openly gay athletes. Key themes derived from the qualitative analysis suggest a lack of overt prejudice against these athletes, but this was linked to suppression and silencing of gay sexualities within the sporting environment. So, while straight sportsmen continue with locker room "chick talk," their gay counterparts have little choice but to stay silent about their own sexual life, or to mask it in other ways. Andersen concludes that this amounts to tolerance rather than acceptance, and that much more work needs to be done before spaces within sport can be opened up where gay as well as straight masculinities can flourish. It is worth noting, for example, that out gay athletes tend to converge on individual sports rather than more prestigious (and more conventionally masculine) team sports, and there is some evidence that many gay sportsmen remain in the closet for fear of their status, and in some cases careers, being irreparably damaged.

The small but significant body of qualitative research on the experiences of gay athletes is yielding in-depth, "inside" analyses which complement existing questionnaire and survey research. Moreover, this qualitative research offers valuable material for psychotherapists who may be working with gay athletes. For example, the difficulties faced by gay athletes, within a culture that breeds mundane (Peel, 2001), indirect and ostensibly inoffensive forms of prejudice and discrimination such as the use of heterosexist terminology and jokes, are brought to life by qualitative data extracts and associated analysis. In addition, qualitative research presents some success stories of gay athletes coming out, and information about key events, relationships and social contexts germane to these positive cases can help psychotherapists support gay athletes who may seek professional support.

Yet, the potential of qualitative research in this area has not yet been fully realized. There is a clear need for more qualitative work which carefully documents the experiences of gay men in sport and which raises awareness of the often subtle reproduction of homophobia and heterosexism. One interesting and potentially revealing focus for qualitative data analysis in this area is websites that offer information and support to gay athletes. As previously stated, these websites are most visible in North America; indeed, an initial trawl of UK websites relating to either gay issues and sport (or both) failed to uncover anything directly relevant. Perhaps the most prominent and influential website is outsports.com, a North American site which offers extensive sports coverage for gay fans and which highlights stories of relevance to the gay sporting community. This website also provides profiles of and interviews with out gay athletes and it is these features which this study uses as data for qualitative analysis.

The present paper, then, is based on a qualitative analysis of accounts provided by gay athletes presented on outsports.com. The spotlight is on the athlete's own words in an attempt to gain "insider" perspectives, and the specific focus is on tales of "coming out" as gay athletes, as this process dominated the accounts presented. As well as being a series of personal stories, it must also be noted that these accounts are also public testaments broadcast over the Internet. As such, they can be considered cultural texts regarding issues of sexual identity and prejudice in contemporary sport. This study should also be regarded as preliminary–an in-depth analysis of internet data which will generate themes to be discussed in relation to other work and to be further elaborated and refined in future research.

METHOD

A commitment to qualitative research methods is typical in particular areas of UK psychology, such as critical social psychology (Gough and McFadden, 2001) and feminist social psychology (Wilkinson, 1996). A general concern here is to locate personal lives within wider social and political contexts in order to foster sophisticated understandings of phenomena. This social constructionist approach (Burr, 1995) acts as a counterpoint to mainstream psychological explanations that reduce phenomena to individual or intra-individual processes (e.g., personality, cognitive mechanisms). Lesbian and gay psychology in the UK is similarly concerned with examining psychological issues across social contexts and has drawn upon (but is not limited to) qualitative research methods such as discourse analysis (Coyle and Kitzinger, 2002; Clarke and Peel, 2007). It must also be noted, however, that such critical qualitative work is not confined to the UK (Andersen, 2002; Hekma, 1998). The present study, then, accesses qualitative data in the form of Internet accounts posted by gay athletes, and develops themes that situate these accounts within prevailing social representations of sport, gender and sexuality.

Data

The data analysed below derives from outsports.com. This site is designed by gay sports fans for gay sports fans and celebrates the achievements of gay athletes. It offers a range of services, including chat rooms, discussion lists, athlete and activist profiles, and information about relevant national and local events. The various athlete profiles, interviews and features certainly provide a rich source of data for exploring gay (and lesbian) experiences in sporting contexts. After sifting through the website, eight texts were identified which seemed to offer important insights into being a gay male athlete. This somewhat modest sample size is common in qualitative research, where richness of the data and depth of the subsequent analysis are prioritised (Potter and Wetherell, 1987; Smith, 2004).

These texts were selected mainly because they offered the most substantial accounts of gay athletes' experiences, which is not to say that other available texts, such as letters and e-mail discussions, do not also provide valuable sources of data. It must be acknowledged that texts presented in media such as websites will likely have been subjected to some editing, and that the stories selected for analysis here may depart somewhat from the version originally supplied by interviewees. However, the texts selected for analysis were those where athlete quotations were more prominent, and journalistic input seemed minimal. As shown in Table 1, eight selected texts featured gay athletes participating, often at a high level, in sports ranging from skiing to tennis and basketball.

Seven of the texts are journalistic profiles based on an interview with the protagonist and one text is entirely penned by an openly gay athlete who was invited to tell his story (Athlete 1 [A1]). All but one of the men featured (A2) have come out as gay in their sports environment.

Qualitative Analysis

Although quantitative methods such as content analysis can be used to analyse qualitative data, it is generally accepted that qualitative methods of analysis produce more detailed and contextualised understandings (Smith, 2004; Camic, Rhodes and Yardley, 2003). Some qualitative methods are informed by social constructionism (Burr, 1995) and are oriented towards situating personal accounts within wider soci-

TABLE 1. Athletes Featured and Their Details

ATHLETE	SPORT	LEVEL	AGE
1	Skiing	College	21
2	Basketball	High School	16
3	Basketball; Volleyball	College	30
4	Snowboarding	Aspiring Olympian	26
5	Motorcycle Racing	Regional champion	45
6	Triathlon	Aspiring Olympian	28
7	Tennis	Aspiring professional	26
8	Gymnastics	National championship	23

etal contexts. Since this study's objective was to produce a sophisticated analysis of gay identity construction within the heterosexist world of sport, qualitative methods were considered ideal. As stated above, the UK qualitative psychology community tends to favour critical approaches such as discourse analysis. However, this study's choice of analytic method relates to the dataset-written Internet accounts rather than the verbal or conversational data preferred by critical discursive approaches. A form of systematic thematic analysis was required akin to grounded theory (GT) procedures (Glaser and Strauss, 1967) in order to generate a set of relevant categories. However, this study does not adopt a full-blown GT approach, since this involves a flexible approach to the sampling of cases on the basis of emerging theory ("theoretical sampling"). As the Internet dataset was "readymade," GT procedures were used in a more selective way that is tailored to the author's objective of understanding and situating gay athletes' accounts (see Willig, 2001, for a discussion of the ways in which GT may be deployed).

Briefly, the qualitative analysis entailed close readings of the first text, segmenting it into sections and generating themes line-by-line, section-by-section. Themes are initially very descriptive, often simply rephrasing the words supplied in the text. This is quite deliberate, as any subsequent theory must be "grounded," hence the term grounded theory. Gradually, as links are made between similar themes, clusters of themes are produced with a higher order status. Theme labels become more abstract and psychological, reflecting the analyst's prior knowledge and engagement with the data.

For example, a line of text such as "my friends had no reason to suspect I was gay" could be coded as "suppression of sexuality" or even "passing as straight." It is worth noting that any one piece of text may be allocated to more than one category—this is the principle of "open coding." This approach quickly offers up many themes but it is important to move from the many to the few by a process of clustering up as analysis gathers momentum. From an initial pool of hundreds of themes, four master themes were produced which are hypothesized to summarise and explain the dataset.

To reiterate, these themes must not simply be taken at face value. The assumption is not that thematic methods like GT see beyond language to "truth" or "experience"; rather, GT is used in a constructionist sense (Charmaz, 1995) and relate themes to, in this case, the heterosexist institution of sport. Social constructionist writing and discursive psychological research have alerted us to the active, performative and variable nature of accounts (Burr, 1995; Edwards and Potter, 1992), so it is likely that the athletes featured would present differing accounts in other contexts. Moreover, the themes presented here are but one interpretation of the data, inevitably coloured by the analyst's preconceptions and engagement with the texts (for a discussion of reflexivity in qualitative research, see Finlay and Gough, 2003). In conducting the analysis, the author was ever mindful of the context in which the accounts were produced, i.e., a gay-centred website dedicated to the promotion of gay men and lesbian women in sport. Indeed, it was noted that positive outcomes were generally emphasised in the published accounts. However, there were examples of stories where outcomes were not completely resolved or straightforward in the data-set in question here, and all accounts alluded to significant obstacles on the road to success and contentment. As well as illustrating key themes, then, the functions of particular stories and phrases deployed in the accounts will be noted where relevant.

FINDINGS

The themes identified echo and extend findings cited in the literature on coming out experiences. Difficulties in self-acceptance and telling others are reported and themes of personal suffering and isolation are underlined, highlighting the lack of space within sport for gay men to negotiate their sexuality. In the analysis that follows, the issue of coming out for gay athletes is focused on, and the following interlocking themes are identified:

- Sport as distraction from sexuality
- Invisibility and isolation within sport
- Coming out to the team: difficult but rewarding
- Becoming politicised: challenging heterosexism within sport

These themes can be viewed as broadly chronological, whereby burgeoning sexuality engenders tensions in sports contexts that are ultimately resolved through support from others, including sporting peers. In narrative terms, a pattern of overcoming adversity to attain (self-)acceptance is presented. The following extract captures something of the journey that many participants recount:

> When I look back over the past year, I'm amazed at how much my life has changed. Last year at this time, not only was I completely in the closet, but I had not even accepted myself as being gay. To-

day, though, I've fully accepted myself, and I'm completely out with all of my friends, my family and most significantly, my ski team. (A1)

The narrative structure embodied in this extract, and present in all eight texts, conforms to the modern pattern which Plummer (1995) terms stories of suffering, surviving and surpassing. In his analysis, coming out stories are but one form of a more generic modernist story where, for example, the metaphor of the journey may be deployed, whereby the protagonist works through different stages to arrive at a "home," or a more settled identity. These common narrative patterns and devices notwithstanding, diversity between coming out stories can be noted. One form of difference relates to the source of suffering, and as shown below, the place and meaning of sport in relation to personal suffering and identity does shift for gay athletes.

Sport as Distraction from Sexuality

Generally, participation in sport began early, and was seen as a means of acquiring peer acceptance. The importance of joining the team and becoming successful is reinforced by A2 (Vernon), who felt obliged to get involved in sport:

> "I really hated basketball, and would much rather read, but other boys didn't do that. Everybody played basketball, and I wanted to fit in," he pauses, "so I did too . . . Oh yeah, I am the man all right," Vernon says. "Even back in sixth grade I was. I would, like, score 25 points a game as a sixth grader." (A2)

What is notable here is the lack of enthusiasm or perceived free choice concerning sport participation–it was simply a matter of "fitting in" and acquiring an identity. In other accounts, the normality of a sporting identity is conveyed. It was common to associate sport with being ordinary, as in references to the "all-American teenager" being sport-centred (A6) and the "average American guy . . . just Andre at the track 99% of the time" (A5). Such constructions work to dismiss the relevance of sexual orientation in sporting contexts.

Generally, sport may be conceived as a form of escape from the surveillance of others, as A2 again emphasises:

> They don't want to think about it. Mom says, "Vernon you need to get a girlfriend." I tell her, "Mom I don't want to. I don't have time

... When I'm in the gym, by myself, it calms my nerves," Vernon said. "If I'm upset I'll go shoot by myself." (A2)

Parental policing of sexuality can be evaded temporarily through sporting activity, which at once offers a form of individual therapy or stress relief, and the upholding of a heteronormative façade. The social construction of sportsmen as masculine and heterosexual offers protection against "being found out," as another athlete (A3) suggests. Sport can also work to distract the self from complex feelings about an emerging gay sexuality, as another describes:

> Skiing provided a focus in my life that made it easy to spend time thinking about the sport rather than agonizing over whether or not I was gay. At the time, I didn't think about the fact that my position as an athlete would later be one of the greatest barriers to my coming out. (A1)

Here, sport offers a positive space where issues of sexuality can be safely contained. The sporting environment becomes a form of sanctuary, a site where personal problems may be temporarily forgotten, where "agonizing" can be kept at bay. The literature does point to activities such as work and study performing similar functions of escape and distraction (Cohen and Savin-Williams, 1996). This athlete also points to the irony of sport, an early form of protection, mutating into a major hindrance against the development of sexual identity, as discussed below.

Invisibility and Isolation Within Sport

Over time, an ineluctable and powerful sense of oneself as gay emerges with the result that the sporting environment is now encountered as difficult rather than therapeutic. A conflict between interior experience and the exterior world is conveyed, and the artifice of presenting a "straight" face to others is lamented. The personal costs of suppressing "inner" gay feelings and "acting" straight were noted in a variety of contexts, and themes of denial, guilt, and fear of being found out were evident. These themes are in accordance with other research on coming out to self and others (e.g., Flowers and Buston, 2001).

A stance of vigilance is required to ward off the suspicions of others and to protect the self against potential social rejection. That such difficulty is exacerbated within sporting contexts is underlined in various ways. Reconciling a gay and an athletic identity presented a major challenge, with the strain of a straight façade evident. Coming out to sports peers was invariably deemed problematic: "a big deal" (A7); "[engenders] worry, depression, stress" (A6). Others speak of fatigue and discomfort while colluding with a pervasive "locker room" culture in which heteronormative stories and practices dominated. For example, a gymnast laments how both straight and gay athletes in this minority sport overcompensate owing to prevailing stereotypes of gymnasts: "straight gymnasts overindulge in chick talk . . . as do gay gymnasts!" (A8).

A perceived incompatibility between "gay" and "athlete" is reported in all cases:

> I still had a lot of trouble seeing myself as a gay man, in large part because I was an athlete and I didn't see any other gay male athletes around me. Through this time, I was still completely silent about the subject and none of my friends had any reason to suspect that I was gay. (A1)

The absence of meaningful role models is emphasised, exacerbating isolation and militating against coming out in sport. Indeed, the featured athletes are invariably introduced as "rare" or "unique," thereby reinforcing these cases as exceptional rather than normal. For example, one is introduced as "a rarity–an out, active male athlete" (A8). Many accounts allude to the "stereotype" of non-athletic gays, and how gay athletes are seen as "strange, unexpected" (A3). This myopia around gay athletes is said to hold within the gay community also, which athlete 6 is determined to challenge:

> [I hope to] demonstrate to the gay community that it's possible to be gay and be an elite athlete. We're here to facilitate that and to mentor up and coming athletes.

The dearth of out gay sportsmen is underlined further through comparison with lesbian athletes, who are deemed to be more conspicuous, as in tennis:

> I don't know of any of the top [male] tennis players who have come out–I mean on the women's side there are a lot of lesbians who have come out, but on the men's side it's very rare to hear of any top players in the pros who have come out. (A7)

The strangeness of gay sportsmen is especially acknowledged concerning "macho" sports. For example, Andre (A5), a motorcyclist, mentions his hobby of shooting handguns with other gay men in terms which recognise the perceived incongruity between being gay and "macho" sports: "yes, gay guys shoot guns and race motorcycles!"

Coming Out to the Team: Difficult But Rewarding

With this hostile sports environment in mind, how can a gay athlete begin to dare thinking about coming out? Here, the role of social influences is cited, often coming from unexpected or previously unknown sources. All the athletes alluded to a significant person or people who were instrumental in their decision to come out to others, including sporting colleagues. For example, athlete 1 shares his excitement at discovering another gay man in his sport:

> Finally, in February 2002 (the winter of my junior year), things changed. While looking at Outsports.com one day, I came across the list of out athletes. Reading it over, I found that there was another Nordic skier on the list who was on the ski team at his college out West. This discovery was incredibly powerful. All of a sudden, it didn't seem like I was completely alone in my situation; here was someone else who had really similar interests and who was also gay. I was able to get in touch with him through e-mail, and we began corresponding, which helped me first to accept myself as being gay and then to have the confidence to come out. (A1)

Given the above mentioned lack of visible gay athletes, the impact of learning about other gay sportsmen cannot be underestimated. This kind of "epiphany" was common to the accounts presented, and Plummer (1995) notes that coming out and other stories require such a transformative experience. As more and more gay men come out in sport, the potential for greater support and acceptance is enormous. The athletes also mentioned the influential role of gay coaches (A3), gay friends and acquaintances (A8), and their first gay lover (A2). Most athletes also referred to female friends encouraging and supporting them throughout their trials.

Some also highlighted the Internet as central in encountering other gay men. One athlete cites a chat room as instigating an enduring relationship: "[We] fell in love, moved in, consider ourselves married" (A8). The use of the Internet in this way, where users can remain anonymous, underscores the difficult, marginal position of gay men interested in sport. Yet, when the athletes actually decide to tell their coming out stories to their sports peers, they report few major problems. The stages leading up to and including actual disclosure to peers are universally presented as stressful, but the results are mainly pleasing. Themes of support, interest and loyalty from sports peers are presented throughout the texts, for example:

> "they appreciated me telling them. They also told me that it didn't change their opinion of me at all" (A1);
> "acceptance . . . didn't make a difference as a whole" (A3);
> "I'm just another athlete now . . . sexuality is forgotten" (A4);
> "a lack of personal troubles in coming out" (A6);
> "Coming out to team went smoothly" (A7);
> "a non-issue . . . no big deal . . . 100% support from the team." (A8)

In addition, several athletes also mentioned mild joking and teasing from teammates, viewed unanimously as supportive: "My teammates even joke about my being gay now, which definitely shows me that they're comfortable with it and accept it" (A1). Such jokes inevitably revolve around the relative attractiveness of colleagues and classic camp references (e.g., A4). One athlete claims to be seen as rather exotic ("gay, fast and friendly") but does not register any discrimination (A5).

In general, the principal fear shared by most athletes was that their status and relationships within the team should not change. Athlete 2 discusses his anxieties about members of his school team and wider community discovering his sexual orientation:

> "In all honesty, there will be some people who are not OK with it," he said. "But at the same time, I think it might open a lot of people's eyes. Like the people at my school, they don't have any gay friends. They don't know any gay people at all. They might just look at me and say Vernon has been my best friend since I was little, and he's gay, and he's cool. I just hope they see me as the same goofy Vernon." (A2)

Here, the core self is distanced from sexual orientation, as others are urged to see beyond gay to the essentially unchanged self beyond. Of those athletes who are out and accepted as gay, there seems to be a great effort to discount gay identities and a desire to be treated like (straight) peers. There are various claims of the nature that "relationships didn't change" (A3), and that "[they] treat him same as before" (A5). Contrast this strategy with one cited above whereby the "real" self is equated with being gay in opposition to a publicly performed false heterosexual self. This example highlights the social constructionist point that self-presentation is dynamic, sometimes contradictory, and tied to particular rhetorical and social contexts (Burr, 1995).

Becoming Politicised: Challenging Heterosexism Within Sport

As a consequence of coming out in sport, most athletes professed greater self-confidence:

> I've gained much greater self-acceptance, and I don't have to waste huge amounts of mental energy anymore worrying about it and trying to hide it. The whole process has been incredibly liberating. (A1)

Others speak about being "at peace" (A4) and "more comfortable" (A7). Ultimately, some athletes were galvanised by their experiences into becoming more political within and through their sport. A mission to overthrow homophobia in sport was evident in some accounts:

> "I want to make a difference. I want someone out there, in the same situation as I to read this article and be inspired–at least one person. Gosh, knowing I could make a difference in someone's life, that inspires me," he said. (A2)

Another athlete is described as "out and proud" and a "one man crusader," and his promotion of gay-friendly sponsors on his equipment and his openness to spectators are highlighted (A4). Another wishes to "educate the straight world that gays and lesbians are normal" (A5). Many report huge satisfaction in successfully countering heterosexism within their sport, often with the support of teammates. An example of a success story is a previously homophobic teammate who now sees him as a "regular guy" (P7). The founder of a support network for gay athletes aims to "demonstrate to the gay community that it is possible to be an elite athlete and gay" and invites closeted athletes to "come out and come together" (A6).

FINAL REMARKS

The positive elements of the stories recounted suggest that barriers can ultimately be overcome and that gay men can experience a level of acceptance within sport. This aspect of the analysis provides some grounds for optimism that the hypermasculine institution of sport will not evade change. This optimistic tone should be tempered, though, since the participants also underline the various difficulties which gay men must confront in the world of sport which uphold this institution as heteronormative and homophobic. As such, the analysis confirms existing research that draws attention to continuing heterosexism and homophobia within sport (Andersen, 2002; Krane and Kauer 2007).

At the same time, as Andersen suggests, the accounts presented by the athletes can be seen as constructed and rhetorically organised. That is, in recounting their experiences within a media environment that promotes the involvement of gay men and lesbian women in sport (outsports.com), it is rather inevitable that editors will privilege success stories so that readers may be encouraged to enter sporting establishments. However, Plummer (1995) emphasizes that some form of successful personal transformation is an inevitable component of coming out stories, regardless of the context in which stories are presented. Yet transformation is not limited to the individual level–I have noted that contact with supportive communities and organizations produces a more collectivist change. Other studies also highlight the potentially transformative effect of bonding with similar others, such as Krane, Barber and McClung's (2002) analysis of the impact of participating in the Gay Games for lesbian and bisexual athletes on subsequent involvement in political campaigns.

It must also be borne in mind that acceptance by teammates might be overstated, as Andersen (2002) speculates. Indeed, there are some indications in the accounts that acceptance is not unconditional. For example, many participants here recounted a "joking" response of teammates regarding their sexuality, which can be seen in terms of trivialising, even erasing, active gay sexualities within sport. The ubiquitous talk of sexuality "not making a difference," "being forgotten," "putting it aside," etc., encountered in this analysis reinforces the point that being gay is acceptable in sport, but *acting* gay is certainly not. Thus heteronormative talk and practice continue to thrive.

Andersen's (2002) work also suggests that acceptance might be linked to sporting prowess, i.e., critique and abuse is much more likely where the gay athlete's contribution is deemed peripheral to the team's goals. Messner (2001) also makes the general point that acceptance by sport peers is contingent on ability, regardless of issues of difference and identity. The importance of competition and winning should not be underestimated in the heteronormative sport environment. It is possible, however, that the emergence of new sports such as surfing, snowboarding and mountain-biking offer an alternative to rule-bound, hierarchical and "masculinised" sport cultures (Wheaton, 2000). Further research into such sports could investigate the potential for gay men and lesbian women to practice sport in an arguably more convivial environment, where performance levels and locker room culture matter less.

Psychologists and psychotherapists might contribute to greater understanding and challenging of heterosexism and homophobia in sporting contexts in a number of ways. An obvious contribution would be to conduct research in this area. The foregoing analysis constitutes a preliminary step and much more work needs to be done to examine gay identities and experiences across a number of sporting-related contexts. Certainly there is little UK-based research in this area, and a lack of attention to cultural influences on perceptions and experiences of gay men in sport. Qualitative research has a particular role to play in illuminating diversity and complexity within different sporting domains, while still attending to the reproduction of and resistance to wider social and political ideologies founded on heterosexuality and masculinity. For example, one can imagine a number of action research projects involving straight and gay athletes and key personnel such as coaches and teachers. The aim here would be to document and discuss issues around sport, gender and sexuality with a view to raising awareness of prejudice and developing programmes to tackle it. For ideas about topics and methods, researchers might look to work in feminist and critical social psychology for guidance (e.g., Gough and McFadden, 2001; Wilkinson, 1996) and to recent texts on lesbian and gay psychology, such as Clarke and Peel (2007).

In terms of other, more direct, interventions, psychologists could advertise their services in sporting domains and offer seminars about heterosexism and homophobia in sport to amateur and professional clubs and associations. Perhaps out gay athletes could be enlisted to facilitate workshops in this regard. Further, the results of pertinent research could be summarised and reports sent to relevant policymakers and gatekeepers. Classroom sessions in schools and colleges could help young people develop an understanding of the issues and acquire confidence in tackling prejudice and discrimination.

Relating to this preliminary study, and some other qualitative research (Krane et al., 2004; Andersen, 2002), there are specific themes that psychotherapists could consider in their work with gay athletes. Given that isolation within sport is a common experience, psychotherapists could recommend a number of dedicated support groups and websites to facilitate a sense of belongingness and build self-esteem. In some cases, as the above findings suggest, becoming involved with other gay athletes can raise consciousness of heterosexism and homophobia more generally, which may prompt participation in collective, political campaigns. As well, qualitative research highlights the often subtle, indirect prejudice leveled against gay athletes by sports peers, which may be veiled by superficial acceptance and seemingly innocuous joking. Psychotherapists can help gay athletes appreciate the problematic nature of such treatment, and perhaps to reject it. However, it must also be noted that not all gay athletes will be inclined towards such critical dialogue with their peers. As seen in this and other studies (Andersen, 2002), a prevalent anxiety after coming out to team colleagues concerns being regarded as "different," and some of these athletes may well prefer not to express their sexuality openly in a sports context. Qualitative research, like psychotherapy, alerts us to the unique aspects of individual lives; and an appreciation of the personal as well as the more cultural issues relating to the masculinist, heterosexist world of sport can help psychotherapists do effective work with gay athletes on a case-by-case basis.

REFERENCES

Andersen, E. (2002), Openly gay athletes: Contesting hegemonic masculinity in a homophobic environment. *Gender & Society*, 16(6):860-877.

Ben-Ari, A. (1995), The discovery that an offspring is gay: Parents,' gay men's and lesbians' perspectives. *J. Homosexuality*, 30(1):89-112.

Borhek, M.V. (1993), *Coming Out to Parents: A Two-Way Survival Guide for Lesbians and Gay Men and Their Parents*. Cleveland, OH: Pilgrim.

Bryant, M. (2001), *Gay Male Athletes and the Role of Organized Team and Contact Sports*. Unpublished master's thesis, Seattle Pacific University.

Burr, V. (1995), *An Introduction to Social Constructionism*. London: Routledge.

Camic, P., Rhodes, J.E. & Yardley, L., eds. (2003), *Qualitative Research in Psychology: Expanding Perspectives in Methodology and Design*. Washington, DC: American Psychological Association.

Charmaz, C. (1995), Grounded theory. In: *Rethinking Methods in Psychology*, eds. J. Smith, R. Harré & L. Van Langenhove. London: Sage, pp. 27-50.

Clarke, V. & Peel, E. (2007), Out in Psychology: Lesbian, gay, bisexual, trans and queer perspectives. Chicester: Wiley.

Cohen, K.M. & Savin-Williams, R.C. (1996), Developmental perspectives on coming out to self and others. In: *The Lives of Lesbians, Gays, and Bisexuals: Children to Adults*, eds. R.C. Savin-Williams & K.M. Cohen. Orlando, FL: Harcourt Brace, pp. 113-152.

Connell, R.W. (1995), *Masculinities*. Cambridge: Polity.

Coyle, A. & Kitzinger C., eds. (2002), *Lesbian and Gay Psychology: New Perspectives*. Oxford: BPS Books/Blackwell.

D'Augelli, A.R. (1994), Attending to the needs of out youth. *Division 44 Newsletter*, 16-18.

Davies, P. (1992), The role of disclosure in coming out among gay men. In: *Modern Homosexualities: Fragments of Gay and Lesbian Experience*, ed. K. Plummer. New York: Routledge, pp. 75-87.

Dworkin, S.L. & Wachs, F.L. (1998), "Disciplining the body": HIV-positive male athletes, media surveillance, and the policing of sexuality. *Sociology of Sport J.*, 15(1):1-20.

Edwards, D. & Potter, J. (1992), *Discursive Psychology*. London: Sage.

Finlay, L. & Gough, B., eds. (2003), *Doing Reflexivity: Critical Illustrations for Health & Social Science*. Oxford: Blackwell Science.

Flowers, P. & Buston, K. (2001), "I was terrified of being different": Exploring gay men's accounts of growing up in a heterosexist society. *J. Adolescence*, 24:51-65.

Glaser, B. & Strauss, A. (1967), *The Discovery of Grounded Theory*. Chicago: Aldine.

Gough, B. & McFadden, M. (2001), *Critical Social Psychology: An Introduction*. Basingstoke: Palgrave.

Greene, B. & Herek, G.M., eds. (1994), *Lesbian and Gay Psychology: Theory, Research and Clinical Applications*. London: Sage.

Griffin, P. (1998), *Strong Women, Deep Closets: Lesbians and Homophobia Within Sport*. Champaign, IL: Human Kinetics.

Hekma, G. (1998), "As long as they don't make an issue of it . . . ": Gay men and lesbians in organised sports in the Netherlands. *J. Homosexuality*, 35(1):1-23.

Kimmel, M.S., ed. (1987), *Changing Men: New Directions in Research on Men and Masculinity*. Beverly Hills: Sage.

Krane, V., Choi, P.Y.L., Baird, S.M., Aimar, C.M. & Kauer, K.J. (2004), Living the paradox: Female athletes negotiate femininity and muscularity. *Sex Roles*, 50(5-6): 315-329.

Krane, V. (2001), We can be athletic and feminine, but do we want to? Challenging hegemonic femininity in women's sport. *Quest*, 53(1):115-133.

Krane, V., Barber, H. & McClung, L.R. (2002), Social psychological benefits of gay games participation: A social identity theory explanation. *J. Applied Sport Psychology*, 14(1):27-42.

Krane, V. & Kauer, K.J. (2007), Out on the ball fields: Lesbians in sport. In: *Out in Psychology: Lesbian, gay, bisexual, trans and queer perspectives*, eds. V. Clarke & E. Peel. Chicester: Wiley, pp. 273-290.

Louganis, G. & Marcus, E. (1995), *Breaking the Surface*. London: Orion.

MacDonald, G.J. (1984), Identity congruency and identity management among gay men. *Dissertation Abstracts International*, 45:1322B.

McKay, J., Sabo, D. & Messner, M., eds. (1999), Men and sport (Special Issue). *Men & Masculinities*, 1(3).

Markowe, L. (2002), Coming out as lesbian. In: *Lesbian and Gay Psychology: New Perspectives*, eds. A. Coyle & C. Kitzinger. Oxford: BPS Blackwell, pp. 63-81.

Messner, M. (2001), Boyhood, organised sports, and the construction of masculinities. In: *Men's Lives*, eds. M. Kimmel & M. Messner. Boston: Allyn & Bacon, pp. 88-100.

Messner, M. (1992), *Power at Play: Sports and the Problem of Masculinity*. Boston: Beacon.

Peel, E. (2001), Mundane Heterosexism: Understanding incidents of the every day. *Women's Studies International Forum*, 24(S), 541-554.

Plummer, K. (1995), *Telling Sexual Stories: Power, Change and Social Worlds*. London: Routledge.

Potter, J. & Wetherell, M. (1987), *Discourse & Social Psychology: Beyond Attitudes and Behaviour*. London: Sage.

Price, M. (2000), *Rugby as a Gay Men's Game*. Unpublished PhD Thesis, University of Warwick, Coventry, UK.

Pronger, B. (1990), *The Arena of Masculinity: Sports, Homosexuality, and the Meaning of Sex*. New York: St Martin's.

Radkowsky, M. & Siegel, L.J. (1997), The gay adolescent: Stressors, adaptations, and psychological interventions. *Clinical Psychology Review*, 17:191-216.

Savin-Williams, R.C. (2001), A critique of research on sexual minority youths. *J. Adolescence*, 24(1):5-13.

Smith, J., ed. (2004), *Qualitative Psychology: A Practical Guide to Research Methods*. London: Sage.

Swain, J. (2000), "The money's good, the fame's good, the girls are good": The role of playground football in the construction of young boys' masculinity in a junior school. *British J. Sociology of Education*, 21(1):95-110.

Wells, J.W. & Kline, W.B. (1987), Self-disclosure of homosexual orientation. *J. Social Psychology*, 127(2):191-197.

Wendel, W., Toma, L. & Morphew, C. (2001), How much difference is too much difference? Perceptions of gay men and lesbians in intercollegiate athletics. *J. College Student Development*, 42(5):465-79.

Wheaton, B. (2000), "New Lads": Masculinities and the "New Sport" participant. *Men & Masculinities*, 2(4):434-456.

Wilkinson, S., ed. (1996), *Feminist Social Psychologies: International Perspectives*. Buckinghamshire: Open University Press.

Wilkinson, S. & Kitzinger, C., eds. (1993), *Heterosexuality: A Feminism & Psychology Reader*. London: Sage.

Willig, C. (2001), *Introducing Qualitative Research in Psychology: Adventures in Theory and Method*. Buckinghamshire: Open University Press.

Woog, D. (1998), *Jocks: True Stories of America's Gay Male Athletes*. Los Angeles: Alyson.

doi:10.1300/J236v11n01_11

Index

Note: Page numbers followed by the letter "t" designate tables.

Mental health problems, in GMLD,
   147-148
"Mental Health Trusts," 146
Merleau-Ponty, M., 49,50
Messner, M., 171
Milton, M., 3,45
Mitchell, S., 78
Mitwelt, 64-66
Morphew, C., 157
Mourning and Melancholia, 77

National Health Service (NHS), 2,4,
   14-15
   of UK, for GMLD, 145-152. *See
      also* Gay men with learning
      disabilities (GMLD), NHS of
      UK for
Neal, C., 13-14
NHS. *See* National Health Service
   (NHS)
Nietzsche, 36
1994 Gay Games, 157

Object relations
   described, 76
   between gay therapists and gay
      clients, 75-91. *See also* Gay
      therapists, gay clients and,
      object relations between
Oedipus complex, 78,79
Office for Standards in Education
   (OFSTED), 130
OFSTED. *See* Office for Standards in
   Education (OFSTED)
Oswald, R.F., 123
Outline of Psychoanalysis, 77
Own age group, importance of, among
   LGB youth at Summer
   Freedom Summer School,
   138-140

PACE. *See* Project for Advise,
   Counselling, and Education
   (PACE)

Parent(s), coming out to, described, 156
Peel, E., 1,2,7,171
Perez, R.M., 29,30
Phenomenology
   described, 47-49
   hermeneutic, of Ricoeur, 34-36
Physical safety, in coming out, 67-69
Pink Therapy series, 2,14,29
Plummer, K., 167,170
Prejudice, "anti-homosexual," of gay
      therapists, 82
Price, M., 158
Project for Advise, Counselling, and
      Education (PACE), 65,133
   Youth Work Service of, 127
Psychology, critical, described, 17
Psychosocial theory and practice,
      LGBT, in UK, review of key
      contributions and current
      developments, 7-25. *See also*
      Lesbian, gay, bisexual, and
      transgender (LGBT)
      psychosocial theory and
      practice, in UK
Psychotherapy
   with gay male clients, existential
      contributions to, 45-59. *See
      also* Gay men, psychotherapy
      with, existential contributions
      to
   lesbians and gay men in
      issues of importance to, 93-109
      community study of, 97-107
         content analysis in,
            99-100,100t
         discussion of, 101t,103-105
         findings from, 103-105
         hypotheses in, 97
         implications of, 105-107
         limitations of, 105
         measures in, 99
         method in, 97-100
         procedure in, 98
         questionnaires in, 97
         results of, 100-103,100t